The Environment for Aging

The Environment for Aging

Interpersonal, Social, and Spatial Contexts

Russell A. Ward, Mark La Gory, Susan R. Sherman

The University of Alabama Press

Tuscaloosa and London

Copyright © 1988 by
The University of Alabama Press
Tuscaloosa, Alabama 35487
All rights reserved
Manufactured in the United States of America

Library of Congress Cataloging-in-Publication Data
Ward, Russell A.
The environment for aging.
Includes index.
    1. Aged—United States.   2. Environmental psychology.
3. Aged—United States—Dwellings.   4. Aged—United
States—Psychology. I. La Gory, Mark, 1947–
II. Sherman, Susan (Susan R.) III. Title.
HQ1064.U5W363   1988   305.2'6   86-24940
ISBN 0-8173-0342-1
British Library Cataloguing-in-Publication
Data is available.

To our multigenerational supports—
our parents, spouses, and children

Contents

Preface

Aging is a complex and varied experience, influenced by the social context in which it takes place. Riley has noted: "There is no pure process of aging—the ways in which children enter kindergarten, or adolescents move into adulthood, or older people retire are not preordained. In this view, the life course is not fixed, but widely flexible" (1978:41). This statement reminds us that the nature and consequences of aging are shaped by many factors and that there will be variability within the older population in the nature and implications of these factors.

The research reported in this book addresses several dimensions of the complex aging experience. Most generally, it explores the influence of "environment," both physical and social, on the lives of older individuals. Several aspects of this environment are highlighted: (1) residential location and neighborhood context, (2) informal networks and social supports, and (3) images of aging as these are reflected in attitudes toward aging and personal orientations to age and age peers. These are linked to the quality of life of older people, as reflected in their subjective feelings of well-being.

The environmental dimensions noted above are quite wide ranging, of course, and the links among them may at first glance seem rather tenuous. Their confluence here can perhaps best be explained by describing the history of this research project. The collaboration began a number of years ago with our interest in the residential patterns of the older population. Specifically, we wished to find out whether housing was segregated on the basis of age as it is on the basis of race and other social characteristics. When we found that it was, we became interested in accounting for the ecological processes that are responsible for this age segregation.

Having investigated ecological patterns of residential age segregation, we were then faced with a question that is often asked of social research (though perhaps too seldom answered): So what? That is, are there particular advantages, or perhaps costs, associated with residential age concentration for older people? This question led to a consideration of the importance of residential location and neighborhood context, the importance of neighbors within the more general social networks of older people, and the support and socializing functions of social relationships. It became clear that we could not explore the implications of residential segregation without also addressing these more general topics. Thus this book has a more general focus than was originally envisioned, though the consequences of neighborhood age concentration remain a prominent subtheme.

Given the wide-ranging interests and issues addressed by our research, the reader may benefit from a brief map of the text. Chapter 1 introduces a general approach to the "human ecosystem," with particular attention to the relevance of environmental factors in the lives of the elderly. More specifically, the first chapter introduces theoretical and empirical issues concerning various dimensions of the environment for aging—neighborhoods, informal networks, and orientations to aging. The issues introduced in Chapter 1 were investigated in an interview survey of 1,185 community residents aged 60 and over. The characteristics of the sample, operationalization of variables, and logic of data analysis are discussed in Chapter 2. Chapters 3 through 6 report findings of the survey that are relevant to the issues discussed in the first chapter.

Chapter 3 discusses the implications of neighborhood context. It is apparent that the elderly actually have two neighborhoods—a social neighborhood and a service neighborhood. Although both neighborhoods may be characterized by objective problems, our respondents express considerable satisfaction with neighborhoods. This attitude reflects attempts to resolve cognitive dissonance arising from limited housing options as well as a more passive and vicarious mode of spatial experience. The environment is experienced in diverse ways, however. We pay particular attention to the implications of urbanism and environmental docility.

Chapter 4 discusses the nature and consequences of informal network characteristics. The older persons in our sample have relatively robust interpersonal ties and supports, both objectively and subjectively. Objective measures of social support, such as frequency and proximity, have little bearing on subjective well-being, however, whereas perceived sufficiency of ties and supports is more salient to morale. As with neighborhood context, the implications of informal networks vary across subgroups. Personal competence is particularly important, again reflecting an environmental-docility hypothesis.

Chapter 5 presents findings on age-related orientations and behaviors. Our respondents have generally favorable attitudes toward other older people, but their own feelings of age identity reflect a decremental view of aging, and "feeling" old appears to be demoralizing. There is little indication that socializing experiences or age-group solidarity make aging any easier in this regard.

Chapter 6 analyzes the consequences of neighborhood age concentration and more generally of age homogeneity within informal networks. There is moderate age homogeneity in the networks of our respondents to which neighborhood age concentration contributes. Contrary to expectations, however, neither age concentration nor age homogeneity contributes to well-being. Neighborhood age concentration lacks the beneficial features of planned age-segregated housing, and age-group solidarity does not appear to be salient in the lives of most older community residents.

Chapter 7 concludes with general themes and implications from this research. As an overview, three basic themes are underscored. First, age itself is of limited importance and does not loom large in the lives of these community residents. Age, and being "old," may be made salient (with potentially demoralizing effects) by certain processes and experiences, however. Second, there is great diversity in the nature and implications of the environmental context for aging. The environmental-docility hypothesis is particularly useful in shedding light on this diversity. The variability of aging means that there is no "typical" older person, and planning and policy must carefully attend to the need for person-environment congruence. Finally, aging must clearly be viewed in interactional or transactional terms. Older people are not simply acted upon by the environment; rather, they experience and construct the environment as a subjective entity. We need to recognize this active involvement to understand the environmental experience of aging.

Any project such as this one owes a debt to a great many people. Most obviously, we are grateful to the older persons who gave of themselves to provide the information presented here. We are also indebted to our research assistants, Marc Mucatel and Deborah Traynor, for their valuable contributions throughout the research process. Helen Dees, Debbie Neuls, and Eileen Pellegrino spent many long hours typing the manuscript. Judith Knight gave useful editorial assistance. Richard Alba, and the Center for Social and Demographic Analysis at the State University of New York at Albany, provided 1980 census data on the age composition of tract locations. The State University of New York at Albany facilitated writing by granting Russell Ward a sabbatical leave.

Several of our colleagues deserve particular acknowledgment. Vern Bengtson, Powell Lawton, and Bill Yoels offered valuable comments throughout the research and writing. Data collection was undertaken by the Opinion Research Corporation, with particular assistance provided by Gerri Spiller. Finally, this research was supported by a grant from the Center for Studies of the Mental Health of the Aging; National Institute of Mental Health. We particularly thank Barry Lebowitz for his advice and support throughout the project.

The Environment for Aging

1 Aging in the Human Ecosystem

Human choice and action take place in socially bounded environments that set the conditions under which people must operate in the community. These environments make some acts more possible than others and some choices more plausible than others. Aging, like other aspects of human experience, is affected by these environments. The present book explores the influences of environments on the lives of older individuals.

Until recently the implications of environmental context received limited attention in sociology and gerontology. A Parsonian theory of the social system dominated American sociology for several decades. In this view, human action was the product of an interacting hierarchy of structures in which the culture dominated all other parts of the social system, whereas the physical environment was subordinate. Interactionist perspectives, although critical of Parson's structural functionalism, developed a similarly one-sided conception of the environment's significance for action. To paraphrase the time-worn dictum of W. I. Thomas, people's definitions of their surroundings, rather than the environments themselves, were important for behavior. Even human ecology, which was initially developed to study the relations between populations and environments, has been criticized for its failure to give serious attention to the study of the spatial environment's consequences for community residents. Indeed, spatial environments have been accorded a passive role in ecology, seen either as a medium in which action occurs or as an indicator or product of larger social forces (Michelson, 1976).

Gerontology, although certainly more attentive to the active role that context plays in the life of the older person, has focused most of its interest on planned environments for aging. These "built environments" (retirement communities, housing complexes, and nursing homes) are valuable subjects to study. They do not, however, represent the natural environment for aging (the city neighborhoods, suburban towns, and rural villages) that the majority of elderly call home in the United States.

There are many reasons for the limited research agenda in sociology and gerontology, perhaps the most significant being the complex interplay of forces found within the sociospatial arena. The environment is more than a physical container; it is a social and cultural product as well. Barker (1968) portrays environments as "behavior settings." A behavior setting is bounded in space and time and possesses a structure that interrelates physical, social, and cultural properties to elicit patterns of behavior. Thus it is difficult both conceptually and methodologically to separate the physical setting from the cultural and social system in which it is embedded (Golant, 1984). The complexity of environment-behavior relations can be seen in Lawton's (1982) description of the five components of the human ecosystem: (1) the individual, (2) the physical environment, (3) the interpersonal environment or network of significant others, (4) the suprapersonal environment of spatially clustered individuals, and (5) the social environment, consisting of the norms and institutions operating in the individual's subgroup or culture. These components indicate the significance of scale in the analysis of environmental relations. The environment consists of a hierarchical clustering of physical units ranging from the home and neighborhood to the larger action space of the individual.

The environmental experience is also a product of several interlocking spheres of activity. Rowles (1978) describes four modalities of spatial experience:

1. *action:* the interaction between individuals and environmental resources occurring at three levels—immediate movement, everyday activity, and occasional trips;
2. *orientation:* the differentiation of social spaces through individualized "mental maps";
3. *feeling:* the giving of meaning and sentiment to space through involvement in a common context with shared values and frequent interaction;
4. *fantasy:* the vicarious experiencing of space, representing a complex composite of present and past environments.

Clearly, then, the "environment" is a complex phenomenon, encompassing physical, psychological, and social components. This book attends to the complexities of the environmental experience by addressing the aging individual's relationship to each of the human ecosystem components mentioned by Lawton. In addition special attention is given to the fact that relationships with each of these components are carried out simultaneously on both experiential and mental levels (Michelson, 1976).

The Older Person as Ecological Actor

An ecosystem approach to aging is especially appropriate because the elderly represent a unique set of ecological actors (Lawton, 1980). Current research points to several distinctive features: (1) older persons appear to be more sensitive to environmental variation (Lawton and Simon, 1968; Lawton, 1970; Lawton and Nahemow, 1973; Golant, 1979); (2) the local environment for action and choice constricts with old age (Stea, 1970); and (3) the elderly are more likely to use modes of environmental experience, such as fantasy, that are underused in the general population (Rowles, 1978).

Lawton and Simon's (1968) environmental-docility hypothesis explains the heightened environmental sensitivity of the elderly. In this thesis the reduced physical and cognitive competence associated with aging causes behavior to become more dependent on environmental forces at the very time when the aged are less able to manipulate the environment. In effect, the elderly may become "prisoners of space" (Rowles, 1978). This local dependence can place them at a disadvantage, because the range of modern support networks has expanded beyond localized neighborhoods (Fischer and Jackson, 1976). The reduced mobility of some older people and the tendency of many inner-city elderly to be "block bound" means that the aged are more likely to "rely on the local area and its inhabitants to support their needs, while most of today's society reach far from home to meet the needs of everyday life" (Carp, 1976:249).

The docility hypothesis has been incorporated into a more general model of environmental effects—the theory of environmental press (Lawton and Nahemow, 1973). In this thesis the individual is defined in terms of level of competence (as measured by biological health, sensorimotor functioning, cognitive skill, and ego strength). Environments of all types are described in terms of their "demand character"; that is, environments vary in the behavioral demands with which they confront their occupants. These demands represent the level of "environmental press" placed on the individual. The model suggests that the higher one's competence, the wider the range of press with which one is able to cope. Conversely, low competence reduces the range of environments to which one can successfully adapt. A slight increase in press "might be enough to throw the low-competence person into a negative-outcome state while causing very little behavioral or affective change in the high-competence person" (Lawton, 1980:14). Because competence can be affected by aging, aging itself is also likely to increase environmental sensitivity.

In addition to affecting environmental sensitivity, aging influences the action space or "home space" of the individual. Stea defines home space as "a complex of familiar objects and people distributed in space with meaningful functions sensed by the perceiver" (1970:138). It is the area of normal activity for the individual, defined in terms of patterns of occupancy and usage. Home space is more than individual geography; it has physical, social, and psychological dimensions. Stea suggests that the nature and scope of home space varies over the life cycle. The home space of children is likely to be spatially and experientially constricted, whereas highly mobile, economically active adults have very large home spaces. The accompaniments of aging—role loss, reduced income, and decreased physical and cognitive competence—narrow spatial experience. Hence the home space of the elderly is likely to be more localized.

The constricting action space leads to a shift in environmental experience. Rowles suggests that with aging there is often an increase in vicarious spatial experience through passive observation (such as looking out a window) and fantasy. Although the elderly may sometimes be "prisoners of space," their vicarious experience represents "jails without walls" (Rowles, 1979). Physical limitations thus do not imply psychological retreat, but they do suggest that the meaning, as well as the importance, of "home" is changing. Home space means something different not only in real geographic terms but also experientially. Indeed Unruh (1983) suggests that space-bound elderly often maintain integration in society through communication links to spatially transcendent "social worlds." These invisible worlds are constructed and maintained through watching television, talking on the telephone, writing letters, reading specialized magazines, and so forth. Such worlds may have great symbolic importance for the individual in spite of their absence from the immediate, observable environment.

The unique features of the environment-behavior relation described above suggest the value of studying the impact of context on aging. Although numerous social scientists have argued that the fit between individuals and environments is critical to social and mental health in the general population, the literature in gerontology suggests that it may be even more important for older populations. The analysis of environment-behavior relations for the elderly is necessarily complex, however (Kahana, 1982; Golant, 1984), and environmental satisfaction and action will not be a simple function of the features of the context. Rather, the psychological and physical state of the person experiencing these features is expected to be critical. Environmental satisfaction results from a complicated process involving ecological, biological, psychological, and social components, but this description is also too simple. As Karp and Yoels (1982) have noted, the environment for aging is a symbolically constructed one. Environmental actions are thus products of "an ongoing interpretive process in which persons are constantly trying to make sense of their life situations" (p. 63). Environments are mental constructions as well as physical realities, a fact that is especially significant for elderly with reduced competence.

Ironically, in describing these complexities, we have taken only a first glimpse at the complex dynamics of action in places and spaces. We have suggested that the study of environment-behavior relations for an older population will be both interesting and important because of the unique qualities of the older ecological actor. So far our discussion has focused on only one agent in the ecological relation, the individual actor. As Lawton's description of the human ecosystem indicates, however, the forces external to the actors are themselves complex. The environment is composed of a nested hierarchy of systems varying in scale and abstraction, each impinging on the individual actor in some more or less determinate fashion. It includes the local spaces and places that Stea calls the "home space" but that might more commonly be called the *neighborhood*. These local residential areas have physical, social, and economic dimensions. The neighborhood is a space consisting of neighbors and services. The environment also consists of an *interpersonal environment* in which the individual is embedded. These social networks make up the basic affective and instrumental ties between person and society. Such ties may be localized or wide ranging.

At a more abstract level, further removed from the individual, are two additional environmental types, the social and the suprapersonal. The *social environment* consists of the norms and values operating in the individual's subgroup, society, or culture. It places more abstract but nonetheless real limitations on the individual's behavior. The term *suprapersonal environment* refers to the population characteristics of a residential area. Although Lawton (1982) uses this term with reference only to the modal characteristics of "all the people in physical proximity to an individual" (p. 40), we shall use the concept more broadly to capture the geography of the larger local community. Our usage is closer to what the urban sociologist Louis Wirth (1938) described as the "urban mosaic," a structured environment of neighborhoods, or a patchwork of social and physical resources, whose general pattern can affect the aging experience. Together with the individual actors themselves, these four environmental factors constitute the human ecosystem within which action and choice occur.

Aging happens in the context of this ecosystem. The research reported in this book details the process. Each aspect of the ecosystem is analyzed separately at first, with primary focus on the older actor's use and fit to this environmental component. The various dimensions are then linked to the issue of quality of life, as reflected in the subjective feelings of well-being. Quality of life is the subject of ultimate interest in much gerontological research and social policy. "The relationship between aging and successful adaptation (variously morale or life satisfaction or mental health) is perhaps the oldest, most persistently investigated issue in the social scientific study of aging" (Maddox and Wiley, 1976:15). Our intent is thus to explore in the fullest detail possible the theoretical and empirical linkages between context and quality of life. In the rest of this chapter we shall outline this relationship as it has been delineated by the social sciences and by gerontology in particular.

The Neighborhood for Aging

The significance of the neighborhood in the modern metropolis has been much debated. The debate centers on two specific issues: the declining sense of community in the modern mass society and the growing insignificance of location and place in the automobile-age city. Although some social scientists have already pronounced the metropolitan neighborhood dead, the neighborhood is clearly far from dead (Lee et al., 1984) and plainly has special significance for the elderly (Stea, 1970; Rowles, 1978).

Wellman notes that the effects of macrosocial processes such as urbanization on the organization and content of primary ties have "set the agenda for much of sociology" (1979:1201). Social networks, embedded in residential neighborhoods and local communities, are seen as a mechanism for transcending the isolation of individuals in mass society (Laumann, 1973), but there has been debate about the nature and viability of these social networks. There have been three dominant approaches to what Wellman (1979) calls the community question.

The "community lost" approach asserts that people are now bound to the city by secondary affiliations that are neither localized nor interconnected. This approach assumes that an "authentic community" can be only local and that lack of attachment to such places results in personal and social disorganization (Fischer and Stueve, 1977; Gerson et al., 1977). The decline of the local community purportedly arises because modern societies have increased individual choice while at the same time limiting access to intimate social ties and encouraging spatially dispersed networks. Individuals have far-flung networks that are shallow and instrumental rather than deep and communal.

Although this is a classical view of urban life, it seems to overstate the disconnectedness of city residents. Fischer (1981) notes that, although urban life may represent a "world of strangers," one must distinguish between public and private worlds. Urbanism, for example, seems related to distrust of most people in the city but not to distrust of neighbors, at least partly because residential segregation produces homogeneous neighborhoods. The "community saved" approach asserts that localized communal attachments persist within "urban villages" (e.g., Gans, 1962; Suttles, 1972).

Wellman (1979) criticizes both of these approaches for over-emphasizing local primary ties. Studies have demonstrated that most urbanites have important interpersonal ties and channels of informal support that have not been destroyed by either formal assistance patterns or secondary social ties. According to the "community liberated" approach, the spatial range of networks has expanded to include the entire metropolitan area. Fischer and Stueve (1977) note that proximity and frequency are not critical to sustaining intimacy because networks can be mobilized in the absence of face-to-face contact, and close relationships have latent rights and responsibilities that need not be exercised regularly. Because nonlocal ties are retained for the reason that they continue to be rewarding, one would anticipate only a weak association between distance and intimacy. Freedom from place has supplanted constraint to place; people are better able to construct and maintain nonlocal ties, and the influence of neighborhood has declined.

It should not be inferred that the neighborhood has become socially irrelevant, however. Hunter (1975) notes that the urban neighborhood can function as a community in three ways: to meet sustenance needs (as a functional spatial unit); as a unit of patterned social interaction; and as a cultural-symbolic unit of collective identity. His study found a decline over time in the use of local facilities close to home but an increase in informal interaction and sense of community. Local involvements, including friendships, are important in fostering neighborhood satisfaction and attachment (Gerson et al., 1977). Although locational constraints may be reduced in modern societies, they are still evident. Strong ties exhibit a gradient effect, with ties declining as distance increases (Fischer and Jackson, 1976; Wellman, 1976), and intimate social ties tend to be confined to sectors of the city (Johnston, 1972).

Neighborhood attachments differ across subgroups, of course. Social losses and mobility limitations associated with aging may heighten the importance of all three dimensions of neighborhood-as-community that were noted by Hunter. Environment, particularly the localized environment, may be especially influential in the lives of the elderly. Although Wellman characterizes the urban community as spatially liberated, it may not in fact be so for the elderly. Lawton and Nahemow (1979), for example, discover that environmental characteristics are better predictors of well-being than personal characteristics in a sample of older persons. Similarly, a study of the extent to which older people feel victimized or vulnerable finds that the major problems expressed are consistently related to neighborhood problems (Kahana et al., 1977). In addition, distance to services has been found to be a major predictor of service use (Regnier, 1975, 1976; Newcomer, 1976), and there appears to be an association between morale and proximity to services (Schooler, 1969; Lawton and Kleban, 1971). Services have "critical distances" for optimal use, and viable neighborhoods need both a minimal core group of services and accessible transportation for other services. Hence neighborhood fit can be described as having a direct bearing on the quality of life of an older population.

A critical element in neighborhood fit and quality of life is the extent to which the local area either supports or retards individual automony. Several dimensions should affect this autonomy—feelings of familiarity and security, access to localized facilities and services, the "service richness" of the local area, and access to friendly neighbors. In addition the salience of neighborhood for personal autonomy is likely to vary across subgroups of the older population. Salient dimensions may include socioeconomic status, environmental docility, and place of residence (city, suburban, or rural).

It is ironic that, although the neighborhood is likely to mean more for the elderly, most theory and research on the environment for aging focuses on built environments rather than on neighborhoods. We need to know more about the neighborhood life-styles, expectations, and experiences of the elderly. In Chapter 3 we address this issue in detail.

The Interpersonal Environment: Networks and Supports

The neighborhood is not simply a physical environment but is also an interpersonal one. The interpersonal environment for aging, however, includes more than local neighborhood. It is, by definition, aspatial and individual—consisting of the social networks and supports of the individual actor. These networks and supports are presumed to be important determinants of individual well-being throughout the life course.

Critical to the definition of the interpersonal environment is inclusion of both access to social ties (networks) and the individual's use of these ties in meeting needs (supports). Having and maintaining access to a network is only the first step toward having social support; "the final step depends on the quality of the relations one is able to find within the network" (Pearlin et al., 1981:340). To distinguish social support from social networks more clearly, Thoits defines social support as "the degree to which a person's basic social needs are gratified through interaction with others" (1982:147).

Social supports, and the networks that provide them, may contribute to well-being in two ways. The contributions of social support are, in part, indirect, mediating the effects of stressful life events (Dean and Lin, 1977; Kessler, 1979; Pearlin et al., 1981). These mediating resources help sustain self-esteem and feelings of mastery in the face of stress. Cobb (1979) suggests that social support reduces stress by improving person-environment congruence, as people who feel esteemed are more confident and are better able to manipulate the environment. Social support may also make direct contributions to well-being. Some research indicates that low support may be stressful in itself (Cobb, 1979). In addition there are sound theoretical reasons why social supports should be directly related to psychological well-being. She cites two in particular: (1) symbolic interactionism, linking social interaction to self-evaluation and social identity, and (2) Durkheimian anomie theory, stressing the importance of social integration.

If social support affects well-being through either of these pathways, access to social networks that provide support and variability in such access become important empirical questions. Characteristics of informal social networks are likely to vary across population subgroups. Social ties, especially those that are intimate, are chosen, but the choices represent a "bounded rationality," as they are made within social constraints (Jackson et al., 1977). Position in the social structure influences (1) values, expectations, and needs brought to social exchanges; (2) capacities for meeting the costs of exchange; (3) access to contexts in which friendships are formed; and (4) social pressures on the selection of friends (Jackson, 1977). Of particular interest here, of course, is the role of age.

Life cycle stages, and associated age stratification of roles (Riley et al., 1972), present social opportunities and constraints associated with changing needs, resources, and contexts (Shulman, 1975; Stueve and Gibson, 1977). Later life involves changes in network structure. Mobility limitations associated with declining health and income, and role losses such as retirement and widowhood, may disrupt existing networks and may alter the basic functions of such ties (Kahn, 1979; Lopata, 1979). Reduced mobility creates greater dependence on the local area and on cross-generational kin groups (Dono et al., 1979). This is not to say, however, that older persons exhibit a disengaged pattern of interpersonal involvement. Indeed, older people generally exhibit robust social ties with family, friends, and neighbors that provide both instrumental and expressive support.

Do such ties make general contributions to well-being in later life? Theory and research in gerontology has provided no clear answer to this critical question. Activity theory and disengagement theory represent opposing arguments, the former arguing that "activity provides various role supports necessary for reaffirming one's self-concept" (Lemon et al., 1972:515), and the latter arguing that social and emotional disengagement are mutually functional for the aging individual and for society (Cumming and Henry, 1961). There has been much criticism and little support for disengagement theory (Ward, 1979). These arguments assert that independence and positive affect depend at least partly on the availability of social support. Although this reasoning seems straightforward, however, evidence concerning the benefits of social networks is far from clear-cut. Informal ties can link the elderly to needed services, for example, but they may also isolate and block proper access to more effective formal services (O'Brien and Wagner, 1980; Wagner and Keast, 1981). Similarly, empirical research on the relationship between social involvement and subjective well-being is neither clear-cut nor consistent. There appears to be little relation between family availability and interaction on the one hand and subjective well-being on the other (Larson, 1978; Hoyt et al., 1980; Glenn and McLanahan, 1981; Montgomery, 1982). Participation in voluntary associations also appears to show little independent association with well-being (Ward, 1979). Friendship interaction seems most consistently related to well-being, but even this link is not universal (Larson, 1978; Wood and Robertson, 1978; Hoyt et al., 1980).

That the contributions of interpersonal involvement are not clearly connected to the well-being of older persons reflects the complexity of such patterns in the older population. Different ties (family, friends, neighbors, and confidants) may provide different functions, with varying degrees of importance, and the contributions of these ties may vary across different subgroups. It must also be recognized that social support has both an objective and a subjective dimension. Interpersonal environs, like neighborhood surroundings, are mental constructions as well as objective resources.

Three issues become particularly relevant. First, different types of relationships may involve different qualities and consequences. Paradoxically, family ties may dominate the support networks of the elderly, but friends, and perhaps particularly friends who are neighbors, may contribute more to subjective well-being. Second, subgroups of the older population may vary in the structure and consequences of social supports. This variation reflects mediational effects of social support as well as varying degrees of environmental docility (if we recognize both physical and social dimensions of environment). Third, the usual objective measures of social support may be less relevant to subjective well-being than subjective definitions of "sufficiency" of social support. Each of these issues is addressed in the research reported in Chapter 4.

The Social Environment: Orientation to Aging and Age Peers

Thus far our discussion has focused primarily on what might be termed microenvironments—the place of residence and the interpersonal networks of the elderly actor. The social environment involves one aspect of a more encompassing macroenvironment. It includes the norms and values operating in the individual's subgroup or subcultures (Lawton, 1982). All environmental experience is filtered through the lens of the individual's society and culture. In particular, orientations toward age constitute a social psychological dimension of the environment within which individuals age. These individual orientations arise from and reflect the broader social environment for aging.

The social context for aging has been a traditional concern in gerontology and has been directly linked to the study of well-being. Although there have been suggestions that societal images of aging are becoming more positive or are at least mixed (Seltzer and Atchley, 1971; Tibbitts, 1979), societal stereotypes about aging and the aged are still largely negative (McTavish, 1971; Bennett and Eckman, 1973; Branco and Williamson, 1982). Such stereotypes reflect the social structure and age stratification system in a society that places a high value on independence and achievement; they also reflect a fear of problems presumed to be associated with aging. Streib indicates that "old age is not valued highly because it is associated widely with decline in physical attractiveness, vigor, health condition, sexual prowess, and perhaps some mental abilities. And . . . it is associated with the expectation of fewer years of life itself" (1976:162).

It appears, then, that old age may be regarded as a stigma, a discredit to the person who bears it (Goffman, 1963). If age categories such as *middle age* or *old age* are central to self-concept, as many have argued, then identifying oneself as old will be equivalent to internalizing this stigma. In this sense, age identity should be central to feelings of well-being. Indeed, research supports the point. Hoyt et al. (1980), for example, found that self-identification as old was associated with lower life satisfaction, even after the researchers controlled for objective conditions such as health, social class, marital status, retirement, and social activity. It is not surprising, then, that people resist identifying themselves as elderly (Ward, 1977a; Bultena and Powers, 1978).

Such resistance, however, has significant political and social consequences. As a great many students of inequality have suggested, identification with the stigmatized status is necessary before an objective social inequity can produce social and political result. Marx, for example, saw class consciousness as necessary for the emergence of "true social classes." If the old resist such identifications, it stands to reason that aging-group consciousness will be unlikely to emerge. Rose defines persons with "aging-group consciousness" as elderly persons who become aware, not merely that they are old, but that they are subject to certain deprivations because they are old, and they react to these deprivations with resentment and with some positive effort to overcome the deprivation. Further, they are aware that most, or all, older persons are subject to these deprivations, and they feel a positive sense of identification with other elderly persons for this reason. For them, the elderly are a group, and not merely a category. [1965b:19]

He argues that a subculture of the aged has developed from such consciousness.

Nonetheless, the existence of such consciousness, and of activism based on it, has been a topic of considerable debate (Ward, 1977c; Williamson et al., 1982). Streib (1976), for example, suggests that the aged have stratum awareness, or a perception of separateness from other age groups, but that they lack a sense of belonging to an age stratum, an identification of interests in conflict with those of other strata, or activism as a stratum. Thus it is often argued that the aged lack an interest in organizing on their own behalf and have not identified common political interests. Binstock has concluded that "there is no evidence to indicate that aging-based interest appeals can swing a bloc of older persons' votes from one party or candidate to another" (1974:202–203). Many reasons have been given for this phenomenon, including old age perceived as a stigma, lack of age identification, the greater salience of other bases for identification (race, sex, and class), cross-generational contacts, and limitations on mobility (Williamson et al., 1982; Ward, 1984a).

A sense of identification with age peers is itself unlikely to be sufficient to stimulate political activism. A recent study of subjective group affiliation by older people found that 28% felt "closest" to older people (in a list of social categories), and another 46% felt "close" (Miller et al., 1980). Although racial and ethnic affiliation is typically associated with greater political participation, Miller et al. found a negative relationship between voting and this measure of age-group identification. They attribute this relationship to lack of economic resources and feelings of both individual and age-group powerlessness among age-group identifiers.

It appears, then, that aging-group consciousness has not yet coalesced into a political force. Dowd (1980a) suggests that both young and old attach legitimacy to the current age stratification system. He asserts that age inequality does not produce age-group consciousness because cross-age social exchange is governed by a rule of rationality rather than a rule of distributive justice.

If we put aside political implications, however, a more restricted view of aging-group consciousness can be seen as having social-psychological benefits for older persons. Aging-group consciousness can be more simply defined as a positive sense of identification with age peers and a perception of the elderly as a group, not merely a category. Ward (1977c) found evidence that such attitudes are positively associated with subjective well-being. Such patterns may stem from the potential benefits of a "subculture" of older people: (1) allowing older persons to pursue their own interests (such as leisure) without concern for society's expectations; (2) reducing the isolation and marginality potentially associated with exclusion from other groups; and (3) providing meaningful roles and a more positive definition of "old person" (Ward, 1984a).

Because reference groups mediate society and culture through the evaluative information they provide about such categories as "old person" (Woelfel and Haller, 1971), a subculture of age peers could provide more positive definitions of aging and could circumvent feelings of relative deprivation and self-derogation arising from comparison with middle-aged standards. It would then be easier to identify oneself as "old" and to share in aging-group consciousness and activism. Visible and supportive age peers can also provide role models to assist in socialization to old age.

These considerations suggest two general questions. First, what are the "costs" and "benefits" of age identity and aging-group consciousness for the individual? On the one hand, self-identification as "old" would seem detrimental to well-being, given the stigma of old age. At the same time, if aging-group consciousness emerges, it can serve as a buffer between the individual and such imagery.

A second issue is: How do self-identification and consciousness emerge? The socialization literature suggests that access to age peers is critical. Thus there is a need to investigate the consequences of age-dense neighborhoods and networks for identification and consciousness. Both of these issues are addressed in Chapters 5 and 6.

Together, these issues suggest the reciprocal nature of ecosystem relationships. In one sense the social environment represents the ultimate source for the meaning of age and the aging experience. People understand their lives by fitting their experiences into preexisting expectations and interpretations. At the same time, the social context, and people's relations to its content, depend on sets of environmental forces encountered in the residential places and social spaces that make up the local community. Socialization occurs in places, and the nature of these places affects one's exposure to a culture's content.

The Suprapersonal Environment: The Urban Mosaic and Aging

Exposure to, and relations with, the social environment are greatly affected by the nature of the *suprapersonal environment*. We use this term to describe the mosaic of residential places and social spaces whose patterns ultimately contain and constrain the aging experience. More specifically, *suprapersonal environment* is used here to refer to the metropolitan spatial structure—the patterned distribution of population, social categories, and activities across the space in which the local population's daily requirements are met. This usage differs from that in Lawton (1982), but it more appropriately captures the sociospatial container for everyday life.

Although neighborhood represents the immediate place for residential behavior, the metropolis is the ultimate containing environment for daily action. Everyday choices concerning daily life take place within its boundaries, hence the manner in which population, activities, and resources are structured there should affect the individual. The metropolis can be viewed as a human-made resource system in which the ease of access to resources (goods, services, and people) is unequally distributed. In this sense, the spatial structure presents the individual with a range of choices that will narrow or widen, depending on one's location within this matrix of choices. Having greater access to a variety of areas or resources presents the individual with a wider array of choices. The degree of access does not determine choice, but it does constrain it. The constraints will be significant if spatial boundaries, both real and imagined, can disrupt movement between areas. Such a situation can exist when people find social relations in their localities more rewarding than those outside this area. At least two conditions can produce this effect:

1. a high degree of life-style *segregation* in which other overlapping ties exist to foster strong social support networks; for the elderly a highly age-segregated setting may encourage such a condition of social homogeneity;
2. a limitation in the array of *choices* produced by logistical difficulties; for the elderly this limitation can occur with reduced mobility and increasing environmental docility (La Gory, 1982).

Studies in factorial ecology clearly suggest that neighborhoods are segregated along a series of life-style dimensions (La Gory and Pipkin, 1981). If people of various life-styles are spatially bounded in the city, then social networks are, at least to a degree, spatially bound as well. Socially homogeneous individuals in close proximity to one another are likely to develop social ties. As a result, segregation often insulates individuals from the urban "world of strangers." This isolation fosters and maintains life-style differentiation and close-knit social areas in the city (Fischer, 1975), and so normative structures and the dynamics of socialization vary spatially. The costs of such isolation, however, may be high (Granovetter, 1973). In segregated communities social ties are "encapsulated in decoupled little worlds," limiting ties to the larger metropolitan network (Wellman, 1979). For the elderly this absence of weak ties to other areas may limit the problem-solving capacity of the age-segregated central-city neighborhood.

Such weak ties may be absent in any case, however, and segregation may increase the local density of potential choices of people or services, heightening the social quality of the neighborhood. A major assumption of both geography and ecology is that spatial movement is costly; that is, one must expend energy, time, and money to traverse space. Because people typically operate in terms of a "principle of least effort" (Zipf, 1949), the choice of a given object of satisfaction will be a function of distance. High "choice densities" (La Gory, 1982) within a neighborhood, then, reflect a situation in which decision making (whether it be in friendship choice, shopping behavior, or recreation) is less constrained. As Lawton and Nahemow (1973) suggest, environmental constraints are more significant for some individuals than for others. Because the elderly may experience limits in mobility, the distance constraint will be greater and the local level of "choice" will be more critical in shaping patterns of social behavior.

Thus a choice perspective on the effects of location on social ties and service usage would seem to suggest benefits attached to age segregation, as noted by Rowles:

> Residential settings of statistically "normal" age composition may be excellent instruments for inadvertently alienating and demoralizing the elderly. With the attrition of ties with their family, friends and other groups, the dispersal of their age peers in a normal neighborhood reduces the number of potential friends available to them. The field of eligibles is thin and scattered, and

the isolating effects may be intensified by declines in health and physical mobility. [1978:26]

Similarly, Rosow (1967) has argued that social integration of the aged is weakened by role loss and role ambiguity. An age-concentrated environment, on the other hand, would presumably foster patterned interaction and shared values and roles to create social integration.

Indeed, much has been written on the benefits of age segregation, but little of this research or theory pertains to the evolved patterns of neighborhood segregation that characterize the metropolis. Research has focused on the age segregation in built environments—retirement communities, old-age apartment complexes, and so forth—but the age segregation found in the residential areas of the metropolis differs both quantitatively and qualitatively from that of built environments. The extent of age segregation is much less pronounced, with less clear boundaries around social territories. This fact raises some doubts as to whether social benefits present in built environs are easily translatable to the urban mosaic.

Rosow (1974) suggests that the formulation of a distinctive new role, expectations and norms appropriate to it, and a set of eligible role models will be promoted by large concentrations of elderly people who are socially homogeneous (i.e., on social class, race, marital status, etc.). Neighborhood age segregation may represent insufficiently large concentrations of age peers compared with the more complete segregation of retirement communities. Retirement communities and old-age apartments are also typically quite homogeneous on social characteristics other than age, perhaps more so than age-segregated neighborhoods. The fact that such neighborhoods are also embedded in more heterogeneous, age-integrated surroundings may further limit the emergence of age-group solidarity. Blau (1977) indicates that heterogeneity in the social and physical environment increases the probability of intergroup relations (in this case, cross-age interactions).

Nor are age-segregated neighborhoods chosen as such; rather, they are a product of ecological processes. There is no built-in incentive to construct a "community" and no structural facilitators for its emergence. Such neighborhoods lack the special design features, physical security, and congregate facilities (dining, activities, etc.) found in retirement communities and public housing for the elderly. Similarity alone is not sufficient for the emergence of social solidarity. Feld (1981) suggests that the relevant aspects of the interpersonal environment are "foci" around which individuals organize their social relations. Activities, and therefore interactions and sentiments, are organized around foci. If individuals share many foci, they are also likely to have multifaceted exchange relationships. Such foci are more likely to be present in specifically age-segregated settings—shared physical spaces and opportunities for common activities.

Furthermore, age-segregated settings should not be expected to have similar consequences for all segments of the older population. Kahana's (1982) theory of congruence outlines the dynamics of person-environment fit for older populations. In this model, individuals with certain types of needs are most likely to be found in and to seek environments that meet these needs. In later years, however, environmental choices are reduced, as is the ability to maintain preferred environments. Hence person-environment congruence becomes particularly salient. Segregation is an important aspect of the environment, with people needing either more or less of it, depending on their social and psychological characteristics.

Rosow (1967) specifically addressed the significance of age segregation for person-environment fit. He suggested that age-integrated settings work well for long-term residents of stable, homogeneous neighborhoods whose local ties have remained relatively intact. Such persons may neither need nor desire access to networks of age peers. Apparent benefits of age segregation may reflect choices and preferences that are atypical in the older population. Teaff et al. (1978), for example, found positive consequences of age concentration in a sample of public housing tenants in which 83% expressed a preference for living exclusively among age peers. Thus the benefits of age segregation here would seem to reflect a "cultural" or "choice" model of segregation. As we shall see in Chapter 6, however, the forces which produce the "urban mosaic" are complicated and do not simply reflect a choice process.

In summary, it can be argued that age segregation is a powerful environmental force in older people's lives. Nonetheless, research addressed to this point is unclear. A useful analysis of the age-segregated, suprapersonal environment requires emphasis on three related issues. First, research is needed on the functions and dysfunctions of age-segregated settings in residential neighborhoods. Second, some effort must be made to detail differences in the consequences of age segregation for different subgroups of elderly. Third, to reconcile potential contradictions in findings between the built and natural settings, it is necessary to outline the processes whereby the age-segregated urban mosaic evolves. Chapter 6 deals with these and other relevant topics.

Conclusions

Aging occurs in contexts that in turn shape the aging experience. The relationship between context and experience is complex, particularly for the elderly (Kahana, 1982; Golant, 1984). The present chapter has outlined an approach to the study of this complicated process. The approach, which we have termed an *ecosystem analysis*, generally follows the earlier work of Lawton (1970, 1982). In this view the environment is conceptualized as both a multidimensional phenomenon and a multilevel phenomenon. As a result of this complexity, individuals occupying the same environment will not necessarily experience the same environment. Because the environ is multilevel, we can speak of it as being both inside and outside the actor (Golant, 1984). At the same time the environment is a multidimensional system. The environs affecting action involve an intricate, complex hierarchy of increasing scale and remove from the individual. Each of these environments interacts with the other components and with the actor to set limits and to mold possibilities for individual meaning and experience. Individuals must adapt to these contextual conditions, but the adaptations that they make will themselves be complex. If there is a single lesson to be learned from this book, it is that environmental relations are complex and that this intricate web of relations is played out in the everyday lives of older populations. Such complexities make choices and variability in action and meaning possible and lead to a variety of aging experiences.

2　Methods of Study

Chapter 1 introduced a wide range of theoretical issues organized around the five components of the human ecosystem. These issues were addressed in an interview survey, with both the sample and the interview constructed to allow depth and detail. This chapter describes the sample, the variables incorporated in the interview, and the analytic techniques used to address the issues in Chapter 1.

The Sample

In the fall of 1980, interviews were conducted with noninstitutionalized adults aged 60 and over residing in the Albany-Schenectady-Troy, New York, Standard Metropolitan Statistical Area (SMSA). The areal range of the SMSA is as defined in 1970 and includes

Table 2.1　Characteristics of Tract Strata Defined According to Percentage Aged 60+

	Range of percentage aged 60+	Number of tracts
1. Age-concentrated young	0–12.9	35
2. Age integrated	13.0–20.9	88
3. Age-concentrated old	21.0+	31

Note: Data from the 1980 census were not available at the time of sampling. Tract characteristics are based on 1970 data used for sampling.

Albany, Schenectady, Rensselaer, and Saratoga counties. The sample included persons aged 60 and over, rather than the more typical age of 65, to encompass the period and events that lead into "old age." Such persons constituted 18.6% of the SMSA population in 1980. The sample was multistage stratified to the block level. A central interest of the original study and of this book is the impact of residential age concentration. To ensure inclusion of respondents across the range of neighborhood age structures, the 154 census tracts in the SMSA were first stratified into three groups, according to the percentage of the tract aged 60 + : (1) "age-concentrated young," or tracts in which older people are underrepresented (less than 13% aged 60 +); (2) "age-integrated," or tracts in which older people are represented more in proportion to their share of the total population of the SMSA (from 13.0% to 20.9% aged 60 +); and (3) "age-concentrated old," or tracts in which older people are overrepresented (21% or more aged 60 +). Characteristics of these tract strata are indicated in Table 2.1.

Within each stratum, households were sampled according to one of two methods. In tracts for which block statistics (and corresponding maps) were available for the entire tract, blocks were systematically sampled according to size (number of households). In tracts lacking complete block statistics, a grid was imposed over maps obtained from the New York State Department of Transportation, with areas ("blocks") sampled randomly from the grid. If the area selected appeared in block statistics, a specific block was randomly sampled. Interviewers were given a random starting household on each sampled block and were instructed to continue around the block until up to three eligible respondents (aged 60 +) had been interviewed (one per household). In households containing more than one eligible

Percentage of SMSA population		Percentage aged 60 +
Total	Aged 60 +	in stratum
25.0	15.1	9.7
59.0	60.7	16.4
16.0	24.1	23.9

respondent, a random selection procedure determined which household member was to be interviewed. Interviewers were selected, trained, and supervised by Opinion Research Corporation, a professional survey organization based in Princeton, New Jersey.

A total of 12,103 households were sampled, yielding 2,463 households with eligible respondents. Of these, 12.9% of eligible respondents were not available despite two callbacks, 39.0% were unwilling or unable to be interviewed, and 48.1% completed interviews (55.2% of eligible and available respondents). A total of 1,185 respondents were interviewed. This total includes 455 respondents in Stratum 1 ("age-concentrated young"), 387 in Stratum 2 ("age-integrated"), and 343 in Stratum 3 ("age-concentrated old"). Central-city tracts are primarily in Strata 2 and 3. Higher refusal rates in city tracts account for the lower numbers of respondents in these strata. Areal coverage is substantial, as respondents are drawn from 140 of the 154 tracts in the SMSA, with no more than 25 coming from any single tract.

Average age of respondents is 70.6, with 52% in their sixties, 34% in their seventies, and 14% in their eighties and over. The sample is overwhelmingly white (96%), and 61% of the respondents are female. Nearly half (46%) reside in one of the three central cities, 28% are "suburban" residents (urbanized area or noncontiguous urban, including the cities of Saratoga Springs and Mechanicville), and the remainder (26%) are "rural" (tracts with population of largest place less than 5,000). Respondents are long-term residents—52% have lived at their current residence for 20 years or more, whereas only 8% have lived there for less than 2 years. In addition, 61% reside in single-family dwellings, and 71% own their house, apartment, or mobile home. Half (50%) are currently married, with 39% widowed. Nearly two-thirds (64%) define themselves as retired; 11% are in the labor force; and the remainder (25%) identify themselves as housewives.

The relatively high refusal rate noted above raises some concern about the representativeness of the sample. The sample was drawn for theoretical and analytic purposes, and we make no claim that descriptive response distributions reflect population parameters. Although sample representativeness is not directly relevant to the research issues addressed here, we can nonetheless use 1980 census data for the SMSA (U.S. Bureau of the Census, 1983) and selected national data to assess possible bias in the sample. Comparisons indicate that the sample is representative on a number of counts:

1. Sixty-one percent of the SMSA older population and 62% of the sample are women.

2. Ninety-seven percent of the SMSA older population and 96% of the sample are white.
3. Sixty-five percent of the SMSA older population and 71% of the sample reside in owner-occupied housing units.
4. Seventy-three percent of older males are married and 17% widowed in the SMSA, compared with 73% and 19% in this sample; 34% of older females are married and 52% widowed in the SMSA, compared with 36% and 52% in the sample.
5. Seventeen percent of older males and 7% of older females in the SMSA are employed, compared with 16% and 9% in this sample.
6. Median length of occupancy nationally for older persons is 22 years (Struyk and Soldo, 1980), compared with about 20 years in the sample.

These patterns indicate that the older populations in the SMSA and the sample are quite congruent. Similar congruence was evident in comparisons made with national data on the older population. Descriptive information presented in subsequent chapters will also be seen to be consistent with other research. Thus there appear to be no obvious biases in the sample.

Two differences are worth noting, however. The sample is somewhat better educated than the SMSA older population; 51% and 40%, respectively, have at least a high school education. The sample also appears to be somewhat healthier; for 45% of the older population nationally, activity is at least somewhat limited owing to health impairment (U.S. Public Health Service, 1981), whereas only 29% of this sample indicate difficulty with any of four indicators of functional health (described below). This disparity may partly reflect differences between the measures used for the national figures and our own measures of functional health. The "advantages" in education and health may also reflect the fact that national data are based on the population 65 and over, whereas our sample begins with people aged 60.

Instrumentation

The interview, which was pretested on a small community sample, was approximately 1 hour in length and ranged widely across topics discussed in Chapter 1: personal characteristics of the ecological actor, the neighborhood environment, the interpersonal environment of networks and supports, orientations to aging and age peers, patterns of age concentration in neighborhoods and networks, and general assessments of well-being. Each group of variables is discussed in the following sections, and the interview schedule appears in Appendix A.

Personal Characteristics of the Ecological Actor

A good deal of literature suggests that older persons represent a rather unique set of ecological actors. The problem with such an observation, however, is the implication that the elderly are unidimensional actors. Indeed, the elderly represent a heterogeneous group, with diverse personal characteristics. In understanding the person's relationship to his or her environment, it is essential to examine these personal characteristics.

The personal characteristics incorporated into the interview include age, sex, race, ethnicity, religion (both type and importance), marital status (and length of current status), employment status, socioeconomic status, health, and housing. Measures of socioeconomic status include education, occupation (and husband's occupation for female respondents), and income. Occupation was coded into both three-digit census classifications and prestige scores employed by the National Opinion Research Center. Composite measures of family occupational status are based on the respondent's occupation for males and never-married females and on husband's occupation for ever-married females. In some analyses, a distinction is made between white-collar respondents (professional, technical, and kindred workers; managers and administrators; sales staff; clerical and kindred workers) and blue-collar respondents (craftsmen and kindred; operatives; laborers; service staff). Measures of income include subjective rating of financial adequacy (from "can't make ends meet" to "money is not a problem") and self-reports of family income and assets. There were relatively high rates of nonresponse on income (37%) and assets (46%), reflecting an unwillingness to divulge such information that is not unusual among older persons. For this reason, education and occupational prestige are generally used as socioeconomic indicators; both are strongly correlated with income ($r = .44$ and $.37$, respectively). Such indicators probably also better reflect life-style differences over the life cycle than does current income.

Health is a critical characteristic of older persons, affecting a wide range of behaviors and attitudes. Self-reported health has been shown to correlate highly with more objective indicators and therefore represents a valid, economical means of assessing the health status of older persons (LaRue et al., 1979; Ferraro, 1980). Two self-report measures of health were included in the interview. Repondents rated their health "at the present time" from "excellent" to "very poor." Functional health was assessed by items similar to the Physical Incapacity Index (Shanas et al., 1968). Respondents were asked whether they could engage in each of the following activities by themselves without difficulty, with some difficulty but still by themselves, or not without the help of another person: going outdoors, walking up and down stairs, getting around the house or apartment, and doing cleaning and other household chores. These four measures were combined into a scale of functional health ranging from 4 to 12, with 12 indicating no functional impairments. As noted earlier, most respondents exhibited little functional impairment ($M = 11.1$; $SD = 1.8$). Functional health is strongly correlated with subjective health rating ($r = .50$). As a further indicator of respondent health, interviewers were asked to indicate whether respondents exhibited any of nine physical difficulties (such as visual impairment or need for a cane). A composite score of interviewer-rated health is strongly associated with the self-report scale of functional health ($r = .49$).

Functional health is an important aspect of individuals' environmental competence (see Chapter 1). Another dimension is the actor's perceived ability to deal with environmental challenges and changes. Our research utilizes a seven-item mastery scale developed by Pearlin and Schooler (1978), measuring the "extent to which one regards one's life chances as being under one's own control" (p. 5). Pearlin and Schooler (1978) define *mastery* as a basic psychological resource constituting a critical dimension of coping. The scale has a range of 7 to 28, with a mean of 21.1 ($SD = 4.1$); reliability (Cronbach's α) is .70.

Housing information includes type of dwelling, household composition (number of residents and relationships to respondent), and whether the respondent owns, rents, or lives with others. Respondents indicated how long they had lived at their current address and in both the neighborhood and the metropolitan area, their type of previous dwelling (if less than 20 years in the current neighborhood), and the size of the place in which they had spent most of their adult life.

The Neighborhood Environment

Neighborhood denotes many things, including: (1) a small inhabited area with distinct physical boundaries, (2) the inhabitants of such an area, (3) the relations that exist among the inhabitants, and (4) friendly relations among the inhabitants (Gould, 1964). Thus both physical and social characteristics characterize the neighborhood. As a result Glass (1948) suggests that neighborhoods are distinct territorial groups with specific physical characteristics that coincide with distinct social institutions and networks. Both objective and subjective techniques have been used to delineate such areas. Glass, for example, used such objective indicators as population density, age and condition of dwellings, and ethnic, religious, and occupational composition. An alternative approach uses behavioral information about places to shop, work, and play (Keller, 1968). Subjective techniques, on the other hand, define neighborhood according to collective mental maps or boundary definitions of residents (Lee, 1970). Each of these procedures yields a somewhat different areal unit and provides a different understanding of the local neighborhood, and each is incorporated in this study.

Tract characteristics were incorporated into the data for each individual, including population characteristics (e.g., racial composition and income of the tract population) and housing characteristics (e.g., housing age and value); more precise definitions of these variables are presented in Appendix B. Interviewers were also asked to characterize the nature of housing in the area in which each respondent lived. Drawing on earlier approaches to the assessment of neighborhood use and the richness of local facilities (Cantor, 1975; Newcomer, 1976; Taub et al., 1977), respondents were asked to indicate their frequency of use, proximity, and mode of transportation with regard to each of five facilities—grocery store, drugstore, church, doctor or clinic, and bank. They also indicated whether they considered each to be "in your neighborhood." In addition respondents rated proximity and frequency of use of a bus stop, whether this bus stop was in the neighborhood, and the proximity of a club or organization for older persons. These measures assess individual mobility, behavioral definitions of neighborhood, and neighborhood convenience (or facility "richness") and usage. Finally respondents were asked to define their neighborhoods by indicating how many blocks and minutes they could "walk in any one direction before the people there would not be considered your neighbors." This question sought to measure the cognized social neighborhood.

Respondents were asked to rate their neighborhoods on a number of dimensions. Using items from the Annual Housing Survey, respondents were asked to rate the neighborhood as a "place to live," in terms of its convenience for getting together with friends and for obtaining services and in terms of the "condition of the other houses." They were also asked how happy they were "about the kind of people who live in your neighborhood" and how safe they felt "being out alone in your neighborhood." Open-ended questions assessed the "best" and "worst" things about "living in this neighborhood" and whether and how the neighborhood had been changing. Finally, several items measured the extent of "local attachment." Respondents were asked how they would feel about leaving the neighborhood, whether they were seriously thinking of moving, and how easy they thought it would be to find a new place to live.

Another locational characteristic for sample members involves urban, suburban, or rural residential contexts. As noted earlier, the sample includes representation from all three, allowing comparisons of patterns related to neighborhood satisfaction, support networks, and other characteristics. It should be noted, however, that our "rural" elderly are nonetheless residents of a metropolitan area. We cannot speak directly to issues concerning rural elderly in nonmetropolitan areas, who would perhaps represent a more "pure" form of rural residence.

The Interpersonal Environment of Networks and Supports

Support systems fulfill three major needs—socialization, carrying out tasks of daily living, and assistance during times of illness or crisis (Cantor, 1979). These functions represent both an instrumental and an expressive dimension of support. In turn, there are three basic sources for such support—kin, close friends or intimates, and neighbors. Each of these dimensions and components of support is addressed in the interview. Instrumental support is measured through availability of helpers for hypothetical situations. Expressive support is measured through items about confidants. Other questions were asked more specifically about children, other relatives, neighbors, and non-neighbor friends. In addition, Thoits (1982) indicates that social networks have both structural properties (size, accessibility, frequency, and stability) and functional properties (perceived amount and adequacy of aid), corresponding to objective and subjective dimensions. Our network variables include both objective and subjective indicators.

Instrumental support. Instrumental support was assessed by asking respondents to whom, other than a spouse, they would turn in each of

4 hypothetical situations—for someone to look in on you, to give you a ride, to get something for you at the store, and to look after your home while you are away. Cantor (1979) asked a similar question about 10 hypothetical situations, but these included both instrumental and expressive support. Our situations focus on instrumental assistance, with later questions about confidants addressing expressive support. Respondents also indicated the age and sex of helpers and whether each helper lived "in your neighborhood." More qualitatively and subjectively, respondents indicated whether they had "enough people or places to turn to for help in situations like these."

Although hypothetical measures of instrumental support (who *would* you turn to?) are commonly used, they have some potential dangers. Family members, for example, may be mentioned more often because they are normatively obligated to help. As we will see in subsequent chapters, however, these indicators are related in expected ways to such variables as family proximity; they do not simply measure norms. In addition, our interest primarily concerns available sources of support rather than actual receipt of support.

Expressive support. Expressive support was measured through the study of confidants. Definitions of "confidants" tend to stress intimacy and the sharing of confidences and feelings (Lowenthal and Haven, 1968; Cantor, 1979; Wellman, 1979). Our approach draws on this earlier work. Respondents were asked whether there was anyone "you feel very close to—someone you share confidences and feelings with" and whether any of these reside "outside of your home." A series of questions was then asked about each of the up to three confidants outside the home whom "you feel closest to." These questions included relationship of the person to the respondent (e.g., kin, friend, or neighbor); proximity and frequency of contact (face to face and by telephone and letter); duration of the acquaintance; and various social characteristics of the person (age, sex, education, ethnicity, and religion). Only age similarity between respondents and their confidants is analyzed in subsequent chapters. The other possible bases for similarity (sex, education, ethnicity, and religion) were analyzed, but the analyses are not presented because they are not relevant to our interest in age homogeneity and exhibited no association with well-being (see, e.g., Sherman et al., 1984, 1985).

To assess the subjective dimension, respondents indicated whether they had "enough opportunities" to "share confidences and feelings with another person." Although all respondents were asked the corresponding subjective question for instrumental help, this question was inadvertently asked only of those who had at least one confidant, so the variable is less powerful and meaningful than we would wish.

Family, friends, and neighbors may be cited in response to questions about both confidants and instrumental helpers, but additional questions were addressed specifically to each of these ties. Questions about family and friends were directed at availability. Questions about neighbors were more detailed, however, because the study reflected a specific interest in the neighborhood environment of older people.

Family ties. Respondents were asked whether they had any living children. If so, they indicated number of children, proximity of each child, frequency of contact with any of their children (face to face, by telephone, and by letters), and whether "you see your children about as often as you would like to." Respondents were also asked whether they had any other relatives living in the metropolitan area and how many of these were seen or heard from regularly.

Friends. Respondents indicated how many friends they had in the metropolitan area but not in the neighborhood; thus, the term *friends* is restricted in meaning to persons who are not neighbors. Care was taken to distinguish between neighbors and nonneighbor friends in two ways: (1) specific questions addressed the location of persons named as instrumental helpers and confidants, and (2) the wording of questions about nonneighbor friends stressed the distinction between friends and neighbors (e.g., "your friends who do *not* live in this neighborhood"). Respondents also indicated the age of most of their friends (from "all about 60 or older" to "all younger than 60"). They were also asked how many new friends they had made in the past year (either within the neighborhood or outside it), how many of these were neighbors, and the age of most of these new friends.

Neighbors. More detailed questions involved relations with neighbors, including socialization and both instrumental and expressive support. Respondents indicated how many neighbors they "know well enough to visit with, either in their home or yours." As with confidants, a series of questions was asked about each of the up to three neighbors the person is "friendliest with": age, sex, religion, education, and ethnicity. As with confidants, analysis is confined to age similarity between respondents and the neighbors with whom they are friendliest (analysis of gender similarity is reported in Sherman et al., 1985). Respondents also indicated how many neighbors they could "rely on for help in emergencies" and the age of those neighbors, frequency of contact with neighbors, how much they have "in common" with neighbors, and whether they have found it difficult to make close friends in the neighborhood.

Finally, respondents were asked whether they had received from neighbors or had given neighbors each of six forms of assistance: look in on you/them, give you/them rides, get things for you/them at the store, look after your/their home, talk to you/them about personal concerns and problems, and lend you/them things other than money. The first five items parallel the more general measures of instrumental and expressive support, which were asked earlier in the interview so that respondents would not be sensitized to responses about neighbors. The sixth item has been found to be an important dimension of neighborhood assistance (Sherman, 1975b; Cantor, 1979). Responses were summed into separate scores of help received and help given, each ranging from 0 to all 6 forms of aid.

In combination, both objective and subjective network dimensions were assessed in the interview. In addition to more objective measures of number, proximity, and frequency, more subjective measures related to perceived sufficiency of availability and contact for helpers, confidants, children, and neighbors. Naming kin, friends, or neighbors as helpers or confidants is also an indication of the quality of these social ties. A strength of these data is the detail available in both objective and subjective measures of social involvement and support. Liang et al. (1980), for example, used single composite measures for both objective and subjective "integration." These data differentiate both of these dimensions according to types of relationships and types of support.

*The Social Environment: Norms and
Expectations of Aging*

The older person's attitudes toward aging (both their own and that of others), as well as the person's experiences in making transitions toward the old-age role, are an important component of the social environment for aging. Several items in our survey measure attitudes toward aging and older people.

Respondents were asked to "describe most older people—aged 65 and older" by indicating whether each of a series of 11 adjectives either "very," "somewhat," or "hardly at all" fit the category. The adjectives were *wise, trustworthy, sick, friendly, flexible, tolerant, selfish, effective, active, sad, dependent.* These adjectives represent the attitudinal dimensions found in previous research on attitudes toward older people—Eisdorfer and Altrocchi's (1961) dimensions of "evaluation" (*wise, trustworthy, sick, effective, sad*) and "activity" (*active*), and Rosencranz and McNevin's (1969) dimensions of "auton-

omous-dependent" (dependent), "personal acceptability-unaccep-
tability" (selfish, flexible, sad, friendly, tolerant), and "instrumental-
ineffective" (active). Such attitudes appear to be relatively stable
characteristics; Eisdorfer and Altrocchi (1961) found test/retest stability over a 4- to 6-week period. Items were scored with higher values
for more favorable responses (e.g., "very" wise, "not at all" sad). The
composite scale of attitudes toward "most older people" has a possible range of 11–33. Following the same format, a subset of the adjectives was used to form a scale of attitudes toward "younger people—
those in their 20's"; the adjectives focus on the likely quality of inter-
generational contacts (trustworthy, friendly, selfish, tolerant). This
scale has a range of 4–12.

As a way of measuring attitudes both toward other older persons
and toward their own aging, respondents were asked to indicate
whether they considered themselves "better off, about the same, or
worse off than most other persons your age, with regard to . . . relationships with your family, social contacts other than with your family, your health, your financial situation." Results were combined into
a scale of age-peer comparisons.

Another measure of attitudes toward older persons asked whether
the respondent would "prefer to spend most of your time with people
your *own age*, with people *younger* than yourself, or with people of
different ages," with a followup question asking for the reasons. Related questions asked whether they would prefer to live in housing
limited to people their "own age" or in housing with people of "different ages" and whether respondents see both people their "own age"
and "younger people (that is, younger families, people under 40)" as
much as they would like to.

One item focused specifically on orientations toward one's own
aging. This cognitive dimension of age identification was assessed by
asking respondents whether they think of themselves as "young, middle-aged, elderly, or old" (Ward, 1977a; Bultena and Powers, 1978).

Other items can be regarded as addressing socialization for old age.
Respondents were asked whether they had a friend, relative, or neighbor who they considered "a good example of what a person should be
like in his or her old age." Several characteristics of this role model
were indicated, including age, sex, relationship to respondent, and
aspects admired. Respondents also indicated whether they had
"found people of your own age at all helpful in offering advice and
support about changes in your life such as leisure, health, retirement,
as you have grown older." If so, respondents indicated the types of

concerns for which age peers had been helpful, what types of persons had been most helpful (e.g., family, friends, or neighbors), and whether help had come mostly from persons of the same sex as the respondent.

Finally, to assess the extent to which age peers represent a separate and identifiable social group, we included items that measure involvement with and on behalf of older persons. Respondents indicated their frequency of involvement in clubs and organizations for older people. They also indicated whether they had ever "taken any action on behalf of older people" and what those actions were.

The Suprapersonal Environment: Age Concentration

The significance of metropolitan patterns of age segregation for local neighborhood resources and for personal support systems has already been outlined in Chapter 1. This research pays special attention to the impact of age concentration on physical, interpersonal, and social environments. Several measures of age concentration are used here, including assessments of neighborhood age structure as well as age of members of the network.

The measures of neighborhood age structure include both objective and subjective assessments. First, the percentage aged 60+ in the tract is incorporated in the data for each individual. These tract statistics are based on 1980 census statistics. The age composition of tracts appears to be quite stable, as there is a high correlation between percentage aged 60+ in 1970 and 1980 ($r = .74$). Second, respondents estimated the proportion of people aged 60+ in "your neighborhood." The tract data are more objective but cover a wider area (beyond the "neighborhood"), whereas respondent estimates are more subjective and localized. Respondent estimates also tend to be higher (range = 1–100; $M = 30.5$; $SD = 24.3$) than the tract data (range = 1–48; $M = 18.6$; $SD = 6.4$), a pattern also found by Lawton (1983b). Table 2.2 indicates that both measures of neighborhood age structure are strongly associated with type of tract. Analyses involving these variables were also run separately for the three tract types, to avoid confounding the effects of neighborhood age structure with those of location in the metropolis.

We should again stress that these are measures of *neighborhood* age composition, as distinct from earlier research on planned communities and age-segregated apartment buildings. There are no indications that the measure of age composition at the broad tract level is

Table 2.2   Mean Values of Neighborhood Age Structure by Type of Tract

Type of tract[a]	Percentage aged 60 + in tract	Percentage aged 60 + in neighborhood
Central city	22.5	37.0
Suburban	17.1	28.9
Rural	13.4	22.7
Overall	18.6	30.5

[a]Central city = Albany, Schenectady, Troy. Suburban = urbanized area and noncontiguous urban. Rural = tracts with largest place less than 5,000 persons.

skewed by the presence of nursing homes or retirement homes. In addition, only 14 respondents (1.2% of the sample) reside in housing they describe as "especially for older people." Thus this sample is well suited for investigating the extent to which previous findings from studies of specifically age-segregated housing can be generalized to normal neighborhood settings.

In addition to several measures of neighborhood age concentration, this study also assesses the degree of age homogeneity in the respondent's social networks. Respondents were asked to estimate the ages of friends, of neighbors with whom they are friendliest, and of persons named as confidants or as instrumental helpers.

Well-being

Aging occurs in physical, interpersonal, and social contexts that themselves shape the aging experience. Ultimately, the ecosystem approach taken in this book is useful for examining the outcomes of these contextual relationships. Several potential "outcomes" of neighborhood involvement, social support, age-related orientations, and age concentration are of interest in this study. Two general types of indicators related to well-being were included in the interview, access to services and subjective well-being.

Services. Respondents were presented with a list of five types of services for older people that were known to exist throughout the survey area. The services are indicated in Table 2.3. To assess knowledge of services, respondents were asked "as far as you know" whether each is "now available to older persons in your county." They were also asked to indicate "who or what has been your most impor-

Table 2.3 Knowledge and Use of Five Services for Older People Present in the Metropolitan Area (percent)

	Know of service	Use service
Someone who telephones or visits older persons	46	1
Facilities for group meals or delivery of meals	67	3
Legal services and advice	46	1
Visiting nurses or home health aides	66	9
Special transportation programs	63	6

tant source of information about these programs and services," whether this source (person or agency) was in the neighborhood and (if it was a person) the age and sex of the information source. Finally, respondents indicated whether they had ever used each of the services.

Table 2.3 indicates knowledge and use of the five services. Consistent with the nature of the sample, use of these formal services is quite low; the highest figure is for nursing services, and these have been used by only 9% of the sample. Knowledge that these services exist is substantially greater, however. Respondents are most knowledgeable about such now-common services as meal programs, visiting nursing services, and transportation programs, whereas slightly less than half know of legal aid and telephone/visitation programs. Thus knowledge of services for the elderly is moderately high even in the absence of use (or apparently need, because the sample is relatively advantaged). Nonetheless, between one-third and one-half of the respondents are unaware of each type of service. A summary scale of service knowledge was constructed, ranging from 0 to 5. Mean number of services known is 2.9 (SD = 1.9; Cronbach's α = .85); 31% know of all five services, whereas 20% know of none of them.

Subjective well-being. Subjective well-being has been a major empirical interest in gerontological research (Larson, 1978; George and Bearon, 1980). It can be viewed as an indicator of mental health and "successful aging" and more straightforwardly as an indicator of perceived "quality of life." Although Larson (1978) suggests that scales of morale, adjustment, satisfaction, and the like represent interrelated measures of a general underlying dimension, other observers suggest that the conceptual domain is multidimensional (Burt et al., 1978; Cutler, 1979; George, 1979; George and Bearon, 1980). Several dimensions of subjective well-being were incorporated in the interview.

One meaning of subjective well-being concerns satisfaction within specific domains (Burt et al., 1978; Cutler, 1979; Lawton, 1983a). We have already noted that the interview incorporated measures of satisfaction for several domains, including health, income, housing, neighborhood, and social contacts and supports. Other indicators represent more global measures of well-being. The global measure of well-being used in this research is morale.

Morale, or overall life satisfaction, is assessed by the 17-item Philadelphia Geriatric Center Morale Scale (Lawton, 1975). This scale taps several dimensions of subjective well-being and is a validated, internally consistent scale that has been widely used with older respondents. The scale has a range of 23 to 68 in this sample, with a mean of 51.9 ($SD = 9.2$); reliability is high (Cronbach's $\alpha = .85$).

One item in the morale scale assesses how often respondents feel lonely (from 4, "not at all," to 1, "a great deal"). Given its obvious relevance to social ties and supports, this item will receive some separate attention. The morale scale also includes an indicator of satisfaction with social involvement ("I see enough of my friends and relatives"). We were concerned that these two items would yield a built-in association between overall morale and characteristics of informal social networks. Analysis indicated that network characteristics had equivalent associations with morale both with and without those items, however, so the full morale scale was used throughout the analyses.

Analytic Techniques

Several forms of statistical analysis are used in presenting results. Simple bivariate relationships are analyzed through the use of contingency tables, correlation coefficients, and analysis of variance. These relationships are explored further using partial correlations and multiple classification analysis (MCA), a variation of analysis of variance. MCA indicates the effects of a categorical independent variable (e.g., sex) on a dependent variable (e.g., morale), net of the effects of covariates (e.g., health). Mean values are presented for the dependent variable within categories (e.g., sex differences in mean morale, controlling for the effects of health); the F test measures the statistical significance of the differences in net means. Two measures of association are generated by MCA: eta is a measure of bivariate association without controls, whereas beta measures the strength of association between the independent and dependent variables net of the effects of covariates. Beta may be interpreted as a standardized partial regression coefficient (Nie et al., 1975:417). Unless otherwise noted, functional health and socioeconomic status (education and occupational prestige) are used as controls (covariates) for both partial correlations and MCA.

Multiple regression analysis is also used in the analyses. This technique provides several types of information. The percentage of the variance in the dependent variable that is explained by the regression model is indicated by the coefficient of determination (R^2), whereas the additional variance explained by the inclusion of variables into a model is indicated by the change in R^2. Standardized regression coefficients (β) indicate the contributions of independent variables net of the effects of other variables in the model and can be compared to assess the relative contributions of independent variables. Standardized coefficients can also be used in conjunction with unstandardized coefficients to compare results of regression analysis for one subgroup with those for another.

One of the strengths of the study is that the large sample size affords unusual opportunities for subgroup analysis. We have noted the complexity of the nature and consequences of aging. The environmental-docility hypothesis, for example, suggests that the effects of environment vary across subgroups of the older population. Thus attention needs to be paid to variation in patterns of association. Particular attention is paid to more "vulnerable" subgroups, for example, people who are widowed or who have functional health impairments. Some analyses use a composite measure of "vulnerability" to heighten subgroup contrast; a low-vulnerability group is composed of persons aged 60–69 who are married and have no functional health limitations, and a high-vulnerability group is composed of persons aged 70 and over who are widowed and have some functional impairment. In a similar fashion, composite subgroups are constructed according to "competence." Competence entails both objective and subjective dimensions. With this characteristic in mind, two sample subgroups were selected to represent extremes of the competence continuum: (1) "high-competence" persons who have no functional impairments and score above the mean on the mastery scale, and (2) "low-competence" persons who have some functional impairment and score below the mean on mastery. This measure of competence can be viewed as an operationalization of the concept of environmental docility.

Analyses reported in subsequent chapters generally utilize all available data (i.e., nonmissing data) for all respondents. Subgroup analyses and multivariate analyses, however, represent some reduction in sample size for specific analyses. Sample sizes for those analyses will be noted, as appropriate, in the relevant tables.

Unless otherwise noted, all associations discussed in the presentation of results are statistically significant at the .05 level. Of course, statistical significance is not equivalent to substantive importance, particularly with a large sample size. Thus little attention will be paid to statistically significant associations that are substantively trivial except where that triviality is itself of interest. Extensive subgroup analysis in a large sample also runs some risk of uncovering essentially random variation in patterns of association. Such analyses are best viewed as exploratory, though one can place greater faith in subgroup comparisons that yield consistent patterns.

Presentation of Results

The next four chapters present the findings from the survey. The chapters are organized around the ecosystem perspective discussed earlier. Chapter 3 describes the neighborhood as a place for aging. It considers the causes and consequences of neighborhood satisfaction and local involvement, exploring the implications of both personal and locational factors in determining neighborhood quality. Chapter 4 analyzes the older person's interpersonal environment, with emphasis on the various components and dimensions of the individuals' support system and their contributions to well-being. Chapter 5 analyzes the patterns, sources, and consequences of the social environment for aging: attitudes toward aging and age peers, age identification, socialization experiences, and aging-group consciousness. Chapter 6 details the nature of age concentration in both neighborhoods and social networks, emphasizing, in particular, its consequences for the older person. Finally, Chapter 7 outlines the implications of the ecosystem perspective presented here for further research and policy.

3 The Neighborhood as a Place for Aging

It is obvious that the death of the neighborhood envisioned by a number of urban soothsayers in the 1960s and 1970s has not come to pass. Residential location still matters. The neighborhood place and space encourages certain behaviors while constraining others. At the same time, it is apparent that social ties and recreation and shopping patterns are less constrained by the friction of space than ever before. This lowered constraint is probably less true for the elderly than for others, however. Because environmental experience and choice constrict with age (Stea, 1970; Kahana, 1982), the neighborhood becomes a critical resource for action and satisfaction.

This chapter presents information concerning the neighborhood as a context for aging. It explores neighborhood usage, perceptions, and evaluations. The introductory section identifies the neighborhood in objective and subjective terms, describing cognitive reconstructions of the local area as well as levels of neighborhood use and satisfaction. The determinants of neighborhood satisfaction and use are discussed in the following sections. The implications of both personal and contextual factors are explored.

Two themes are given special emphasis. The first concerns the environmental "competence" of individuals. Objective dimensions of neighborhood quality should be more salient for the socially and physically more vulnerable segments of the aged population (Lawton, 1980). Kahana (1982) suggests that, as environmental choices are reduced by physical, social, and economic loss, a close fit between residential environment characteristics and personal characteristics and preferences becomes critical. Hence it is important to explore the differences between vulnerable and nonvulnerable groups in terms of objective neighborhood conditions, neighborhood use, and perceptions of neighborhood quality.

The second theme concerns the differences between city, suburban, and rural elderly in terms of neighborhood assessment and usage. Does the level of urbanism in the residential environment interact with other factors to produce unique neighborhood experiences? This question is central to urban sociology yet remains only incompletely answered. Classical urban theorists (e.g., Wirth, 1938) describe the urban space as diverse and potentially pathological. Contemporary social scientists, on the other hand, are divided between those who argue that urban location increases interaction and service choices (e.g., Fischer, 1975; La Gory, 1982) and those who believe that urbanism and location have almost no significance for everyday experience (e.g., Wellman, 1979). This issue is of great importance for gerontology; the elderly are predominantly urban and highly localized because of reduced mobility.

The Neighborhood: Objective and Subjective Components

The analysis of neighborhood quality and satisfaction is complicated. Residential spaces and places are not simply staging areas for human action. They consist of complex bundles of services. They are imbued with intense personal and cultural meanings, and they contain localized networks from which people choose interactions (La Gory and Pipkin, 1981). The neighborhood can also be experienced in a variety of ways, through action, orientation, feeling, and fantasy (see Chapter 1). We cannot hope to unravel all of the complexities here. Indeed, we must start simply. In this section we shall explore the importance of the distinction between the neighborhood of the mind (a place to which people feel some degree of affiliation) and the neighborhood of use (a place whose facilities and services are used by people). Objective and subjective residential spaces, although in reality intertwined, are analytically separable. To understand the significance of the neighborhood for the elderly requires consideration of both dimensions. Adequate residential and neighborhood planning cannot be accomplished without considering both the individuals' perceived fit with the environ (mental congruence) and their actual fit (behavioral congruence; Michelson, 1976). Although a high degree of mental congruence with the neighborhood context should encourage the actualization of defined needs and preferences and should enhance life satisfaction, mental congruence is distinct from behavioral congruence. This distinction is particularly important for the elderly, because aging correlates with both diminishing environmental interaction and high neighborhood satisfaction (Lawton, 1980). The apparent difference between actual use of an environment and mental reconstructions of that environment suggests the value of exploring neighborhood use, neighborhood definition, and satisfaction separately.

Social and Service Neighborhoods

Our own data make clear that individual definitions of the neighborhood are complex. In the research we asked people to think of their neighborhoods in several ways, as a place populated by "neighbors" and as a place containing "services." When respondents are asked to estimate the boundaries of the neighborhood by focusing on the people contained there ("how many blocks . . . before the people there would not be considered your neighbors?"), the mean estimated radius is 3.7 blocks, with a modal response of 1 block. The resulting area is comparable to Regnier's (1981) finding for a sample of persons in Los Angeles who were 60 and above. Average estimated walking time to reach the "edge" of this imaged neighborhood is 13 minutes. The area is delineated by some basic mental affiliation with the others who share the defined space. It is properly both a social area and a neighborhood of the mind and can easily be covered on foot by a reasonably healthy person.

Thus the subjectively defined social neighborhoods of these older respondents are delimited but not strikingly so. It is noteworthy, however, that many respondents found it difficult to define their neighborhoods; 35% could not estimate the number of blocks in their neighborhoods, and 38% could not estimate walking time to the neighborhood edge. Persons with some functional health impairment were more likely to be unable to estimate blocks (42%), and both persons with some health impairment (52%) and city residents (44%) were more likely to be unable to estimate minutes. Health and location otherwise have little significance for neighborhood definition, except that rural residents estimate greater walking time ($M = 15.4$ minutes) than suburban (12.8) and city residents (11.6). Older persons generally, and certain subgroups in particular, appear to be less familiar with this neighborhood, perhaps because they venture out less often and experience the neighborhood in more vicarious fashion. Such findings seem to underline the importance of aspatial social linkages, an idea that gains some support from existing literature. Adams (1986), for example, shows that the elderly were able to maintain close personal relations with old friends in spite of the absence of face-to-face contact. Unruh (1983), in another context, demonstrated the significance of invisible "social worlds" for the lives of certain subgroups of elderly. By watching television, talking on the telephone, writing letters, and reading specialized newsletters and magazines, people can develop and maintain ties with aspatial groupings of others.

When people were asked to focus on their use of services, they drew different neighborhood boundaries than when they were asked directly to describe the bounds of their imaged social neighborhood. Table 3.1 indicates that a large majority of respondents use each of the five basic community services assessed in the interview. In addition, four of the services used are considered to be in the neighborhood by most respondents (the services of a doctor being the exception). This service neighborhood is larger in area than the social neighborhood, however. Although the social neighborhood is easily walkable, the service area is not. Eighty-one percent of the sample describes a service area at least seven blocks in radius. This radius is beyond recommended service distances (Newcomer, 1976). It appears that this does not prevent service use by relatively capable older persons, but such use entails some cost.

In response to a question about travel to the five services, the overwhelming majority of respondents said they use a private automobile. The average number who drive or are driven to the five service facilities is 79%, whereas 18% walk and 3% take some form of public

Table 3.1   Characteristics of Five Basic Community Services (percent)

	Grocery	Church	Drugstore	Doctor	Bank
Ever use	89	74	81	88	86
Use weekly[a]	91	73	20	3	23
Distance[a]					
1–3 blocks	24	22	20	5	17
4–10 blocks	15	18	15	6	14
In "neighborhood"[a]	59	59	55	28	53

[a]Percentage of respondents who ever use each service.

transit. The service area is not a walking neighborhood for this sample, yet a significant portion of respondents consider four of the five services they use to be in their neighborhood. This is true despite the fact that for most respondents these services are beyond the 3–4-block radius of their social neighborhood.

Clearly, people are making rough distinctions between two types of neighborhood areas. The *social neighborhood* is a small, walkable space. It involves mental affiliation with a real grouping of people. The larger, less walkable service territory is a *neighborhood of use.* This area is also recognized as neighborhood, but here people are asked to think about how they use local spaces rather than to consider mental affiliation with local groupings of people. Thus as noted by Stea (1970), home space is defined along multiple dimensions.

Neighborhood Satisfaction

As the discussion of neighborhood use and definition indicates, the neighborhood is a complex cognitive construction. This complexity should be reflected in expressions of neighborhood satisfaction. Layers of cognitive constructs are imposed between the objective neighborhood and the personal experience of the local area. Satisfaction may have little relation to reality.

Lawton (1980) argues that a considerable body of evidence has accumulated suggesting that older persons are generally more likely to express satisfaction with their environment than younger people. This tendency to describe the neighborhood in positive terms is clearly evident in our sample. An overwhelming majority of respondents (85.2%) rate the neighborhood as a "good" or "excellent" place to live. Local attachment is also strong, as 81% say they would feel sorry or very sorry if they had to move away. One important reason for this expressed satisfaction and attachment may be that it reduces cognitive dissonance (the disparity between objective and subjective aspects of the environment). Evidence for this point is twofold. First, most members of the sample (73%) believe that it would be difficult to find a new place to live (27% "fairly" difficult, and 46% "very" difficult). This perception makes it likely that any dissonance between expectations and actuality will be resolved by inflating satisfaction levels. Only 8% of the respondents say that they are "seriously" thinking of moving in the next year or so. Second, not only do the conditions exist to encourage inflated expressions of satisfaction, but this perception of movement difficulty is correlated with satisfaction levels (.11 with general neighborhood rating, .16 with expressed "happiness" about neighbors).

At this point, it is worth asking what factors are associated with perceived difficulty of movement. Location does not seem salient, because type of tract (city, suburban, rural) is not related to movement difficulty. Personal characteristics associated with vulnerability (see Chapter 2) are related, however. Perceived movement difficulty is related to age ($r = .15$), being female (.18), lower income (.15) and education (.12), widowhood (.17), functional health limitations (.08), and lower perceived mastery (.11). Sixty-five percent of respondents in their eighties, for example, say it would be "very difficult" to move, compared with 41% of those in their sixties; similar comparisons yield 55% of persons with health limitations versus 43% of those with none and 54% of widowed versus 39% of married respondents. Thus more vulnerable subgroups of the older population are susceptible to residential dissonance and inflated estimates of neighborhood satisfaction.

Although dissonance plays a role in neighborhood satisfaction, clearly other factors are also at work. Perhaps the most significant factors are what Lawton (1980) terms "age-related" and "cohort-specific" limitations on aspiration levels. The age-related limitation stems from the fact that future chances for change are reduced with age, hence the elderly are more easily satisfied. "Cohort-specific effect" refers to the very different socialization experiences of today's elderly and young. The elderly's childhood socialization with a more traditional family system may have engendered a reluctance to question the status quo, leading to higher expressed satisfaction.

It is also conceivable that the positive valuation of place by the aged may be influenced by a relatively more favorable environment. Sample members do live in tracts with slightly more desirable characteristics than the average in the metropolitan region. Median tract income is $10,729 for the sample, for example, and $10,644 for the Standard Metropolitan Statistical Area, and percentage of vacant units is 3% for the sample and 4.4% for the SMSA. The very high satisfaction of this population, however, cannot be explained by these very small differences in the objective neighborhood environment. This fact will become clearer in the section dealing with the determinants of satisfaction.

Satisfaction, it appears, is characteristic of the elderly. That is not to say that satisfaction levels are uniformly high among the aged. To understand the determinants of satisfaction requires clear conceptualization of the components of stated satisfaction. That is, it is important to distinguish the varied aspects of the perceived neighborhood that could influence satisfaction.

Our interview provides information on a variety of neighborhood attitudes. In a series of Likert-type items, questions were asked about the following aspects of the neighborhood: physical appearance, convenience, neighbors, neighborhood safety, attitude toward moving, neighborhood change, and overall neighborhood rating. Additional information was provided by open-ended questions asking respondents to list the worst and best features about living in their neighborhood.

What aspects of the perceived neighborhood contribute to satisfaction or dissatisfaction? Respondents are most satisfied with the people who make up their neighborhood. Sixty-three percent are very satisfied with the "kind of people" in their neighborhoods, whereas only 3% describe themselves as "not at all happy." The significance of the social environment for satisfaction is underscored when people are asked to list the best and worst things about their residential area. The three most cited neighborhood assets were: neighbors (52%), peace and quiet (41%), and convenience to shopping (31%). The implication is that, while an overwhelming majority of people are happy with their neighbors, this "happiness" is still salient for satisfaction. In other words, "happiness" with fellow residents matters to people and should influence the degree of satisfaction with the environment.

When people are asked to find things wrong with their neighborhood, they seem to respond with difficulty; 43% cannot find anything wrong. Noise level, traffic, and neighborhood maintenance are the most frequent complaints, accounting for 30% of all negative responses. Thus the neighborhood is highly valued by most respondents. Features of the physical environment, when salient, seem to operate to create dissatisfaction as often as satisfaction. The social environment, on the other hand, usually encourages satisfaction when it is a salient feature for the individual.

Indeed, the social environment is both salient and satisfying for this sample of the elderly. Respondents almost uniformly express some liking for their neighbors, and neighbors seem a common source for neighborhood satisfaction. In Chapter 6 we will investigate this issue more closely in looking at the age composition of neighborhoods and social networks.

In addition to neighbors, respondents are overwhelmingly satisfied with neighborhood maintenance, convenience, and security. Only 5%

see their neighborhoods as not very well kept up or as poorly kept up. Similarly, 93% describe their neighborhoods as safe most of the time (including 55% as safe all of the time). Only 17% and 15%, respectively, describe the neighborhood as inconvenient for shopping and visiting. This statistic is significant because we have already noted that service usage generally extends beyond recommended distances (Newcomer, 1976).

The overwhelming satisfaction of the elderly with their neighborhoods seems to suggest a high degree of "mental congruence" or fit with the neighborhood. Is this "fit" rooted in behavioral experiences? The data seem to suggest not, at least not in any simple or straightforward way. Perceived neighborhood quality is basically unrelated to service usage. General neighborhood satisfaction, for example, is unrelated to proximity or frequency of use of neighborhood services.

The lack of relationship between neighborhood use and neighborhood satisfaction coupled with the tendency to inflate satisfaction estimates may seem to suggest that perceptions of neighborhood quality have little bearing on individual well-being. Such is not the case. Neighborhood satisfaction contributes significantly to general feelings of well-being. When health, education, and occupational prestige are controlled, overall morale is correlated with general neighborhood satisfaction ($r = .14$), happiness with the kind of people in the neighborhood (.13), perceived safety of the neighborhood (.16), and the convenience of the neighborhood for shopping (.19) and visiting with friends (.23). Other things being equal, neighborhood satisfaction makes an important contribution to quality of life and is thus a critical policy goal.

Use and satisfaction appear unrelated. What factors influence perceptions of the local residential area? This question is significant to both sociologists and planners. Rapoport (1977) distinguishes between the "potential" environment (the one that is designed) and the "effective" environment. A potential environment becomes "effective" only when it is accepted and used. Acceptance is dependent on both contextual conditions and personal characteristics. Although these factors are related in complex ways to acceptance, we shall examine correlations as an initial exploratory device.

The neighborhood is a physical, social, and cultural context. The objective dimensions of the environment that are considered to be salient for use and satisfaction are diverse (Michelson, 1976; Rapoport, 1977). Several aspects of the residential context, however, are nearly always identified by sociologists as critical to the local environmental experience. One of these is the degree of urbanism in the area of residence. Community sociologists emphasize the role of urbanism in transforming local community life-styles and perceptions. Classical theorists such as Wirth (1938) stress the likely pathological consequences of densely populated residential arrangements characteristic of central cities. Contemporary theorists such as Fischer and Stueve (1977) argue that these urban locales are not necessarily prone to pathology but do differ from other residential contexts in the amount of choice they offer residents. Whichever approach one takes, it is clear that urbanism matters. Persons living in central cities should have levels of neighborhood satisfaction and patterns of service use that differ from those of people living in suburbs or rural areas.

In addition, ecological research in the social area and factorial ecology traditions (Shevky and Bell, 1955; Schwirian, 1974) identify several other contextual conditions that represent bases for life-style variations in local residential areas. These dimensions include socioeconomic status (SES), life cycle status, race, and mobility factors. Census data for residential tracts can be used to identify these dimensions of the objective neighborhood context. The SES of a tract is measured by median household income and median education. Life cycle status is indexed by percentage aged 60 and over in the tract, race by the proportion of nonwhite, and mobility by the percentage of

Table 3.2   Zero-Order Correlations between Neighborhood Context and Neighborhood Satisfaction Variables

	General neighborhood satisfaction	Happy with neighbors	Feelings about moving	Feelin about safet
Urbanism of Neighborhood[a]	−.19	−.12*	−.11*	−.21
Percentage aged 60 +	−.20*	−.15*	−.09*	−.25
Average income	.32*	.20*	.14*	.17
Average education	.30*	.16*	.13*	.14
Percentage of blacks	−.25*	−.15*	−.13*	−.20
Percentage of vacant housing	−.24*	−.20*	−.13*	−.10

*p = .05.

vacant housing units. These factors, along with the level of urbanism in the tract (city, suburb, rural), are primary indicators of neighborhood context.

These "objective" aspects of the local context are, however, not experienced in uniform ways. The individual's environmental experience is the result of cognitive and perceptual filters conditioned by social position, cultural values, and personal biography. Contextual effects are individually experienced. An understanding of the neighborhood experience for the elderly, then, requires consideration of both contextual conditions and individual characteristics.

Contextual Variables as Correlates

Table 3.2 presents zero-order correlations between objective neighborhood conditions (the context variables) and a variety of measures of neighborhood satisfaction. It is obvious from these data that neighborhood context variables are generally related to resident's level of satisfaction. Each of the contextual factors is significantly related to general neighborhood satisfaction, satisfaction with neighbors, reluctance to move, feelings of neighborhood security, and satisfaction with neighborhood maintenance. Only assessments of neighborhood change and convenience have weak associations with the majority of the contextual factors.

Neighborhood maintained	Neighborhood changing	Shopping convenience	Visiting convenience
−.11*	.02	.20*	.14*
−.20*	.02	.09*	.09*
.35*	.06*	.09*	.04
.32*	−.08*	.08*	.03
−.28*	.14*	−.07*	−.00
−.24*	.00	−.09*	−.04

aUrbanism coded: city = 3, suburban = 2, rural = 1.

Convenience seems to be a derivative of metropolitan location. Urban neighborhoods are judged convenient and decentralized neighborhoods inconvenient. Racial composition appears to be the key barometer of the individual's assessment of neighborhood change, as higher proportions of blacks are associated with the perception that the neighborhood is changing. Neighborhoods with higher proportions of blacks may be the neighborhoods that are undergoing racial transition. Not surprisingly, perceived neighborhood quality is associated with more objective measures of quality. Table 3.2 indicates that neighborhood satisfaction variables are positively correlated with the average income and education of tract residents and negatively correlated with the presence of vacant housing.

Of particular interest to us are the relationships of urbanism and age segregation to neighborhood satisfaction. The central-city elderly are clearly less satisfied with their area of residence than suburbanites and ruralites (Table 3.3). Lowered satisfaction manifests itself in the city resident's greater concern for safety and unhappiness with neighbors. These findings seem to support the arguments of classical urban

Table 3.3   City-Suburban-Rural Differences in Neighborhood Satisfaction (percent)

	City	Suburban	Rural
Neighborhood "excellent" place to live	35	60	51
"Very happy" with people in neighborhood	56	73	64
Would be "very sorry" to move	41	53	57
Feel safe "all of the time"	45	62	67
Other houses "well kept up"	49	78	55
Neighborhood changed in past few years	48	40	48
"Very convenient" for shopping, etc.	60	59	36
"Very convenient" for visiting friends	55	57	40

theorists such as Wirth (1938). The diversity of life-styles and the greater exposure to strangers characteristic of the urban world are less likely to produce a sense of trust and predictability among the urban elderly. This lack of trust and predictability may erode the residents' sense of security as well as their general degree of satisfaction with neighbors. Such potential costs of being urban and elderly, however, are partly balanced by the convenience of this location for shopping and visiting friends (Table 3.3). The choice of residential location represents a series of tradeoffs among convenience, space, and other life-style concerns. Although these tradeoffs are undoubtedly real, it is clear from the general differences in satisfaction levels manifested by city, suburban, and rural respondents that residential location is not a simple function of choice. Central-city residents are clearly less satisfied with their location, suggesting that their residential options may more often be closed.

Just as the urbanite is less satisfied with the neighborhood environment, so also are those elderly residing in more age-concentrated areas. Table 3.2 indicates that age density in the tract is negatively correlated with the various indicators of neighborhood satisfaction. The negative association between age concentration and neighborhood satisfaction is surprising. We noted in Chapter 1 that current work in ecology and gerontology hints at the positive effects of life-style segregation, as neighborhood satisfaction is likely to be greater among people similar in status, preference, and needs who reside in close proximity to one another. Homogeneity makes for similar environmental demands and thus greater likelihood that the demands can be met. In addition, such clustering is believed to promote trust and predictability in neighbor relations (Rapoport, 1977). The elderly in our sample who reside in more age-concentrated areas, however, express less local satisfaction.

Age concentration does not occur randomly in the urban space. Age density in the tract, for example, is positively correlated with high concentrations of low-income and black residents. In particular, neighborhood age structure is strongly associated with urbanism (see Chapter 2). Table 3.4 indicates that the apparent negative contributions of age concentration are largely eliminated when urbanism is controlled. Indeed, tract age density is positively correlated with general neighborhood satisfaction, happiness with neighbors, and perceived adequacy of neighborhood maintenance among city residents. Neighborhood age homogeneity may yield unique benefits in the more complex social environment of the city. Recent work in urban ecology (Rapoport, 1977; La Gory and Pipkin, 1981; Lofland, 1985) argues that segregation is a critical adaptation to complex environments. In this view, the environmental complexity of the city produces a greater likelihood of stimulus overload and exposure to strangers and to unconventional norms. This exposure creates a less predictable social environment. As Rapoport (1977) indicates, however, the limited predictability of the urban environment can be alleviated by the development of homogeneous residential areas. These segregated neighborhoods ensure that space will be shared with people of similar backgrounds and interests. In short, urbanism, with its potential crisis of trust and predictability, makes the positive benefits of segregation more salient for its residents. Perhaps complex environments make the positive consequences of age segregation more critical to the resident.

Although age concentration may be beneficial in urban areas, these same positive consequences are not apparent in rural and suburban tracts. In rural areas, there appears to be no relationship between age segregation and neighborhood satisfaction. In suburbs, on the other hand, persons in age-concentrated areas are actually more fearful. We can explain the absence of benefits from age segregation in rural and suburban areas in terms of the salience concept. Suburban and rural communities are less complicated physical and social environments. In such communities, the positive consequences of a segregated neighborhood may be nullified or even outweighed by its dysfunctions. The smaller size of suburban and rural community populations is likely to promote strong community ties to begin with, hence segregation does not contribute a needed ingredient to the social dynamic. In this case, segregation might actually serve to isolate a population from the larger community and increase the resident's sense of vulnerability. Perhaps for this reason, in our sample suburbanites residing in age-concentrated settings are actually more fearful.

This explanation, however, is not completely satisfactory because it predicts no differences between suburban and rural places with regard to the consequences of age segregation. Both are "simpler" environments, and the positive results of age segregation should therefore be less salient, but why suburban age segregation has negative results although rural age segregation shows no effect cannot be explained satisfactorily. The most likely reason for the negative consequences in suburbs is that age-dense suburbs tend to be older, poorer, and located closer to the central city of the metropolis (Fitzpatrick and Logan, 1985). In this case age density may be merely a proxy for a collection of negative environmental factors.

Table 3.4   Zero-Order Correlations of Tract Age Density (Percentage Aged 60 +) with Measures of Neighborhood Satisfaction, by Type of Tract

	City	Suburban	Rural
General neighborhood satisfaction	.16*	− .01	.06
Happiness with neighbors	.19*	− .08	− .00
Neighborhood maintained	.10*	.07	.08
Feelings about neighborhood safety	− .05	− .23*	.09

*p = .05.

On the whole, then, age concentration per se appears to make only weak contributions to perceptions of neighborhood quality. Regarded in another way, such perceptions also appear to have little bearing on preferences for age segregation. Respondents were asked whether they would prefer to live in housing limited to their age group. Such a preference is not related to general neighborhood satisfaction, happiness with neighbors, attitudes about neighborhood maintenance or change, feelings of safety, or perceived convenience of the neighborhood. When critical personal characteristics (functional health, socioeconomic status, and age) are controlled, there is a tendency for persons to prefer age-segregated housing if they feel they have little in common with neighbors (.09) or if they have found it hard to make friends in the neighborhood (.10), but these associations are small. Preference for age-concentrated housing does not appear to be a function of the quality of current residential environment; rather, it represents a response to such personal factors as health, socioeconomic status, and availability of social support (see Chapter 6 for further discussion of this issue).

Personal Characteristics as Correlates

Although ecological and contextual factors are significantly related to neighborhood attitudes, personal characteristics are less consistently associated with perceived neighborhood quality. The zero-order correlations between personal characteristics and measures of neighborhood satisfaction are summarized in Table 3.5.

The basic demographic characteristics of age, sex, and race exhibit only scattered associations with neighborhood satisfaction. Age has little bearing on the various components of neighborhood satisfac-

Table 3.5 Zero-Order Correlations between Personal Variables and Neighborhood Satisfaction

	General neighborhood satisfaction	Happy with neighbors	Feelings about moving	Feeling about safety
Age	.00	.06*	.09	−.06*
Sex[a]	−.01	−.02	−.10*	.20*
Race[b]	.15	.06*	−.05	−.12*
Income	.09	.02	−.02	.15*
Education	.13*	.05	.03	.04
Occupational prestige	.09*	.04	.03	.01
Widowed	−.04	.05	−.01	−.11*
Household size	.01	−.05	−.05	.10*
Dwelling type[c]	−.18*	−.11*	−.08*	−.16*
Years at present residence	−.01	.04	.15*	−.02
Health	.11*	.04	.00	.13*
Mastery	.11*	.05	.02	.14*
Difficult to move	.11*	.16*	.36*	−.01

*p = .05.
[a]Male = 1. Female = 0.

tion. Males consider their neighborhoods safer and more convenient for visiting. Whites are more generally satisfied with their neighborhoods than are blacks, though they perceive their neighborhoods to be less safe. Socioeconomic status has positive associations with neighborhood satisfaction, but the coefficients are not substantial. Widowhood has little bearing on neighborhood perceptions, except that the widowed are slightly more likely to view their neighborhoods as unsafe. For the most part, these associations can be at least partly accounted for by the relations between personal characteristics and urban location; nonwhite and widowed respondents, and those with lower SES, are more likely to reside in central-city neighborhoods that are typically less secure and more complex. Stinchcombe et al. (1980)

Neighborhood maintained	Neighborhood changing	Shopping convenience	Visiting convenience
− .05	− .08	− .09*	− .06*
− .01	− .00	.06	.11
.18*	− .01	− .05	− .03
.18*	.10*	.15*	.07*
.16*	.02	.11*	.10*
.11*	.03	.19*	.10*
.01	.09*	− .09*	− .04
.07*	.05	.05	.02
− .20*	− .01	.05	.08*
.00	.19*	− .02	− .01
.10*	.04	.12*	.10*
.13*	.06*	.23*	.22*
.05	.02	.04	.03

bWhite = 1. Nonwhite = 0.
cSingle-family house = 1. Multifamily house = 2. Apartment building = 3.

suggest that a sense of environmental security or fear is produced by a variety of factors, the most important of which may be the objective risks associated with one's most often used environments. The authors show that people who spend the majority of their day in urban neighborhoods that are racially integrated run a disproportionately higher risk of being exposed to harmful situations. If those same people spend much of their days and nights alone (as in the case of the widowed), these risks are even greater. In essence, Stinchcombe would argue that a sense of insecurity is caused by dangerous settings more often than by fearful people. The evidence, however, is far from clear.

Other personal variables show only mixed effects on neighborhood attitudes. Respondent's housing experiences, for example, exhibit scattered associations with neighborhood satisfaction. Not surprisingly, length of residence is positively related to the perception that the neighborhood is changing. Length of residence is also related to local attachment, as persons who have lived at their current address for a long time tend to be more likely to express sorrow at the prospect of moving. Finally, apartment dwellers express less satisfaction with the neighborhood in all aspects. This relationship disappears, however, when residential location is controlled, reflecting the tendency for apartments to be concentrated in the central city.

Although the age of the respondent appears to have little bearing on neighborhood satisfaction, Table 3.5 indicates that certain characteristics associated with aging (functional health and mastery) are related to neighborhood attitudes. These two factors represent significant dimensions of what Lawton (1980) has called the environmental docility of a subset of the elderly. We shall examine the significance of docility for environmental attitude formation later in this chapter. One additional relationship bears mention. Older persons who say it would be hard to move from their home express greater general satisfaction with their neighborhood and their neighbors and are more negative about the prospect of moving. Ease of movement is an indicator of the potential for cognitive dissonance; dissonance, in turn, was mentioned earlier as one possible explanation for the tendency of older persons to inflate their level of environmental satisfaction.

An Overall Model

To this point we have reviewed the correlates of neighborhood attitudes without considering the determinants of attitude formation. What factors contribute to the older person's view of the local area of residence? Table 3.6 reports multiple regression results for a model of overall neighborhood satisfaction. This regression was initially run with all the contextual and individual variables listed in Tables 3.2 and 3.5 as well as with four neighborhood attitudes—safety, happiness with neighbors, neighborhood maintenance, and neighborhood change. Only variables with significant coefficients are reported in Table 3.6. (All subsequent regression models reported in this chapter follow the same format used for Table 3.6. Because the strategy here is to explore relations, stepwise regressions are run in two stages, an initial exploration stage and a final model stage. Initial variables in the model include the contextual variables in Table 3.2 and the individual variables in Table 3.5 as well as the neighborhood attitude variables mentioned above.)

Table 3.6 Multiple Regression Analyses of General Neighborhood Satisfaction

	General neighborhood satisfaction
Neighborhood maintained	.32
Happy with neighbors	.34
Safety	.12
Neighborhood change	−.12
Median income	.12
R^2	.44

Note: The standardized regression coefficients reported are statistically significant at $p = .05$. $N = 1,079$.

As Table 3.6 indicates, overall satisfaction with the local area is the result of both perceived and objective conditions in the neighborhood. Favorable perceptions are most significantly influenced by the respondent's positive views of the neighborhood as physical context (neighborhood maintenance) and social context (happy with neighbors). Perceptions of local change and safety, although important to overall satisfaction, contribute less significantly to general neighborhood satisfaction than do these perceptions of local physical and social context. Surprisingly, contextual variables, although related to satisfaction (see Table 3.2), show little causal influence. Only neighborhood income contributes significantly to neighborhood satisfaction, with an R^2 change of only 1.2%.

It is of interest to note that neither personal status variables nor objective neighborhood conditions play much direct role in the evolution of an overall attitude about the neighborhood. This fact lends support to the contention of Rowles (1978) that the elderly respond to a mentally constructed environment rather than to an objective one. Although the environment to which all people respond is cognitively constructed rather than "real," we might ask whether cognitive reality, and indeed "fantasy," is not more significant for the aged population, as they are more likely to experience space vicariously through passive observation.

Environmental Docility

The suggestion that mental constructions of the neighborhood are important to neighborhood satisfaction leads inevitably to larger

Table 3.7 Zero-Order Correlations of Selected Personal and Contextual Variables with Neighborhood Satisfaction, by Vulnerability

	Not vulnerable		
	General neighborhood satisfaction	Happy with neighbors	Feelings about safety
PERSONAL:			
Education	.17*	.13*	.10
Occupational prestige	.22*	.04	.05
No. of neighbors known	.03	.16*	.10
Frequency of seeing neighbors	.07	.11	.11
Number of neighbors for emergencies	.19*	.17*	−.00
Years at current address	.05	.11	.02
Difficult to move	.23*	.15*	.02
CONTEXTUAL			
Percentage aged 60+	−.07	−.05	−.20*
Urbanism[a]	−.19*	−.15*	−.23*
Housing type[b]	−.30*	−.25*	−.11
Neighborhood type[c]	.08	−.09	−.06
Percentage of blacks	−.21*	−.13*	−.12*
Tract income	.29*	.14*	.01
Percentage vacant	−.21*	−.21*	.02

*p = .01.
Note: Not vulnerable = 60–69, married, no health limitation. Vulnerable = 70+, widowed health limitation.

questions about the role of environmental competence in the formation of neighborhood perceptions. The concept of environmental docility asserts that certain subsets of the elderly will be more affected by the environmental context than others (Lawton, 1980). The less competent the individual (socially, psychologically, and economically), the greater the impact of environmental factors on that individual. Although the elderly as a social group are more environmentally vulnerable, some are more vulnerable than others. Lawton and Nahemow's theory (see Chapter 1) predicts an interaction between

| | Vulnerable | |
General neighborhood satisfaction	Happy with neighbors	Feelings about safety
.05	.16	.03
.06	.05	.00
.03	.13	.09
.11	.26*	.07
−.03	.17	.15
−.03	.06	−.03
.09	.28*	−.03
.06	−.03	−.18*
−.25*	−.25*	−.22*
−.31*	−.31*	−.17
−.24*	−.22*	−.12
−.36*	−.36*	−.24*
.36*	.32*	.24*
−.28*	−.30*	−.09

[a]City = 3. Suburban = 2. Rural = 1.
[b]Mostly single-family houses = 1. Mostly apartments = 2.
[c]Entirely residential = 1. Mostly residential = 2. Mostly commercial = 3.

environmental docility and objective tract conditions in the determination of neighborhood perceptions and behaviors.

To operationalize environmental docility, we categorize respondents into composite subgroups along two dimensions. The first, which we term *vulnerability*, compares persons aged 60–69 who are married and have no functional health limitations with persons aged 70 and over who are widowed and have some functional health limitation. The second, which we term *competence*, compares persons who have no functional health limitations and score above the mean in mastery with persons who have some functional health limitation and score below the mean in mastery. When we combine objective (functional health) and perceived measures of competence (mastery), this last group is closest to Lawton's (1980) description of those who are likely to be environmentally docile.

Table 3.7 presents zero-order correlations of indicators of neighborhood satisfaction (general satisfaction, happiness with neighbors, and feelings of safety) with selected personal and contextual variables for the two "vulnerability" subgroups. The data in Table 3.7 indicate that neighborhood perceptions are more sensitive to contextual factors in the "vulnerable" group, supporting the docility hypothesis. In particular, the commercial-residential mix of the tract (neighborhood type), percentage of blacks in the tract, and average family income in the tract exhibit considerably higher correlations with neighborhood attitudes in the vulnerable group. Vulnerable persons living in low-income or racially mixed areas are generally less satisfied with the neighborhood and with neighbors and express greater concern for safety. In addition vulnerable elders in neighborhoods with a higher concentration of commerce are more dissatisfied with the neighborhood, the security it offers, and their neighbors.

The salience of context for the vulnerable category may not be a simple function of the group's docility. It is possible that the residential context for this group may be less desirable, because the group has fewer resources to use in responding effectively to environmental change. In fact, zero-order correlations suggest that the vulnerable live in a more "ideal-typical" urban environment portrayed by classical city theorists. The percentage of older persons in a tract is more strongly correlated with percentage black for the vulnerable subgroup ($r = .31$) than for the nonvulnerables ($r = .05$). Furthermore, tract urbanism is more strongly correlated with percentage black ($r = .38$ for vulnerables, $r = .25$ for nonvulnerables), with the concentration of high-density housing ($r = .65$ vs. $r = .54$) and with commercial concentration ($r = .31$ vs. $r = .14$). The vulnerable group is thus concentrated in places that could be labeled *transitional and mature urban areas*.

The contrast between vulnerable and nonvulnerable subpopulations becomes even more apparent when multiple regression results are analyzed (Table 3.8). This regression was initially run in exploratory fashion, with all the personal and contextual variables in Table 3.2 and 3.5 included. The patterns in Table 3.8 suggest clear differences in the determinants of neighborhood ratings for the two groups.

Several variations are worth particular mention. The perception of change is a significant force in the formation of neighborhood ratings for the vulnerable group, offering support to the environmental docility hypothesis. The perception of environmental change produces strong negative definitions of the local area by more vulnerable elderly. The vulnerability of this subgroup also appears to prevent the typical reaction to cognitive dissonance created by the conflict between environmental options and environmental evaluations. Although the nonvulnerable population responds to its limited environmental options (difficult to move) by redefining the neighborhood in positive terms ($B = .16$), the sense of limited options has no such effect on the vulnerable group. Indeed, the perception of limited options may actually increase the negative definition ($B = -.08$), serving to reinforce this group's sense of helplessness.

Finally, social networks are of particular significance to the vulnerable subgroup. Children nearby and neighbor friends positively

Table 3.8   Multiple Regression Analyses of General Neighborhood Satisfaction, by Vulnerability

	Nonvulnerable	Vulnerable
Happy with neighbors	.37	.41
Neighborhood maintenance	.29	.25
Neighborhood change	−.09	−.31
Urbanism of tract[a]	−.10	—
Average income of tract	—	.09
Difficult to move	.16	−.08
Occupational prestige	.15	—
Number of neighbors for emergencies	—	−.19
Number of neighbors who visit	—	.11
Proximity of children	—	.10
Number of friends outside neighborhood	—	−.11
R^2	.48	.60
N	379	137

Note: The standardized regression coefficients reported are statistically significant at $p = .05$.
[a]City = 3. Suburban = 2. Rural = 1.

influence neighborhood satisfaction. At the same time, social networks do not have uniformly positive consequences for environmental assessments. The number of nonneighbor friends and of neighbors
available for emergencies is negatively related to neighborhood satisfaction. Such networks may reinforce a sense of environmental impo-
tence. Clearly these relationships are nonrecursive; negative environmental assessments produce the need for greater local instrumental
support and extralocal ties. At the same time, this protective social
shell reinforces the earlier negative definition.

Let us now turn to the "competence" subgroups, our other operationalization of environmental docility. Table 3.9 reports results of
multiple regression models of general neighborhood satisfaction for
the two competence subgroups. (As before, this model was initially
run in exploratory fashion, with all the personal and contextual variables in Table 3.2 and 3.5 included.) Comparison with the vulnerability subgroup models (Table 3.8) is instructive.

As with the vulnerable subgroup, neighborhood satisfaction for the
less competent subgroup is strongly affected by neighborhood
change. In addition urbanism and the sense of limited environmental

Table 3.9 Multiple Regression Analyses of General Neighborhood Satisfaction, by Competence

	Low competence	High competence
Neighborhood maintained	.31	.36
Happy with neighbors	.35	.25
Felt safe	.22	—
Neighborhood changing	−.19	—
Average income of the tract	.13	.14
Urbanism[a]	—	−.16
Percentage aged 60 +	.11	—
Difficult to move	—	.11
Commonality with neighbors	—	.10
R²	.54	.45
N	226	499

Note: The standardized regression coefficients reported are statistically significant
at p = .05.
[a]City = 3. Suburban = 2. Rural = 1.

options (difficult to move) have significant coefficients only in the more competent group. Several differences also become apparent in these comparisons, however. The less competent elderly's evaluation of neighborhood is strongly influenced by security concerns, but the same is not true for the vulnerable subgroup. In addition, although the vulnerable group's view of the neighborhood is affected by social networks, the less competent subgroup's neighborhood satisfaction is unaffected by such resources.

These similarities and differences between the two sets of docility subgroups permit us to identify unique attributes of these two categories of docility while at the same time providing general understanding of the importance of docility for environmental satisfaction. Let us first consider what we can say generally about docility. The two groups of "docile" elderly hold views of the neighborhood that are more predictable than the views of the less docile (for the vulnerable subgroup $R^2 = .60$; $R^2 = .48$ for the nonvulnerables; $R^2 = .54$ for the low-competence subgroup; $R^2 = .45$ for the high-competence group). This finding supports Lawton's (1980) contention that docile elderly are more sensitive to environmental factors and respond to these factors in more predictable ways. This sensitivity is most apparent with regard to their response to perceived change; change is salient for satisfaction only in the docile groups of elderly.

Although the docile elderly are generally more sensitive to environmental conditions, however, they are unaffected by the urbanism of the neighborhood. Only the nonvulnerable and high-competence subgroups' attitudes toward the neighborhood are affected negatively by the urbanness of the area. The urban pathology and distress predicted by classical theorists is apparently not experienced by the elderly with reduced physical, social, and psychological resources and abilities. Perhaps a more active life-style is necessary for the individual to experience the press or overload of the city. In this sense, restricted and more vicarious spatial experience may serve a protective function.

Although the two docile subgroups exhibit similarities, there are also important differences between them. The vulnerable group has reduced social resources. People in this group are widowed, and hence social networks are salient for the formation of neighborhood satisfaction. The same is not true for the less competent older population. This group is categorized as docile because of its self-defined inability to control and master the life situation—a situation of reduced psychological resources. The less competent elderly person's evaluation of place is strongly affected by security concerns, as reduced psychological resources make security more salient for satisfaction. For less competent individuals, social ties are insignificant for neighborhood satisfaction.

Lawton and Nahemow's (1973) docility thesis proves useful in predicting person-environment relations. Indeed our findings suggest that docility has profound impact on the neighborhood experience. The very nature of the neighborhood is different for docile and non-docile elderly; for docile groups in particular the threat of neighborhood change looms large. In spite of the utility of the docility thesis, one might quibble with the details of the portrait. The thesis assumes a "machine-based" model of environment-behavior relations. The richness of the environmental experience is seen as a function of the "quality" of the machine processing environmental inputs. In the model, machine quality (the individual's level of docility) intervenes between the objective environmental inputs. The data in Table 3.9 do not entirely support this metaphor. The significant environmental inputs are both objective and subjective. Indeed, mental portraits of the neighborhood are the most significant source of neighborhood satisfaction. This finding indicates some support for a synthesis of symbolic interactionist and traditional input-output models of environmental behavior. We shall return to this point at the end of this chapter.

Urbanism

Just as gerontological theory predicts an interaction effect between docility and neighborhood satisfaction, ecologists would argue for the uniqueness of the urban neighborhood experience. At a simple descriptive level the significance of urban residence for neighborhood satisfaction seems straightforward; urbanites are less satisfied with their neighborhood than other people. Central-city residents are less likely to describe their neighborhood as an excellent place to live, to say that they are very happy with their neighbors, or to view their neighborhood as safe. These data should not be treated as evidence for the detrimental impact of urban environments for aging. Indeed, there are several reasons for caution here. First of all, it is obvious from our earlier analysis that city residence provides certain advantages as well as disadvantages (see Table 3.3). A clear advantage is its convenience to shopping and friends. This advantage may or may not outweigh the losses of urban residence entailed in such factors as reduced security and lowered involvement with neighbors. In short, although zero-order correlations between city residence and neighborhood satisfaction suggest that urbanism influences neighborhood satisfaction, the relationship may be complex and is not necessarily additive in nature. Second, as both Gans (1962) and Fischer (1975) argue, urban residence is complicated by the fact that urbanites are sociologically different from ruralites and suburbanites. These personal factors must be controlled before we say anything definitive about the urban experience.

To demonstrate the uniqueness of urban residence, it is necessary to ask whether the degree of urbanness in the area of residence interacts with other sets of forces to produce unique determinants of satisfaction in each of three types of residential tracts. Table 3.10 reports regression models of general neighborhood satisfaction for each of three types of location—city, suburban, and rural. Only two factors are associated with satisfaction in all three places: happiness with neighbors and happiness with neighborhood maintenance. This fact suggests several things about the neighborhood experience. First, neighborhoods, no matter what their level of urbanism, are assessed in terms of neighbors and maintenance. This assessment indicates that

Table 3.10   Multiple Regression Analysis of General Neighborhood Satisfaction, by Urbanism of Tract

	City	Suburb	Rural
Happy with neighbors	.35	.33	.26
Neighborhood maintenance	.34	.14	.35
Feelings of safety	.10	.14	—
Neighborhood change	−.12	−.19	—
Tract income	.14	—	—
Percentage black	—	—	−.10
Neighborhood type[a]	—	−.11	—
Occupational prestige	—	.25	—
Mastery	—	—	.12
Married[b]	—	.10	—
R^2	.23	.31	.39
N	491	298	272

Note: The standardized regression coefficients reported are statistically significant at $p = .05$.
[a]Entirely residential = 1. Mostly residential = 2. Mostly commercial = 3.
[b]Married = 1. Not married = 0.

the neighborhood is viewed universally as both a social and a physical environment and that satisfaction on both dimensions is critical for overall residential satisfaction. Second, beyond this similarity of perspective, there are abiding differences between the three places.

It is clear that each location offers different resources and experiences and that each in turn attracts and retains populations with slightly different expectations. Table 3.10 shows no consistent relationships across areas between neighborhood satisfaction and contextual or personal background variables. Let us consider differences in contextual factors first. In cities, tract income influences neighborhood satisfaction, with persons living in poorer areas exhibiting lower levels of satisfaction. Tract income, however, has no bearing on neighborhood satisfaction beyond the central city. In rural neighborhoods the racial composition of the area influences the level of satisfaction. Evidently, such Gemeinschaft-like locations promote a sense of community and predictability in people's lives (as evidenced by the insignificance of security and change concerns), but they also encourage a degree of cultural intolerance. Finally, in suburban locations, the extent of commercial activity in the neighborhood (neighborhood type) negatively affects satisfaction, perhaps indicating that suburbanites prefer homogeneous, single-purpose residential places.

There are also differences between places in terms of the personal background factors that affect a respondent's expressed level of neighborhood satisfaction. When aspects of the perceived environment are controlled for, personal background factors (such as age, sex, marital status, and health) have no bearing on satisfaction for city residents. In the suburbs, on the other hand, several indexes of personal resources—occupational prestige and marital status—influence neighborhood satisfaction. Suburban respondents who are married or who have higher prestige tend to be more satisfied with their neighbors. In the rural place a psychological resource, perceived mastery, is important for neighborhood satisfaction. Here a feeling of control and independence is beneficial. The differences between rural and urban location with regard to personal background effects fit well with generally accepted characterization of the two places. In the suburbs family and consumption are salient to life-style; in the rural areas control or mastery is critical.

The differences in the dynamics of environmental satisfaction for various locations have significance for policy and planning. In recent years the gerontology literature has been building a case for the advantages of urban location, particularly residence in age-segregated suburban communities (Carp, 1975; Lawton, 1980). These advantages are by no means clear in Table 3.10. Although the elderly are generally satisfied with their area of residence, urban residents are clearly less satisfied with their environment than others. Furthermore, segregation by age generally exhibits no relationship with satisfaction.

Use of Neighborhood Services

To this point, we have largely confined our discussion to patterns of neighborhood perceptions. The resources available in a local area, and the use of those resources, are also important dimensions of environmental quality and well-being (see Chapter 1). This statement is particularly true for the elderly because, according to Kahana (1982), environmental options are more likely to be constrained in later years. Local satisfaction is only one aspect of the person-environment fit. Michelson (1976) suggests that "behavioral congruence" is analytically separable from mental fit or stated satisfaction. That is, the question of person-environment congruence is complicated by the fact that "saying" and "doing" are separate acts. Although the forces that determine satisfaction and use should be similar, it is necessary to treat the two separately. In this section we deal with the question of neighborhood service use and its determinants.

The neighborhood acts as the resource base for the provision of various publicly and privately supplied services. Local availability of services is of critical importance to persons who find the cost of traversing space high. The elderly, for a variety of reasons, may be especially sensitive to the "friction of distance." Reduced physical health, more limited sources of income, and widowhood tend to constrain mobility and to narrow consumption patterns spatially.

Our analysis cannot address the quality of services consumed. Clearly the friction of distance experienced by various categories of elderly will to some extent constrain the quality of services used. We cannot assess the relation between quality and mobility here, but we do look at a related issue, the question of the efficiency with which local services are used.

Data for service usage include composite information on use patterns for grocery stores, drugstores, churches, doctors, and banks. On the basis of this information, two variables were constructed that relate to the issue of efficient service usage: (1) the average frequency of service use for the five services (frequency) and (2) the average distance traversed to obtain these services (distance). These variables

Table 3.11 Zero-Order Correlations of Contextual and Personal Factors with Indicators of Neighborhood Service Use

	Frequency	Distance
CONTEXTUAL		
Urbanism[a]	−.04	−.42*
Percentage aged 60	−.05	−.36*
Percentage black	−.06	−.17*
Tract income	.05	−.25*
Percentage vacant	−.05	−.04
PERSONAL		
Age	−.15*	−.08*
Functional health	.38*	.16*
Mastery	.17*	.06
Education	.14*	.00
Widowed[b]	−.15*	−.12*
Years at current address	−.06	.02
Number of neighbors for emergencies	.06	.12*
Proximity of children	−.04	.00
Distance of service used	.18*	—

*p = .05.
[a]City = 3. Suburb = 2. Rural = 1.
[b]Widowed = 1. Married = 0.

measure one important dimension of behavioral congruence with the neighborhood environment. Simply put, they assess the degree to which costs of travel are minimized by the individual service consumer. They cannot, however, measure the degree to which the profits of travel (in terms of quality of consumed services) are maximized by that consumer.

Table 3.11 presents zero-order correlations of selected personal and contextual factors with the indicators of neighborhood service use (frequency and distance). Frequency of local service use is most strongly related to personal factors, especially functional health. The distance traveled to services is largely a function of contextual factors, however. City neighborhoods and neighborhoods with larger populations of older people tend to have smaller service territories. These are usually areas with services sufficient to meet the special needs of the population, hence service territories are smaller and service consumption does not demand large expenditures of energy in terms of number of trips and time traveled. These areas minimize travel costs and are therefore more efficient service territories. Territorial efficiency is more critical for some elderly than others, of course. Most important, functional health is a critical determinant of service consumption capacities. Good health permits a wider-ranging service territory and a greater frequency of service usage. Hence urban locations and age-segregated areas are more efficient locations for the less healthy elderly.

Environmental Docility

The data presented in Table 3.11 indicate that the most consistent and significant determinants of service use patterns are the neighborhood context and environmental competence variables. In particular, the significance of functional health for the various aspects of service consumption underscores the theme of environmental docility that is prominent in this chapter. We have already seen the significance of docility for neighborhood satisfaction (mental congruence). Because docility involves sets of personal circumstances that are likely to reduce the possibility of environmental manipulation and action, one would expect it to be even more significant for experiential congruence.

Table 3.12 presents regression models of service distance and frequency of service use for the competence subgroups. (Results for the "vulnerability" subgroups are not presented because the patterns are similar to those for the "competence" subgroups.) Neighborhood age structure (percentage aged 60 + in the tract) is the most significant determinant of distance of services used for the low-competence elderly; a high concentration of older persons appears to encourage more localized service consumption. Limited environmental options (difficult to move) also produce more local service use, whereas high socioeconomic status and perception of neighborhood change produce an expanded service territory. Of these factors, only neighborhood age concentration has any significance for the high-competence group, and its effect is comparatively weak. Although age concentration's influence on service radius is weak, urbanism plays a major role for nondocile elderly; the more urban the neighborhood, the more localized the service area. Although this relationship is certainly not surprising, significantly it does not hold for the low-competence group. Urban location per se does not confer direct service concentration advantages on more environmentally docile elderly. Urban location's indirect effects are particularly notable for this group,

Table 3.12 Multiple Regression Analyses of Distance and Frequency of Service Use, by Competence

	Distance	
	High competence	Low competence
Urbanism[a]	−.30	—
Housing type[b]	—	−.21
Neighborhood type[c]	−.13	—
Tract income	.13	—
Percentage aged 60+	−.10	−.25
Neighborhood change	—	.13
Happy with neighbors	−.10	—
Occupational prestige	—	.16
Number of neighbors for emergencies	.13	.13
Difficult to move	—	−.20
Distance of services used	—	—
Neighborhood maintained	—	—
Commonality with neighbors	—	—
Widowed[d]	—	—
Number of neighbors known	—	—
Education	—	—
Years at current address	—	—
R^2	.29	.28
N	472	211

Note: The standardized regression coefficients reported are statistically significant at $p = .05$
[a]City = 3. Suburb = 2. Rural = 1.
[b]Mostly single family = 1. Mostly apartments = 2.
[c]Entirely residential = 1. Mostly residential = 2. Mostly commercial = 3.
[d]Widowed = 1. Married = 0.

however. Two factors characteristic of cities, high concentration of elderly and neighborhood change, exert opposite effects on the radius of the service area. These mixed effects of urban location are of particular importance to planners. Urban residential location does not, by itself, confer advantages on older people with reduced competence.

As with distance of services used, Table 3.12 indicates that urbanism is the most significant determinant of frequency of service use for the high-competence subgroup; city residence is associated with

Frequency	
High competence	Low competence
.14	—
—	—
—	—
—	—
—	—
—	—
—	—
—	—
—	—
—	—
.12	.34
—	−.13
.10	—
—	−.18
—	.13
.14	—
−.09	—
.07	.20
475	220

greater use of services. Education is also of particular importance for this more able category, with higher-status persons using services more often. Such findings are not surprising or particularly noteworthy by themselves. What is interesting, however, is the near absence of these relationships for the low-competence subgroup. For the docile elderly, frequency of use is best described as a function of radius and the number of neighbors who are known. Persons who have a wide-ranging service area and a large neighborhood support group (number of neighbors known) use services most frequently. The relationship between service area radius and service utilization in the docile groups appears to reinforce Lawton's (1980) suggestion that docility enhances the significance of environment. The absence of an urbanism effect for this group also tends to support the earlier observations about urban residence. City residence confers no automatic advantage on the less able elderly. Indeed, such residence may actually negatively influence consumption patterns.

Urbanism

The significance of urbanism for service utilization raises questions about service usage in the variety of neighborhoods in the metropolitan area. Do the variety of places and spaces we call rural, suburban, and urban offer unique configurations of resources that might make service consumption patterns different in each area? Are there unique consumption styles and habits in each? Urban areas are clearly more convenient locations in a purely geometric sense. This convenience translates directly into more localized service areas, with urban places being the most compact and rural areas having generally decentralized service areas. This relation between urbanism and distance to services does not, however, mean that ruralites use services less often than others. In fact, ruralites and urbanites travel about as often for services, whereas suburbanites make the most frequent service trips.

Table 3.13 presents regression models of the determinants of distance from services used and frequency of use by type of neighborhood. The patterns suggest interactions between service utilization and type of neighborhood. Distance is primarily a function of age concentration (or percentage aged 60 + in the tract) and age of respondent in rural areas. Age concentration is also critical to distance in suburbia, with commercial mix and average income having additional import. Although age concentration in the neighborhood encourages localized service consumption in these areas, city neighborhoods are not influenced by age concentration. Indeed, persons in city neighborhoods show little patterned variation in distance. Only the type of residential area (predominance of apartments) and functional health have any relationship to distance, and their effects account for only 4% of the variance. Age concentration appears to benefit elderly in rural and suburban areas, reducing the need for extensive mobility. The advantage of age concentration, however, is not apparent in cities. The generally more convenient shopping ar-

Table 3.13 Multiple Regression Analyses of Distance from Services Used and Frequency of Service Use, by Type of Tract

	Distance			Frequency		
	City	Suburb	Rural	City	Suburb	Rural
Percentage aged 60+	—	−.21	−.25	—	—	—
Neighborhood type[a]	—	−.27	−.11	−.10	—	—
Housing type[b]	−.16	—	—	—	—	—
Tract income	—	.17	—	—	—	—
Neighborhood maintained	—	—	−.14	—	—	—
Number of neighbors for emergencies	—	—	.11	—	—	—
Number of non-neighbor friends	—	.11	—	—	—	—
Health	.12	.11	—	.46	.36	.29
Age	—	—	−.16	—	—	—
Percentage vacant	—	—	—	—	—	−.10
Distance of services used	—	—	—	.18	.17	—
Household size	—	—	—	—	.10	—
Years at current address	—	—	—	—	—	−.15
Commonality with neighbors	—	—	—	—	—	.15
Neighborhood safety	—	—	—	—	—	−.13
R^2	.04	.21	.13	.26	.16	.17
N	451	273	257	479	288	261

Note: The standardized regression coefficients reported are statistically significant at $p = .05$.
[a]Entirely residential = 1. Mostly residential = 2. Mostly commercial = 3.
[b]Mostly single-family dwellings = 1. Mostly apartments = 2.

rangements of cities (with their reduced service-area radii) are un-affected by the social characteristics of the neighborhood. Such characteristics are apparently significant only in less convenient locations such as suburbs and rural areas.

The strong service resources of the city may also be used to interpret the differences in frequency of use. Functional health is the primary determinant of the frequency with which services are used in all these areas. The significance of this force, however, increases with urbanism; health is most significant for use in the city and least important in rural areas. We might conclude that, if people are able, they will use services frequently in the city, a fact that is less true in suburban or rural areas. Indeed, in rural areas use is complicated by a variety of neighborhood attitudes and neighborhood characteristics.

Conclusions

Age-related constraints, and the greater likelihood of "environmental docility," make the neighborhood a critical resource for choice and action in the older population. The issue of primary importance in this chapter has been the role of neighborhood context in the behavior and perceptions of older persons. A variety of analyses have been performed that produce a picture of neighborhood perception and behavior for the elderly population. Older people can be described as having two neighborhoods, a "social" area of neighbors and a "service" area of local facilities. The social neighborhood is more delimited, though not strikingly so. It is noteworthy that the self-defined service neighborhoods typically extend beyond recommended service distances (Newcomer, 1976), yet these respondents go out into the community on a regular basis and generally view the neighborhood as convenient.

These older respondents are generally quite satisfied with their neighborhoods. Their relative satisfaction may partly reflect cognitive dissonance associated with limited alternatives. Physical quality and neighborhood maintenance are important dimensions of neighborhood perception, reflecting a more vicarious, observational mode of neighborhood involvement (Rowles, 1978). Indeed, mental constructions of the neighborhood are critical determinants of neighborhood satisfaction. Both personal characteristics and objective neighborhood conditions have little direct influence on neighborhood satisfaction. Happiness with the "kind of people" in the neighborhood is an important dimension of neighborhood satisfaction, for example, but neighborhood age concentration has little effect. The "neighborhood of the mind" seems central for older people, who have reduced resources for direct neighborhood involvement. This underlines the earlier findings of Unruh (1983) and Adams (1986), who find symbolically constructed environments to be important for the well-being of older persons.

Environmental docility and urbanism were treated as subthemes throughout the chapter. It is clear that the forces shaping neighborhood perception and behavior depend upon both neighborhood context and individual competence and vulnerability. The environmental experience of older people, and the effects of environment on the elderly, are complex. City residence, for example, represents a mix of costs and benefits. City residents are generally less satisfied with their neighborhoods, but their neighborhoods are also more convenient in both objective and subjective terms. Each environment offers different experiences and resources, and the environmental requirements of individuals are quite diverse.

Of particular note are the findings that bear on the environmental-docility hypothesis (Lawton and Nahemow, 1973; Lawton, 1980). As this framework suggests, older persons with reduced competence are more sensitive to contextual, environmental factors. Neighborhood change, for example, has greater influence on neighborhood satisfaction for more vulnerable, less competent respondents. Such persons are also likely to have been left behind in processes of neighborhood change and succession (La Gory et al., 1980). The environmental experiences of such persons should be of particular concern to gerontologists and planners.

Findings related to the effects of urbanism, however, caution us against too facile a generalization. City residence per se has less influence on neighborhood perceptions and use among persons with reduced competence. The convenience of city neighborhoods, for example, confers no particular advantage on environmentally docile older persons. Such persons constitute a special case in experiencing urban life. A more active life-style may be required to experience the benefits or the "pathologies" of the city. The environmentally docile elderly live more encapsulated lives that limit their exposure to the surrounding area, for better and for worse.

In terms of a general environment-behavior model, the research indicates the value of a modified "press" model. Docility clearly matters in terms of both mental and behavioral congruence with the environment. The docile elderly are generally more sensitive to environmental conditions. These environmental conditions, and their import for satisfaction and behavior, cannot be understood on the basis of a simple machine-based model of human action, however. Environmental conditions include both objective and subjective components. The environment is both outside and inside; it is not just something "out there," dictating responses to sensory machines. The environment is a "symbolically constructed phenomenon" (Karp and Yoels, 1982). Indeed, for our models of neighborhood satisfaction, the most significant determinants of satisfaction are the meanings people attribute to their area of residence. Such findings support the notion of symbolic interaction.

The patterns of findings have significance for policymakers. The gerontology literature has been slowly building a case for the positive functions of urban residence and age-segregated neighborhoods. Although the elderly as a whole are satisfied with their area of residence, urban residents are less satisfied than others and age segregation generally has little bearing on satisfaction. Nevertheless, urban neighborhoods and age-segregated residential areas do provide some benefits. In particular, they represent more efficient service areas. Urban residence and residence in age-segregated places provide a mix of costs and benefits. Although residence in these areas may benefit some categories of elderly, it has clear costs for others.

Age is not by itself a meaningful social category identifying common environmental requirements. Planning for the elderly cannot be done simply, for there is no single population of elders with shared needs and perceptions. We cannot plan environments for "the elderly," just as we cannot plan environments for "the poor," because there are no such unidimensional social beings. Planning requires careful assessments of the life-style expectations and needs of the populations planned for. To say that urban residence or age homogeneity should be functional for the elderly is to revive the disastrous social engineering prescriptions of the 1960s. Ecological understandings have matured significantly since that period.

4 The Interpersonal Environment: Characteristics and Consequences of Support Networks

Chapter 3 focused on the ecological significance of residential and neighborhood context. In addition to spatial dimensions of the environment for aging, Lawton's (1980) five components of the human ecosystem (discussed in Chapter 1) remind us of the significance of the interpersonal environment or network of significant others. Informal networks and supports have been receiving increased attention from sociologists and have also been of interest to gerontologists for some time (Antonucci, 1985; Ward, 1985). This interest reflects an assumption that informal networks and the support they provide are important determinants of individual well-being throughout the life course. Heightened well-being may flow quite directly from the gratifications of social involvement. The linkages between informal networks and the formal care system are also important to well-being, as they may complement each other (Litwak, 1985). Empirical evidence of the contributions of social involvement to the well-being of the aged remain unclear, however. This chapter seeks to clarify the complex relationships between interpersonal ties and supports and the well-being of older persons.

We first discuss the extent to which older persons are embedded within networks of interpersonal relationships (family, friends, and neighbors) and the extent to which those ties afford instrumental and expressive support. We will see that the older persons in this study are not socially isolated in either objective or subjective terms. This is consistent with other studies of the older population. There is subgroup variation, however, in the size and content of informal networks.

The second section of this chapter assesses the sources of both instrumental and expressive support. Different interpersonal ties function in different ways, reflecting the varying qualities of relationships with family, friends, and neighbors. There are also patterns of compensation and substitution in the provision of instrumental and expressive support.

The last section of the chapter investigates the contributions of informal networks to well-being. We assess knowledge of services, reflecting more indirect contributions of informal networks to well-being, and morale, which is perhaps a more direct indicator of the benefits of social involvement. This section analyzes both interpersonal ties (family, friends, and neighbors) and social support (instrumental and expressive), using both objective and subjective indicators of network "adequacy."

In Chapters 1 and 3 we discussed the concepts of environmental docility and person-environment congruence (also see Lawton and Nahemow, 1973; Lawton, 1980). These approaches emphasize variability in the environmental needs of the elderly and particularly the heightened influence of the environment on the lives of older persons with reduced competence. Such considerations are relevant to interpersonal dimensions of the environment for aging. In recognition of this complexity, we pay attention throughout this chapter to variation in interpersonal ties and their consequences across subgroups of the older population. We will see that the relationship between social involvement and well-being is far from simple.

Informal Relationships and Supports

The informal networks of individuals are complex throughout life, encompassing three major types of interpersonal relationships—family, friends, and neighbors. The characteristics and composition of these networks are also likely to vary across population subgroups. As we noted in Chapter 1, age and the age stratification of roles affect the mix of social involvements of individuals; for example, there are fewer childhood friends as age increases, with neighbors and co-workers substituting for them as marriage and parenting pull people apart. Interaction with neighbors tends to increase after children are born and to decrease after they leave home. Turnover in friends occurs early in adulthood, though there is relative stability thereafter (Stueve and Gibson, 1977). Although older married adults have particularly stable social networks, such persons also have fewer social needs outside the home (Shulman, 1975).

The studies just cited involved respondents aged 18 to 65. Later life should also involve changes in network structure. Mobility limitations due to declining health and income, and role losses such as retirement and widowhood, may disrupt existing networks. Indeed, it has been suggested that aging may be associated with fewer, more unstable ties, with changes in the functions of existing ties, and with changes in the types and locations of ties that are needed (Wood and Robertson, 1978; Dono et al., 1979; Kahn, 1979; Antonucci, 1985). Dono et al. (1979) have noted that reduced mobility creates greater dependence on the local area for social contacts. They also suggest that the cross-generational kinship group becomes a more viable source of support, as long-term friends experience similar reductions in resources.

Some of these comments might seem to imply that aging necessarily involves impoverished social support networks. Such is not the case, however. Contrary to stereotypes of social isolation and loneliness in old age, gerontological research has demonstrated the robust nature of the social networks of most older persons. Indeed, in this area gerontologists have debunked some of the myths about aging. Our respondents exhibit a similar picture of social involvement for each of the three types of interpersonal ties—family, friends, and neighbors.

It should be noted that the following analyses do not explicitly deal with the role of spouses in social support. Like other researchers of support networks (e.g., Wellman, 1979), we narrow our focus somewhat to ties outside the household. In so doing we do not deny that marital status is an important element of support; Litwak (1985), for example, stresses the importance of the "marital household." The consequences of marital status, however, represent issues that are distinct from, although related to, those concerning support networks. Thus networks of extrahousehold relationships are the focus here. Many of the analyses presented below, however, were done separately for married and widowed respondents to assess the implications of marital status. We refer to those analyses as appropriate.

Family Ties

There is evidence of substantial interaction and assistance within the extended family of older persons, with assistance patterns focused on children and their spouses and on siblings (Cantor, 1975, 1979; National Council on the Aging, 1975; Wood and Robertson, 1978; Shanas, 1979; Bengtson and DeTerre, 1980; Golant, 1984). Cantor (1975), for example, found that one-half of her New York City sample saw a child weekly, and 87% received some assistance from children.

Access to family and involvement with kin is also considerable for the respondents in our survey. Access to children, for example, is high. More than three-fourths (78%) have at least one living child ($M = 2.6$). Approximately one-third live with or within walking distance of one of their children, and another 31% have a child living in the metropolitan area; only a small minority of the sample (13%) have children who are living but none of whom are residing within the metropolitan area. In addition 45% of the respondents see a child at least several times a week, with another 14% seeing one on a weekly basis. Indeed, only 15% of those with children neither see a child weekly nor name a child as a confidant or instrumental helper. Telephone contact may partly substitute for face-to-face interaction. Among those who have children but do not live in the same house or building with a child, 56% talk with children at least several times a week.

Although access to children is substantial among these respondents, parent-child relationships are not without problems. Indeed, a sizable minority express some dissatisfaction with the amount of contact with their children. Among those with children, 61% see them as often as they would like to, but 39% would like to see some or all of their children more often. As we will see later, such feelings have a bearing on morale and loneliness.

Most respondents (64%) also have other relatives living in the metropolitan area, with 55% regularly seeing or hearing from at least one other relative. If we combine children with other relatives, only 16% of the sample have no family members in the area ($M = 3.5$). In sum, these patterns indicate considerable accessibility and involvement in family ties.

Friends outside the Neighborhood

Older people are also not isolated from friendship ties, though friends are generally seen less than in the past and less often than family members (Cantor, 1975, 1979; National Council on the Aging, 1975; Bild and Havighurst, 1976; Wood and Robertson, 1978; Golant, 1984). Our respondents generally have extensive friendship networks outside their neighborhoods. Although 24% indicate that they have no nonneighbor friends, 38% indicate that they have 10 or more such friends, and the median number of friends is 6.3. Approximately one-third had made a new friend within the past year, and those who had more friends were also more likely to have made new friends.

Neighbors

Of particular interest in this study is the role of neighbors within the informal networks of older persons. We have suggested a heightened significance of localized support in later life. Some research indicates that informal neighboring declines with age (Kasarda and Janowitz, 1974; Hunter, 1975). Still, there is other evidence of neighborhood support systems among older people (Cantor, 1975, 1979; Carp, 1975). In her New York City study, for example, Cantor found that 62% knew at least one neighbor well, with over one-half involved in support relations with neighbors. Neighborhood relationships exhibited high reciprocity, involving both instrumental and expressive support; socializing was the most important feature. Similarly, Lopata (1979) indicates that, although little support is exchanged with neighbors who are not considered "friends," neighbors are a primary source of both old and new friends for widows.

Our respondents generally have access to neighborhood ties. Nearly two-thirds (65%) of the respondents know at least one neighbor well enough to visit with him or her. The mean number of neighbors known is 3.5, and it is 5.4 among those who know any neighbors. This trait is quite similar to the pattern found by Cantor (1979) in New York City. One-fourth indicate that they see neighbors daily, and another 37% see them at least weekly. There is less use of the telephone with neighbors than with children, though 13% talk to neighbors daily and another 28% talk at least weekly.

These patterns indicate that older persons are not isolated within their neighborhoods despite feelings on the part of many that they are "out of place"; 35% indicate that they have "not much at all" in common with their neighbors, but only 13% say that they have found it difficult to make friends in the neighborhood. In addition, relatively few persons are dissatisfied with their neighborhood involvement; only 14% would like to get together with neighbors more often (and only 2% would like to get together less often).

The apparent neighborhood integration of these respondents is also reflected in assistance patterns. Only about one-fourth (28%) do not know any neighbors on whom they could rely for help in emergencies. Table 4.1 indicates the frequency of help given to neighbors and received from neighbors. Only 25% have given none of the six forms of assistance and only 27% have received none; most respondents have been involved in several types of aid. These patterns of neighborhood assistance are probably reciprocal, because giving and receiving assistance are strongly correlated ($r = .76$).

Table 4.1   Assistance Given to Neighbors and Received from Neighbors (percent)

	Given	Received
Look in to see how you/they are doing	55	60
Give you/them rides	37	41
Get you/them things at the store	43	46
Talk to you/them about personal concerns	38	38
Look after house when away	52	54
Lend things (other than money)	54	48
Total sample, aid M[a]	2.8	2.9
Respondents giving/receiving any assistance, aid M[a]	3.7	3.9

[a]Mean aid (out of six).

It is evident that these respondents generally have access to a range of interpersonal relationships. As we have noted, previous research indicates that the informal networks of the elderly are quite robust, and this sample is no exception. If we combine family members, friends, and neighbors who are friends, only 2% indicate that they have no interpersonal ties within the metropolitan area, whereas 38% have 20 or more. Furthermore, nearly half (44%) have access to all three types of relationships.

Social Supports

Although most of our respondents, like older people generally, clearly have access to a variety of social involvements, we noted in Chapter 1 that interpersonal ties are not synonymous with social support. As Thoits (1982) has observed, not all interpersonal relationships are necessarily supportive in meeting the social needs of individuals. To what extent do the social ties of the elderly fulfill social support functions?

Social support has been conceptualized in various ways. Cobb (1976) refers to social support as "communicated sharing" that provides information that one is cared for or loved, esteemed and valued, and belongs to a network of communication and mutual obligation. Kahn (1979) describes three functions of social supports—affect, affirmation (construction of meaning), and aid (symbolic and material). Similarly, Kaplan et al. (1977) define support as the degree to which needs for affection, approval, belonging, and security are met by significant others. Our research focused on two broad forms of social support: instrumental assistance, involving more tangible aid, and expressive support, involving confidants who provide the type of "communicated sharing" described by Cobb (1976).

Not surprisingly, given the general accessibility of social ties, few respondents in our survey fail to name someone (other than spouse) to whom they can turn in the four hypothetical instrumental situations; 86% indicate help for all four situations. These helpers are quite proximate, as 64% name a helper who resides in the same neighborhood (either a neighbor or a relative). A large majority (92%) say that they have enough help for such situations.

Although the availability of instrumental aid is widespread, confidants would seem to be a more critical source of social support. Such expressive ties are most likely to fulfill the social needs (e.g., affection, approval, and identity) cited by Thoits (1982) and Kaplan et al. (1977). They are an important source for intimate communication and as such serve to stimulate a sense of solidarity and trust. Such close personal relationships can act as a buffer against age-linked losses (Lowenthal and Haven, 1968).

Most adults have access to a confidant relationship. Wellman (1979), for example, found that 98% of his young to middle-aged sample in Toronto had at least one intimate, with 61% having five or more. The expressive ties of older people appear to be somewhat less robust, although research to date is not entirely clear on this point. Lopata (1979) found that from 10% to 20% of her sample of widows indicated no current confidant or person who made them feel important, useful, secure, self-sufficient, or accepted. Cantor (1975, 1979) found that nearly one-half could name no confidant. Babchuk (1978), in a study of Nebraska residents aged 45 and over, found that only 15% had no confidant (M = 3.0). Rosow (1978), commenting on this research, however, notes that, although relatively few were completely isolated, one-third had either no close ties or only one confidant, making them highly vulnerable.

The patterns exhibited by our respondents are closest to those described by Babchuk (1978). Respondents generally have access to at least one confidant; 83% indicate that they have a confidant, and 77% indicate a confidant outside their households (M = 3.0). It is noteworthy that respondents generally have many interpersonal ties in the metropolitan area but only a few who are considered confidants. This finding underscores the particular quality of this intimate, expressive tie. If we look at the first-named confidant (outside the household), one-fourth see this confidant daily (and 77% at least weekly), and 43% indicate that this person resides in their neighborhood (90% in the metropolitan area). In addition one-half talk on the telephone with their first confidant at least several times a week. If we take into account all confidants, 37% see at least one of their extrahousehold confidants daily (87% at least weekly) and 57% have a confidant in their neighborhood (96% in the metropolitan area). Confidants are thus quite accessible for those who have them. These patterns refer to extrahousehold confidants, and inclusion of confidants within the household would certainly enhance this picture of general accessibility of expressive support among the elderly. Indeed, 95% of those with a confidant indicate that they have enough opportunities to "share confidences and feelings with another person."

To summarize our discussion to this point, it is apparent that most of our respondents have extensive informal networks that provide them with supportive social relationships. We can view this characteristic in another way by considering the potentially heightened significance of proximate social support in later life. A composite measure of proximate assistance was created by combining (1) receiving any of the six types of aid involving neighbors, (2) having an instrumental helper in the same neighborhood (neighbor or relative), and (3) having a confidant in the same neighborhood. Respondents generally have proximate support: 29% exhibit all three forms of neighborhood-based assistance, 39% indicate two of the three (usually the first two), 21% have one of the three, and only 9% have no such proximate assistance.

Most of our discussion has focused on rather quantitative indicators of network structure: size, proximity, and frequency. Quantity is not the same as quality, of course. It is therefore important to note that *subjective* assessments (perceived sufficiency) of involvement with children and neighbors and of access to instrumental and expressive support are also generally quite favorable among our respondents. Older people exhibit a tendency to give more favorable evaluations of their life circumstances than seems warranted by objective conditions (Carp and Carp, 1981). Indeed, Table 4.2 indicates that subjective network assessments are only weakly related to their more objective counterparts. Table 4.2 also indicates, however, that the four subjective assessments are not strongly enough intercorrelated to suggest a general "yea-saying" response set. Objective and subjective measures appear to represent distinct dimensions, and the subjective dimen-

sions appear to be distinct from one another. Thus the social networks
of most of our respondents appear to be adequate in both objective and
subjective terms.

That most respondents evidence both objective and subjective sufficiency of informal networks does not mean that interpersonal ties and
supports are equally robust for all subgroups of the older sample,
however. Let us turn to possible sources of variation in network composition and adequacy.

Subgroup Variation in Network Composition

Both sociologists and gerontologists have investigated subgroup differences in the characteristics of social networks. A number of respon-

Table 4.2   Zero-Order Correlations of Subjective Network Assessments with
Their Objective Counterparts and with Each Other

	Enough contact		Enough help	
	Children	Neighbors	Instrumental	Expressive
CHILDREN				
Number	−.03	−.02	.04	.01
Frequency of interaction	.36*	.02	.13*	.06
NEIGHBORS				
Number known well	−.04	.01	.08*	.07*
Frequency of interaction	.06*	.14*	.12*	.08*
Help received	−.04	−.05*	.10*	−.01
INSTRUMENTAL SUPPORT				
Number of helpers (0–4)	.06*	.02	.14*	.14*
Number of helpers in neighborhood (0–4)	−.01	−.00	.07*	.03
EXPRESSIVE SUPPORT				
Number of confidants	.02	.05*	.06*	.01
Proximity of confidant	.02	.04	.10*	.11*
Frequency of interaction	.08*	.07	.13*	.13*
SUBJECTIVE ASSESSMENTS				
Children	—	.12*	.14*	.13*
Neighbors		—	.15*	.11*
Instrumental			—	.32*
Expressive				—

*p = .05.

dent characteristics are likely to be associated with the nature of social networks and the supports they provide, including age, sex, socioeconomic status, health, role loss (retirement and widowhood), and residential location.

Age. Earlier in the chapter we noted that age may affect the "social convoy" (Kahn, 1979) surrounding the individual; in particular, age-related experiences may reduce the size of informal networks and may increase the aging individual's reliance on kin and on the proximate ties of the neighborhood. Such arguments generally refer to a longer time span, from youth to later life, than is represented in our sample, however. Research on middle-aged and older persons has found little relation between age and network characteristics (Antonucci, 1985). Our data also indicate that age has only scattered relationships with interpersonal ties. Not surprisingly, older respondents are less likely to have living children, but age is otherwise unrelated to proximity or frequency of interaction with children. Age is also unrelated to involvement with other relatives. Older respondents do have slightly fewer nonneighbor friends ($r = -.07$) and new friends ($-.08$). They also know fewer neighbors ($-.11$) and both give ($-.21$) and receive ($-.10$) less assistance from neighbors. Age is generally unrelated to the availability of instrumental and expressive support, however. On the whole, age per se has little bearing on the characteristics of informal networks for individuals already in their older years.

Sex. Some research has suggested that women have more intimate friends and confidants (Lowenthal and Haven, 1968; Booth, 1972; Booth and Hess, 1974; Powers and Bultena, 1976; Babchuk, 1978; Hess, 1979). The data for our older respondents, however, reveal few sex differences in the "quantity" of interpersonal ties and supports. Men and women do not differ in their involvement with children, other relatives, or neighbors or in availability of instrumental and expressive support. Male friendship networks outside the neighborhood are somewhat more extensive. Although approximately one-fourth of both sexes have no such friends, men are more likely to have more than five friends (62% vs. 50%, $p = .0001$).

Sex differences are more apparent in the *content* of informal networks, however. Older men, for example, are more likely to have cross-sex ties in their informal networks (Table 4.3). Although this pattern may partly reflect the sex ratio of the older population, it is not eliminated by controls for age and marital status. It is common to find women central in the informal support networks of older people (Antonucci, 1985; Litwak, 1985). Even among the predominantly male social isolates who occupy single-room-occupancy hotels, women are central in the formation of supportive arrangements (Eckert, 1980).

These patterns may reflect normative constraints. Adams (1985), for example, has suggested that cross-sex friendships by older women are defined as "romance" and that norms inhibit such romance in old age. Litwak (1985) has also suggested that traditional women's roles are better suited to the activity needs of older people.

Of particular interest concerning the content of informal networks are possible sex differences in the use of interpersonal ties for support. Although the literature indicates that older men rely on spouses as confidants, older women more often name children, other relatives, and friends as confidants (Hess, 1979). Some similar patterns are evident in our data. Men and women are equally likely to name children, and men are actually more likely to name any family member (73% to 66%, $p = .05$) and only family members (59% to 46%, $p = .0005$). Women, however, are more likely to name nonneighbor friends (20% to 12%, $p = .01$) and neighbors (39% to 30%, $p = .05$) as confidants. Older women thus exhibit greater variety in their support networks.

The reasons for such patterns are not clear. Hess (1979) suggests that norms direct men to seek intimacy in marriage, making them more dependent on wives as confidants. Friendships, on the other hand, draw women out of the isolation of home into wider social networks, serving an integrative function. Subgroup analyses indicated that the sex differences in support networks noted above were evident regardless of marital status, but these differences may reflect patterns developed earlier in adulthood when these respondents were married. Whatever the reason, the greater variety of support sources gives older women more flexibility in "constructing" their support networks and in adapting to social losses such as widowhood.

Socioeconomic status. Higher socioeconomic status has been

Table 4.3 Sex Differences in the Likelihood of Naming Someone of the Opposite Sex as Closest Neighbor, Instrumental Helper, and First-Named Confidant (percent)

Designation of opposite sex	Male	Female
Closest neighbor*	38	13
Instrumental helper[a]*	53	28
First confidant*	47	19

*$p = .0001$.
[a]"Someone to look in on you and see how you are doing"; patterns are the same for the other instrumental situations.

found to be associated with networks that are more diverse and involve fewer kin or neighbors (Jackson et al., 1977). Gerontological research also indicates that older persons with higher socioeconomic status tend to have larger networks that include more friends, whereas working-class elderly tend to live closer to family and interact more regularly with kin (Antonucci, 1985).

Variations on the basis of socioeconomic status are more pronounced in our data than those linked to age and sex. These differences are summarized in Table 4.4. Higher-status respondents have slightly fewer children and interact less frequently with children, though there is no difference in involvement with other relatives. Such persons have more nonneighbor friends and new friends, however; for example, 68% of professional/managerial respondents have more than five friends, compared with only 52% of those from craft occupations. This distinction may reflect class differences in the meaning of "friendship," however, rather than actual differences in social ties. Higher socioeconomic status is also related to knowing more neighbors and being involved in greater mutual assistance with neighbors. In general, it appears that higher-status (white-collar) older persons have more extensive friendship and neighborhood networks, whereas lower-status (blue-collar) older persons are more involved with children.

These patterns are reflected in instrumental and expressive support relations. Socioeconomic status is not related to having instrumental helpers or the proximity of helpers, but it is related to type of helper. In specifying who would "look in on you," for example, blue-collar respondents are more likely to name a child (55% to 37%) and white-collar respondents are more likely to name a neighbor (43% to 26%). This reflects the closer proximity of blue-collar elderly to their children. Higher status is also associated with having more confidants; 48% of college-educated persons have three or more confidants, for example, as compared with only 32% of those with no high school experience. This characteristic, and the negative association between status and frequency of interaction with confidants, reflects a greater use of nonneighbor friends by the college-educated group (23% to 11%, p = .005). The less-educated group is more likely to name only family confidants (58% to 41%, p = .001), reducing the variety and frequency of confiding relations.

Health. Health problems potentially heighten the importance of some interpersonal ties by restricting access to others. Functional health, however, has little association with involvement with children

Table 4.4 Zero-Order Correlations of Socioeconomic Status with Network
Characteristics

	Education	Income	Occupational prestige
CHILDREN			
Number	−.09*	−.04	−.09*
Frequency	−.19*	−.09*	−.11*
Other relatives			
Number seen regularly	−.03	−.03	−.03
FRIENDS			
Number	.17*	.17*	.11*
Number new	.15*	.11*	.11*
NEIGHBORS			
Number known	.14*	.14*	.12*
Frequency	.04	−.07*	−.05*
Number for emergencies	.07*	.04	.07*
Aid given	.21*	.26*	.04
Aid received	.15*	.12*	.03
INSTRUMENTAL HELP			
Number of helpers	.01	.02	.03
Number in neighborhood	−.01	.06	−.02
CONFIDANTS			
Number of helpers	.08*	.10*	.09*
Frequency for first named	−.13*	−.12*	−.12*

*$p = .05$.

and other relatives, number of nonneighbor friends, or having instrumental helpers and confidants. Still, mobility restrictions may affect
neighborhood relations. Although functional health is not related to
frequency of interaction with neighbors, it is weakly related to number
of neighbors known well ($r = .10$), number who could be called upon
in emergencies (.10), number named as instrumental helpers (.07),
and the amount of assistance both given (.14) and received (.06) from
neighbors. Functional limitations may be particularly disruptive of
neighboring in rural areas. Among rural residents, those with some
functional impairment are nearly twice as likely to know none of their
neighbors as are those with no impairments (41% to 22%, $p = .005$).
Failure to know neighbors may represent an important deficit for
these persons, because friends and neighbors have particular instru-

mental value in rural areas (e.g., for transportation) and also serve to reinforce social roles in the community (Kivett, 1985).

It appears that those who could benefit most from neighbors have less possibility of such help. Such patterns may partly account for a positive correlation (.13) between functional health and perception that one has enough instrumental help. These relationships are generally small, however. Health problems appear not to be terribly disruptive of support networks, at least within the moderate range of disability present in this sample.

Role loss. Role losses such as retirement and widowhood are potentially disruptive of informal networks. They at least threaten relationships, such as those with co-workers or in-laws, that revolve around the lost role. Retirement, however, exhibits virtually no associations with the interpersonal ties and supports investigated in this study. Retirement thus appears neither to disrupt ongoing informal networks nor to trigger any general social withdrawal or disengagement.

Widowhood has only a very small association with involvement with children and none with other relatives; recency of widowhood makes no difference in these patterns. Women who are widowed are more likely to indicate that they have no friends outside the neighborhood (28% to 20%) and are less likely to have more than five such friends (47% to 62%). These differences are reduced when controls are added for health, socioeconomic status, and age, however, suggesting that widowhood itself is only partly responsible for reduced friendship networks. Social disruption may also be a product of the burdens of caring for a sick spouse prior to widowhood rather than being attributable to widowhood as "role loss." Widowhood has little relation to involvement with neighbors except that, among rural residents, widowed persons are twice as likely to know none of their neighbors (39% to 19%, p = .0005). This tendency is similar to the pattern for functional health, again suggesting that the greater residential dispersion in rural areas makes neighboring more susceptible to disruption just when it is most needed. Finally, widowhood is unrelated to the availability of instrumental and expressive support (outside the household). In general, it appears that the support networks of older people are able to "weather" the effects of role loss.

Residential location. Studies of the general population have found that large urban places are characterized by more extensive interpersonal ties than are rural areas (Kasarda and Janowitz, 1974). Suburban residents tend to be more locally oriented than city residents, socializing more often with neighbors and having more friends in the neighborhood (Fischer and Jackson, 1977; Kennedy, 1978). This difference may partly reflect length of residence, because this characteristic is associated with number of local ties and psychological attachment to place (Kasarda and Janowitz, 1974; Gerson et al., 1977).

Only sparse information is available about informal networks of the rural elderly. There is some evidence of greater kinship interaction, but findings are equivocal (Lee and Cassidy, 1985). Indeed, some studies indicate greater interaction with children among urban elderly, reflecting proximity and financial resources. Despite barriers associated with low income and transportation problems, there is some evidence that rural older people have greater contact with friends and neighbors, fostered by long-term residence and the social homogeneity of rural areas (Kivett, 1985). We have already seen some evidence, however, that health problems and widowhood may disrupt interpersonal ties in more dispersed rural areas.

How is location related to the interpersonal ties and supports of older persons in this sample? Two dimensions of location are highlighted here: length of residence and type of location (city, suburban, or rural).

Length of residence is not related to involvement with children or other relatives, to number of nonneighbor friends, or to availability of instrumental assistance. Number of years at current address is also unrelated to frequency of interaction with neighbors, although it is related to number of neighbors known well (partial correlation r = .10, when we controlled for health, socioeconomic status, and age) and both assistance given (.22) and assistance received (.16). Length of residence is not related to number of confidants, but those who have moved within the previous 2 years are twice as likely to name a nonneighbor friend as a confidant (30% to 15%, p = .005); these friends may be former neighbors. Overall, length of residence appears to have little bearing on network characteristics, but this sample includes relatively few recent movers. In this respect, of course, our respondents are representative of the older population as a whole because the elderly are typically long-term residents (a pattern that holds even more for residents of the Northeast).

Table 4.5 summarizes variations by type of location. The clearest pattern in Table 4.5 involves differences between city residents and others (both suburban and rural), although rural residents cite the greatest number of neighbors known and indicate somewhat greater availability of neighbors for assistance. The similarity between suburban and rural residents may reflect the metropolitan nature of the sample, where the suburban/rural distinction is less clear. As we noted in Chapter 2, we cannot speak of patterns for nonmetropolitan elderly who reside in more distinctively rural settings.

Compared with suburban and rural residents, city residents are more likely to have no living children, but they are also slightly more likely to live in the same house or building as children. The primary differences involve neighbors, however. City residents know fewer neighbors and receive less aid from neighbors. This statement is particularly true of those who live in apartments. One-half (49%) of city residents living in apartments know none of their neighbors, compared with 30% of those living in single-family dwellings. City residents are also somewhat less likely to name neighbors as sources of instrumental or expressive support. Despite the potential offered by greater neighborhood density, neighboring seems to be restricted to some extent by the mobility and anonymity of city life.

The Structure and Functions of Support Networks

To this point we have discussed variation in the ties of older persons, stressing both the variety of relationships available and subgroup variation in the content of the informal network. We turn now to another aspect of informal network variation—the varying "value" of relationships to the older individual. This issue we will discuss in greater detail later in this chapter in analyzing the contributions of informal networks to well-being in later life. First, however, we will address questions concerning the functional specificity of interpersonal ties and the degree to which different relationships can substitute for one another in providing instrumental and expressive support.

A number of studies have investigated the composition and structure of informal networks in the general adult population. Wellman's research (Wellman et al., 1973; Wellman, 1979), for example, found quite dispersed networks. Although the great majority of intimate ties were in the metropolitan area and many now-distant ties had local origins, only 13% were in the same neighborhood, and few individuals had more than one intimate in the neighborhood. The strongest ties were usually with immediate kin, and distance appeared to be unimportant for these immediate family relationships. Parent/child intimates provided more support in both emergency and everyday matters; friends, neighbors, siblings, and other relatives were of lesser and roughly equal importance. People also tended to specialize (hav-

Table 4.5 Differences in Network Characteristics of City, Suburb, and Rural Residents

	City	Suburb	Rural
CHILDREN			
Have none (%)	28	21	16
Live in same house/building (%)	26	22	21
NEIGHBORS			
None known (%)	42	30	28
Number known (M)[a]	3.1	3.4	5.5
None for emergency (%)	35	24	21
Number for emergency (M)[a]	2.3	3.0	3.1
No help received (%)	31	26	22
Help received (M)[a]	2.9	3.1	3.3
Neighbor named as instrumental helper (%)	39	48	37
Neighbor named as confidant (%)	31	38	41

Note: $p = .05$ throughout.
[a]Results of multiple classification analyses with health and socioeconomic status as covariates.

ing kin or friends as intimates) but maintained one or two other types of intimate ties as well. Kin interaction does not appear to reduce friendship ties, nor do reduced kinship ties appear to increase friendship or group participation; rather, those rich in one area tend to be rich in others (Booth, 1972; Sherman, 1975a; Babchuk, 1978).

During adulthood, then, informal networks tend to be dispersed throughout metropolitan areas. Kinship ties are prominent in support networks, though friends and to a lesser extent neighbors also provide support. Such age-related experiences as health changes and role loss, however, may alter the roles played by different social ties. Neighbors, for example, may become more salient sources of support for the elderly with limited mobility, so that dispersed networks would be disadvantageous for them. The possibility of compensation and replacement within social networks becomes particularly relevant to older people, as the social convoy changes in response to aging and its accompaniments.

The greatest gerontological research attention has gone to family ties, and family ties appear to dominate the support networks of older persons. Shanas (1979), for example, found the immediate family to be the major source of assistance during illness, and Lopata (1979) found that children and their spouses were the most important sources of help with early problems of widowhood. There has been debate, however, about the relative roles played by different social ties. Two models of network functioning are most prominent: the "hierarchical-compensatory" model and the "task-specific" model.

Cantor (1979), presenting respondents with 10 hypothetical situations in which they might need assistance, found that kin, preferably children, were clearly the first choice for assistance, followed by friends and neighbors, who were used primarily with regard to sociability and sporadic, short-term help. Cantor concludes that networks of older people are "hierarchical-compensatory." According to this model, children and other kin play a central role irrespective of task, with children preferred even when they are "nonfunctional" (living far away or interacting infrequently). The network is also compensatory, however, because the elderly turn to other ties (especially friends and neighbors) when children are not available.

This conclusion, however, may reflect the type of support (instrumental) investigated by Cantor. Others have argued for a "task-specific" model of social support (Litwak and Szelenyi, 1969; Weiss, 1969; Dono et al., 1979; Litwak, 1985). According to this view, the various components of informal networks—kin, friends, and neighbors—are differentiated structurally according to the types of tasks they can handle most effectively. Because relationships become specialized, well-being depends upon the availability of a number of different types of relationships.

The structure of kin groups is characterized by permanent membership but differential mobility. This mobility impedes face-to-face interaction, though modern systems of communication, transportation, and monetary exchange permit maintenance of ties over distances. The persistence of affection and mutual obligation makes family ties particularly well suited for tasks involving long-term ties. The history of reciprocity, for example, makes kin, especially children, a preferred source of instrumental assistance during illness or widowhood.

Family ties appear to be best suited for more tangible, instrumental assistance, particularly aid that is more substantial and is offered over a longer term. Family relationships appear to be less central among expressive ties, however. Indeed, although research indicates a clear preference for kin in instrumental situations, confidants have been found to be more evenly distributed among kin and friends (Cantor, 1979; Lowenthal and Haven, 1968). Friends appear to become a particularly important source of confidants following widowhood (Lopata, 1979). It is thus necessary to consider the functions for which neighbors and nonneighbor friends are particularly suited.

The structure of neighborhoods emphasizes proximity and face-to-face contact, and appropriate functions relate to speed in responding to emergencies, services based on territoriality, and everyday observation for learning (Litwak and Szelenyi, 1969). These functions are likely to be particularly important for the elderly, given their reduced mobility. Access to neighbors who are also intimate friends may be particularly important for older people, as they are more dependent on localized social ties because of their environmental docility.

Friendship ties are weakest structurally in terms of permanence and face-to-face contact but are held together by affectivity and choice (Litwak and Szelenyi, 1969). Friends are contemporaries and equals, qualities both of which contribute to openness and intimacy. Thus friends may be important sources of expressive support (confidants).

To what extent, then, are the interpersonal relationships of older people functionally specific, and to what extent do they combine or compensate for one another? In the most general sense, the interpersonal ties of our respondents do not appear to be compensatory. Persons having no living children, for example, do not exhibit greater involvement with other relatives, nonneighbor friends, or neighbors. Indeed, social "richness" in one area tends to be associated with "richness" in other areas. People who have more family and friends outside the neighborhood, for example, also know more neighbors (partial correlation $r = .19$, when we control functional health and socioeconomic status) and receive more assistance from neighbors (.10). These patterns do not bear on the central issue, however: To which ties do people turn for instrumental and expressive support?

Table 4.6 indicates the helpers named in the four instrumental situations. Children are most prevalent, followed by neighbors. It is noteworthy that the elderly would turn to agencies very rarely (if they were given the choice); informal support is preferred to formal support. The same person may apparently be chosen for each situation; there is little mixing of helpers across situations. Among those individuals naming either kin or neighbors, for example, 58% name only kin and 23% name only neighbors. There is thus little evidence of functional specificity of social ties across these situations.

Table 4.7 indicates the type of helper named as a function of the proximity of a child (the pattern is the same for all four situations). Children are clearly preferred when proximate, with neighbors most

Table 4.6   Helpers Named for the Four Instrumental Situations (percent)

	Look in on you	Give you a ride	Get you something	Look after your house
None	7	9	8	9
Child	42	41	40	38
Other relative	17	17	16	16
Neighbor or friend[a]	30	28	34	34
Other[b]	3	5	2	3
Total	100	100	100	100
N	1,171	1,169	1,169	1,161

[a]These are virtually all neighbors; nonneighbor friends were rarely named as instrumental helpers.
[b]Includes church and social agencies.

likely to substitute when they are not (though "other relatives" are also prominent for those with no children). The long-term reciprocity of ties with children appears to make their assistance preferable, although the aged may turn to neighbors because of their proximity (friends who are not neighbors are seldom used).

Cantor (1979) found that friends and neighbors were the most im-

Table 4.7   Who Would Look in on You and See How You Are Doing, by Proximity of Nearest Child (percent)

	No children	Outside SMSA	In SMSA	Same neighborhood	Same house or building[a]
No one	11	10	5	4	4
Child	—	9	58	80	63
Other relative	41	23	11	6	8
Neighbor	43	55	26	10	23
Other	6	3	2	2	1
Total	100	100	100	100	100
N	255	145	353	177	217

$\chi^2 = 445.7$. $p = .001$.
[a]Respondents could not name a helper living in the same household.

portant elements of the informal support networks of childless elderly. Patterns in Table 4.7 indicate that childless respondents exhibit increased reliance on neighbors, but nonneighbor friends are not prominent. Childless persons also appear to have retained or cultivated other kinship ties. Shanas (1979), for example, has reported greater interaction with siblings and other relatives among childless older persons.

Table 4.8 indicates considerable variety in those named as confidants. Children and neighbors are most prevalent (as they were for instrumental help), followed by siblings and other relatives. This pattern describes only confidants outside the person's household, of course; if household members had been included, spouses would certainly be prominent and children might also be more prevalent. As with instrumental help, friends who are not neighbors are used relatively infrequently for expressive support. Very few name other persons, such as clergy or physicians, as confidants, again indicating a preference for more informal sources of support. Individuals tend to "specialize"; 51% name only family members, 21% name only neighbors, and 7% name only nonneighbor friends. Wellman (1979) found a similar tendency to specialize in intimate ties.

Different types of confidants vary in their accessibility. Let us take first-named confidants as an example; 37% of neighbor confidants are

Table 4.8   Persons Named as Confidants (Outside the Respondent's Household) (percent)

	Confidant			
	First	Second	Third	Any[a]
Child	32	24	20	38
Sibling	16	15	14	23
Other relative	14	19	21	27
Neighbor	26	28	28	36
Friend	11	13	15	17
Other[b]	1	1	2	1
Total	100	100	100	—
N	895	655	439	895

[a]Named as any of the up to three confidants to whom respondent feels closest.
[b]Includes clergy and physician.

seen daily, compared with only 5% of nonneighbor friends; children are seen quite frequently (29% daily and 81% weekly), whereas siblings are less accessible (17% are seen daily and 62% weekly). It is consistent with the intimacy of this relationship that confidants tend to represent long-term bonds. This tendency obviously holds for family ties, but the sample had known 57% of friends and even 47% of neighbors named as confidants for more than 20 years (and three-fourths of each for more than 10 years). These patterns again underscore the unique and intimate quality of the confidant relationship.

Table 4.9 indicates that children tend to be preferred as the closest confidant to the extent they are available. This pattern is much less pronounced than it was for instrumental helpers, however. Furthermore, although neighbors "substitute" for children as instrumental helpers, siblings and other relatives are used more often as confidants when children are less proximate.

Several conclusions are evident from these data on instrumental helpers and confidants. As we noted earlier, research indicates that the informal networks of most adults are quite dispersed. The networks of older persons in this sample are more constricted locationally. In particular, nonneighbor friends are less evident; the implication is that they are replaced by more localized neighborhood ties for older persons. The greater emphasis on proximate sources of social support likely represents an aging effect, reflecting the reduced

Table 4.9 Type of Person Named as First Confidant by Proximity of Nearest Child (percent)

		Nearest child			
	No children	Outside SMSA	In SMSA	Same neighborhood	Same house or building[a]
Child	—	25	48	50	28
Sibling	28	19	10	10	16
Other relative	30	13	9	9	14
Neighbor	28	28	23	25	28
Friend	13	15	9	7	14
Total	100	100	100	100	100
N	181	107	290	149	153

Note: $\chi^2 = 171.1.$ p $= .001.$
[a]Persons in the same household could not be named as a confidant.

mobility and constricted social roles of older persons (and of their friends, who are similarly older). This finding supports Carp's (1976) conclusion that the aged "must rely on the local area and its inhabitants to support their needs, while most of today's society reach far from home to meet the needs of everyday life" (p. 249).

Neither neighbors nor nonneighbor friends dominate the support networks of the older persons, however. Rather, family ties are most prevalent, and many of these ties are proximate and readily accessible. Preference for kin varies by support function, as patterns for instrumental helpers and confidants reflect elements of both the "hierarchical-compensatory" and "task-specific" models of support networks. Children are preferred sources of instrumental support, reflecting the long-term reciprocity of parent-child relationships; the aged are more likely to turn to other ties as children are less accessible.

It might be argued that the prominence of family ties in these measures of support networks reflects a bias toward naming family members because of normative obligations attributed to the family. Other patterns, however, suggest that this is more than a "response set." The preference for children, for example, is less evident for expressive support, which involves greater peership and choice. In addition, "substitutes" for children vary by function, echoing Litwak's (1985) concept of "functional substitutability" among primary group ties. Reflecting their proximity, neighbors are increasingly named as instrumental helpers as children are less proximate. Other kin (including siblings) are preferred substitutes as confidants, however, reflecting the long-term nature of such ties. As we noted, nonlocal (nonneighbor) friends are not prominent sources of either instrumental or expressive support. This is not attributable to measurement problems; the person named for support and the location of that person were measured separately.

These patterns indicate that access to children is particularly important in the provision of social support for the elderly. Patterns of compensation and replacement, however, also support a view that older persons are best served by a diverse informal network (Litwak, 1985). Indeed, one might ask which interpersonal ties most indicate a supportive network. Those who have no children or see them infrequently are less likely to have instrumental helpers; 78% of those with no children indicate helpers for all four situations, compared with 91% of those who see children at least weekly. Still, availability of children is not related to number of confidants or to the proximity or frequency of interaction with confidants. Access to other relatives

Table 4.10   Partial Correlations of Involvement with Neighbors with Instrumental and Expressive Support

	Number of neighbors known well	Neighbor interaction frequency	Assistance from neighbors
INSTRUMENTAL			
Number of helpers	.09*	.06*	.17*
Number of neighbor helpers	.10*	.18*	.35*
EXPRESSIVE			
Number of confidants	.20*	.10*	.17*
Number of neighbor confidants	.11*	.19*	.22*

Note: Functional health, education, and occupational prestige were controlled.
*p = .05.

bears little relation to either type of support. Number of nonneighbor friends is unrelated to instrumental assistance. It is related to number of confidants (r = .19) but is otherwise unrelated to confidant variables, including whether a friend is named as a confidant. Involvement with neighbors exhibits the most consistent associations with support. Table 4.10 indicates that knowing and interacting with neighbors and having received assistance from them is associated with general availability of both instrumental and expressive support, as well as with naming neighbors as either helpers or confidants. Neighborhood involvement may thus be most indicative of the extensiveness of an informal network and the social supports it provides. Once again, this possibility suggests that the neighborhood is a critical social resource for the elderly.

Informal Networks and Well-being

The informal network represents the basic social resources available to the individual, the ties that bind the person to the larger social order. Since Durkheim, social scientists have emphasized the relationship between these ties and the individuals' own sense of well-being. Indeed, the special attention that gerontologists accord to the networks of older persons reflects the assumption that networks contribute to well-being in later life (Antonucci, 1985; Ward, 1985). We now examine this assumption, focusing on two potential contributions: knowledge of resources and services and subjective well-being.

Knowledge of Services

Informal networks represent linkages by which individuals receive information and assistance. Such networks have been found to play an important role, for example, in job-seeking behavior (Granovetter, 1974) and to influence the manner in which individuals define and act upon symptoms or life crises (Freidson, 1961; McKinlay, 1973). Similarly, interpersonal ties may constitute a "lay referral" network for older people. Knowledge is an important determinant of service utilization by the elderly (Ward, 1977b; Snider, 1980),and Sussman (1976) notes that social support systems, especially kin, play a mediating role in assisting older people to obtain appropriate services.

This mediating role reflects the "shared functions" of informal and formal networks (Litwak, 1985). Just as various informal ties can be viewed as "task-specific," informal and formal networks are best suited to provide particular forms of assistance. This sharing of functions heightens the value of cooperation and coordination between them. More generally, Golant (1984) suggests that interpersonal ties enhance well-being through the provision of linkages to the "outside" environment. Lay referral represents one such linkage.

To what degree do informal networks actually operate as a lay referral system? It can first be noted that the most common sources of information about the five services discussed in Chapter 2 are relatively formal: media sources (television, radio, and newspapers) were indicated as the "most important source of information" by 57%, senior citizens' clubs were indicated by 13%, and social agencies were indicated by 8%. Other professionals, such as physicians and clergy, were also cited by 5% of the sample. This item suggests that the informal network of kin, friends, and neighbors is apparently not a major source of information: 10% name friends and neighbors, and only 4% name relatives.

Having living children is not related to either knowledge or use of services. Among individuals with children, however, frequency of interaction with a child is negatively related to both service knowledge (partial correlation $r = -.06$, when we control health and socioeconomic status) and use of services ($-.08$). These associations are quite small, of course, but they suggest that children may serve as substitutes rather than as mediators for formal services. Access to other relatives has no association with service knowledge. These patterns, combined with the fact that only 4% name kin specifically as information sources, offer little evidence that the family network is a source of awareness about formal senior services.

Having more friends outside the neighborhood is weakly related to greater awareness of formal services (partial correlation $r = .10$, when we control health and socioeconomic status). In particular, persons with no nonneighbor friends are least knowledgeable (services known $M = 2.2$ if no friends, 2.8 if one–five friends, and 3.0 if six or more friends). Naming friends as confidants and/or instrumental helpers is also associated with somewhat greater service knowledge ($M = 3.2$) than having friends but not naming them for such support ($M = 2.9$). These patterns thus offer some support for a view of nonneighbor friends as a "lay referral" network.

In general, number of neighbors known well and frequency of interaction with neighbors exhibit little association with service knowledge, though there are some exceptions. Frequency of interaction with neighbors is related to knowledge (partial correlation $r = .18$, when we control health and socioeconomic status) among respondents with some functional health impairment, and knowledge is related to both number known (.14) and frequency of interaction (.14) for apartment dwellers in central cities. Involvement in mutual assistance patterns with neighbors displays stronger and more consistent associations, however; knowledge is related to both help given to neighbors (.20) and help received from neighbors (.13). These associations are particularly evident for rural residents (.25 and .23, respectively) and city residents (.32, .19).

Table 4.11 indicates average number of services known as a function of combinations of interaction and assistance involving neighbors. The pattern underscores that actual assistance from neighbors, rather than frequency of contact, is related to service awareness. The pattern is more pronounced among rural residents. Localized information sources appear to be particularly valuable in rural areas, which tend to be characterized by fewer and more dispersed services (Coward and Rathbone-McCuan, 1985). More generally, the patterns in Table 4.11 suggest that neighborhood assistance networks are also referral networks.

Both having instrumental helpers and the proximity of helpers are related to service knowledge but in opposite directions. Having little assistance for instrumental situations is related to less knowledge of services; persons naming no helpers or only one helper (out of four situations) know of significantly fewer services ($M = 1.8$) than do those who name at least two helpers ($M = 3.2$). This pattern reflects isolation from both formal and informal supports for persons lacking instrumental helpers. Proximate helpers may reduce the need to know

Table 4.11 Multiple Classification Analyses of Service Knowledge by Nature of Relations with Neighbors

| | Services known | | | |
| | Total sample | | Rural | |
Neighbor relations	M	N	M	N
See weekly, get expressive help	3.1	289	2.7	81
See weekly, get instrumental help	3.1	201	2.6	60
See less than weekly but get expressive and/or instrumental help	3.1	240	2.7	75
See weekly but get neither type of help	2.7	77	1.7	10
See less than weekly and get neither type of help	2.7	115	1.8	30
β	.08	—	.18	—
p	.05	—	.05	—

Note: Functional health, education, and occupational prestige were covariates.

about formal services, however, as persons who have all their helpers in the neighborhood exhibit slightly less knowledge (M = 2.9). A similar pattern is evident with confidants. Knowledge of services is greater among those who have a confidant (M = 3.0) than among those who do not (M = 2.6); however, those who have their first-named confidant residing in the neighborhood know of fewer services (M = 2.9) than do those whose first-named confidant is in the metropolitan area but not the neighborhood (M = 3.3).

The informal networks of older people appear to make both positive and negative contributions to knowledge of formal services. Involvement with friends and neighbors is associated with greater knowledge (albeit modestly), whereas children, confidants, and instrumental helpers have more complex relationships to service knowledge. These are more apparent in Table 4.12, which combines the effects of presence and accessibility. The pattern for children is one of reduced knowledge when children are quite proximate. Having helpers and confidants appears to increase service knowledge, but easy access to such helpers again appears to reduce knowledge. These patterns are particularly pronounced for children and confidants among more "vulnerable" elderly—those who are widowed or have health problems. Some ties may thus substitute for formal services, potentially hindering access to such assistance instead of providing "lay referral."

These patterns may be understood by considering Granovetter's (1973) distinction between "strong" and "weak" ties. Children, confidants, and instrumental helpers represent strong ties characterized by intimacy and mutual obligation. These sources of assistance are often preferred to more formal services and, when they are available, substitute for formal services, though they may serve a referral function when they are less available. This role has both positive and negative elements. On the one hand, valuable support and assistance is

Table 4.12   Multiple Classification Analyses of Service Knowledge by Access to Children, Confidants, and Instrumental Helpers by Marital Status and Functional Health

| | Total Sample | | Marital status | | | |
| | | | Married | | Widowed | |
	M^a	N	M	N	M	N
CHILDREN						
None	3.09	245	2.89	85	3.23	82
See weekly or less	2.93	364	2.97	224	2.85	120
See several times a week	3.07	231	2.79	130	3.43	95
Same house/building	2.64	254	2.81	127	2.50	115
β	.09*		.04		.19*	
CONFIDANTS						
None	2.57	261	2.58	147	2.45	83
See weekly or less	2.97	320	2.90	179	3.04	107
See several times a week	3.23	214	3.10	114	3.37	86
See daily	2.91	302	2.91	129	2.83	137
β	.12*		.09		.16*	
INSTRUMENTAL HELPERS						
None	1.89	49	1.67	31	2.03	13
None in neighborhood	3.17	173	3.11	98	3.28	64
1–3 in neighborhood	3.33	141	3.45	58	3.20	58
All 4 in neighborhood	2.85	559	2.85	285	2.78	221
β	.16*		.20*		.15	

Note: Functional health, education, and occupational prestige were covariates.
*$p = .05$. ^{a}Mean number of services known.

provided, potentially reducing or eliminating the need for formal services. On the other hand, awareness and access may be reduced despite a heightened need for formal services that may be more appropriate and of higher quality. Indeed, accessible strong ties appear to be associated with lower awareness of formal services among more disadvantaged respondents (e.g., those who are widowed or who have functional impairments).

The "weak" ties of friends and neighbors involve less intimacy and obligation. Although they may (and often do) provide short-term assistance of a limited sort, they are neither expected nor preferred sources of more regular or major assistance. Granovetter (1973) suggests that weak ties are valuable because they link individuals to

Functional health			
No limitation		Some limitation	
M	N	M	N
3.16	174	2.92	71
2.98	261	2.83	103
3.26	174	2.56	57
2.78	170	2.30	84
.09		.13	
2.77	178	2.12	83
2.95	229	3.06	91
3.32	162	3.05	52
3.08	212	2.49	90
.10		.21*	
1.86	42	2.47	7
3.18	124	3.12	49
3.45	97	3.06	44
3.02	403	2.38	156
.18*		.18*	

wider-ranging networks, thereby serving as a more effective source of information. Friends and especially neighbors (because of their proximity) are often in a particularly good position to become aware of the needs of older individuals. Friends and neighbors are thus in a strategic position to make "referrals" to other sources of assistance, whether other interpersonal ties (such as children) or the formal service network.

To this point we have considered the contributions of network characteristics in isolation. Table 4.13 presents results of multiple regression analysis, adding variables in stages to a model predicting service knowledge. We analyzed a number of regression models. The final model reported here includes variables with the greatest theoretical and empirical importance. One distinction involves access to instrumental and expressive support, regardless of source. Instrumental help is measured by an index of proximate instrumental help (1 = name a helper in the neighborhood, either relative or neighbor, for all four situations; 0 = name a helper in the neighborhood for fewer than four situations). Two measures of expressive assistance were incorporated: number of confidants and a composite measure of frequency of interaction with any confidant (5 = daily; 4 = 2–6 days a week; 3 = weekly; 2 = less than weekly; 1 = has no confidant). The type of person (kin, friend, or neighbor) named as helper or confidant proved

Table 4.13   Stepwise Multiple Regression Analysis of Service Knowledge

Health	.04	.03	.03	.03
Education	.15*	.16*	.15*	.14*
Occupational prestige	.07*	.06*	.06*	.07*
Instrumental helpers in neighborhood		−.05	−.05	−.05*
Confidants (number)		.03	.01	−.00
Confidants (frequency)		.06	.06*	.06
Children (frequency)			−.05	−.05
Other relatives (number)			.03	.03
Nonneighbor friends (number)			.05	.05
Neighbors (frequency)				−.04
Neighbors (assistance)				.09*
R^2	.039	.046	.051	.058
ΔR^2	—	.007	.005	.007

Note: N = 775. Cells show standardized regression coefficients.
*p = .05.

to have little empirical importance and is not included in the final models. Other measures, however, assess the various types of relationships composing the informal network. Measures incorporated in the model are: (1) a composite measure of interaction with children (4 = see a child daily; 3 = see a child weekly; 2 = see a child more than annually; 1 = see a child once a year or less or has no living children), (2) number of other relatives in the metropolitan area who are seen regularly, (3) number of nonneighbor friends in the metropolitan area, (4) frequency of interaction with neighbors, and (5) number of types of assistance (out of 6) received from neighbors. Variables were added to the regression equations in the following order: (1) functional health, education, and occupational prestige, serving as controls; (2) indicators of instrumental and expressive support; (3) indicators of family ties and nonneighbor friendships, to assess the contributions of nonneighbor social ties; and (4) frequency of interaction and assistance received from neighbors, to assess the contributions of involvement with neighbors.

Network characteristics account for only 1.9% of the variance in service knowledge. Indeed, there are only two rather small significant coefficients, a positive association with aid received from neighbors and a negative association with proximity of helpers. The model as a whole explains only 5.8% of the variance in knowledge of services, with education having the only coefficient that is even modest in size. It appears that such knowledge reflects processes not tapped by these variables. This finding is perhaps not surprising, given the dominance of mass media as sources of information for these respondents.

We have noted that one of the strengths of this large sample is the possibilities it provides for subgroup analyses. Interpersonal ties and supports may play varying roles with regard to service knowledge for different segments of the older population. This possibility is examined in Table 4.14, which presents results of multiple regression analyses by functional health and the composite indicator of "competence." These analyses parallel that in Table 4.13, but coefficients are presented only for the social variables.

In general, involvement with neighbors appears to be associated with greater knowledge of services for more vulnerable elderly— those who have health problems and reduced competence. Proximate helpers are also associated with reduced knowledge for low-competence respondents; such persons may substitute informal for formal assistance and may thereby reduce service knowledge. More generally, the results lend support to the view that informal networks func-

Table 4.14   Multiple Regression Analyses of Service Knowledge, by Functional Health and Competence

	Functional impairment		Competence	
	None	Any	High	Low
Instrumental helpers in neighborhood	−.02	−.11*	−.00	−.15*
Confidants (number)	−.04	.06	−.03	.17*
Confidants (frequency)	.07*	.01	.08	−.00
Children (frequency)	−.06*	−.01	.02	−.01
Other relatives (number)	.06*	−.03	.06	−.02
Nonneighbor friends (number)	.05	.01	.03	−.00
Neighbors (frequency)	−.12*	.14*	−.14*	.18*
Neighbors (assistance)	.08*	.02	.08	.08
N	569	206	340	154

Note: Standardized regression coefficients are italicized when corresponding unstandardized coefficients differ by more than their combined standard errors.
*p = .05.

tion in different ways for different groups of older people, a point that will be more apparent in the next section.

Subjective Well-being

Social supports, and the networks that provide them, may contribute to subjective well-being in two ways. Some researchers view the contributions of social support as being indirect, mediating the effects of stressful life events (Dean and Lin, 1977; Kessler, 1979; Pearlin et al., 1981). These mediating resources help sustain self-esteem and feelings of mastery in the face of stress. Cobb (1979) suggests that social support reduces stress by improving person-environment congruence, as people who feel esteemed are more confident and better able to manipulate the environment.

Social support may also contribute directly to well-being. Cobb (1979), for example, suggests that low support may be stressful in itself. Thoits (1982) also indicates that there are sound sociological reasons why social supports should be directly related to psychological well-being. She cites two in particular: (1) symbolic interactionism, linking social interaction to self-evaluation and social identity, and (2) Durkheimian anomie theory, stressing the importance of social integration. Thoits reviews a number of studies indicating direct effects of social support on psychological well-being.

There has been debate about whether interpersonal ties make more general contributions to well-being in later life, however. We noted in Chapter 1, for example, that disengagement theory and activity theory have presented quite different views of the nature and value of social involvement in later life. We have already noted that older people do not generally exhibit a disengaged pattern of social involvement. Many gerontologists have argued that the maintenance of positive affect and independence among the elderly depends at least partly on the availability of social support. Lowenthal and Robinson (1976), for example, assert that "intimacy and the capacity for mutuality continue to be vital resources through very old age" (pp. 433–434). Similarly, Lopata (1975) defines a support system as a set of relationships involving the giving and receiving of objects, services, and social and emotional support for *maintaining* a style of life. Indeed, Snow and Gordon (1980) have noted the policy relevance of strengthening "natural networks," identifying points of intervention to mobilize informal support.

Although this reasoning seems quite straightforward, however, evidence concerning the benefits of informal networks is far from clear-cut. Informal ties can link the elderly to needed services, for example, but they may also isolate and block proper access to more effective formal services (O'Brien and Wagner, 1980; Wagner and Keast, 1981). This was the implication of some patterns reported in the previous section. Similarly, empirical research on the relationship between social involvement and subjective well-being is neither clear-cut nor consistent. There appears to be little relation between family availability and interaction and subjective well-being (Larson, 1978; Hoyt et al., 1980; Glenn and McLanahan, 1981; Montgomery, 1982). Voluntary participation in associations also appears to bear little independent association with well-being (Ward, 1979). Friendship interaction seems most consistently related to well-being, but even this relationship is not universal (Larson, 1978; Wood and Robertson, 1978; Hoyt et al., 1980).

The lack of clarity concerning the contributions of social involvement to the well-being of older persons reflects the conceptual complexity of social networks and the supports they provide. Three issues related to this complexity can be identified: (1) the relative importance of different types of interpersonal relationships, (2) subgroup variation in the implications of social support, and (3) the distinction between objective and subjective dimensions of social support.

We have already noted the varying qualities and functions of relationships with family, friends, and neighbors. In particular, although family ties are often preferred sources of social support, the quality of family relationships may be problematic. Lowenthal and Robinson (1976), for example, note that the literature on family ties of the elderly has focused primarily on quantity rather than quality and leaves a sense of sterility and formality. Although family members assume primary responsibility for the dependent aged, the extent to which family interaction is rewarding may decline with age because of dependence, role reversal and conflict, and generational distance (Berghorn et al., 1978).

These arguments suggest that family involvement should not necessarily be expected to increase overall feelings of well-being among older persons. Interaction with friends may be valued more highly because it is voluntary (Adams, 1967). The obligatory nature of kin relations, on the other hand, detracts from their quality, and kin may be estranged by generational differences in interests and experiences. Indeed, some research supports the notion that interaction with friends and neighbors is more generally associated with morale than is interaction with family (Pihlblad and Adams, 1972; Arling, 1976).

The particular value of friends and neighbors may also reflect what Granovetter (1973) calls "the strength of weak ties." Although "strong" ties, such as those with kin, involve the intimacy and reciprocity usually felt to be beneficial characteristics of social networks, Granovetter notes that one's strong ties can also be expected to show links with each other, yielding a relatively closed network. "Weak" ties, such as friendships that are less intense and intimate, are likely to serve as links to wider-ranging networks. Such ties, even though they are less intimate, may help counteract feelings of social isolation and marginality associated with retirement, poor health, and other concomitants of aging.

The contributions of informal ties to well-being, then, apparently may vary across types of interpersonal relationships. Friends, and perhaps local friends in particular, may be most valuable because of their expressive functions. It is also likely that the importance of social ties generally and of particular types of social ties varies across subgroups of the older population.

The view that social supports affect well-being indirectly, by buffering or mediating the effects of stressful life events, suggests that interpersonal ties will be more important for persons who have experienced such events. Larson (1978), for example, cites evidence that they are less salient for older persons with good health or higher socioeconomic status. Blau (1973) suggests that the importance of social interaction may increase with role loss and the reduction of activities. Loneliness appears to be a particular problem for widows (Lopata, 1979), the chronically ill, and the institutionalized older person (Montgomery, 1982). In addition to stressful life events, environmental docility is also relevant to understanding the role of informal networks. Support networks are themselves a dimension of the older person's environment. People who are environmentally "docile" are thus likely to be affected most by the nature of their social involvements. Localized ties are also likely to exhibit heightened importance for such persons. Reduced income and health, for example, limit mobility and create greater dependence on the local area for social contacts.

Clearly, the relationship between well-being and interpersonal ties is complex; different ties may fill different functions, with varying degrees of importance, and the contributions of these ties may vary across subgroups. The complications do not stop there, however. It must also be recognized that social support has both objective and subjective dimensions. As we stated earlier in this chapter, the quantity and quality of ties are two different issues. Quality is, of course, a subjective dimension of networks. Indeed, Thoits's (1982) definition of support emphasizes the *gratification* of needs, implying that the social network has a subjective component. The significance of subjective definition is further highlighted by research suggesting that low social involvement does not necessarily produce low morale (Lowenthal and Robinson, 1976). The point of view of the individual should thus be taken into account.

Just as objective measures of the quantity of social involvement have yielded inconsistent findings, however, more subjective approaches to the quality of involvement have not yielded a clear pattern of results. Liang et al. (1980), for example, investigated both objective and subjective dimensions of social integration. They found that the subjective sense of integration (perceptions of integration vs. loneliness and isolation) was an intervening variable between morale and objective integration (which had no direct effect on morale). Schooler et al. (1981), however, found that subjective integration exerted little effect on morale, whereas objective integration had a modest direct effect. Thus it remains unclear whether "sufficiency" of social support is best conceptualized in objective terms or in subjective terms.

In the following analyses we address the complications and complexities of the relation between informal networks and well-being outlined above. We examine the associations between network characteristics (interpersonal ties and supports, including both objective and subjective dimensions) and three indicators of subjective well-being: morale, mastery, and loneliness.

Let us begin with a global view of these patterns. Table 4.15 summarizes the associations between our indicators of well-being and selected characteristics of the informal networks of our respondents. With the exception of the more subjective network characteristics (seeing children and neighbors enough, having enough instrumental

Table 4.15 Partial Correlations of Selected Network Characteristics with Morale, Mastery, and Loneliness

	Morale	Mastery	Loneliness[a]
CHILDREN			
Have any	−.02	−.02	.02
Frequency	.08*	.06*	.09*
See enough	.18*	.15*	.15*
RELATIVES (number seen regularly)	.05	.06*	.05*
FRIENDS			
Number	.08*	.09*	.15*
Number new	.06*	.10*	−.05
NEIGHBORS			
Number known well	.05	.04	.02
Frequency	.09*	.06*	.08*
Aid received	−.00	−.01	−.03
See enough	.17*	.14*	.14*
INSTRUMENTAL HELPERS			
Number of helpers	.06*	−.01	.03
Number in neighborhood	.06*	.02	.06*
Enough help	.23*	.16*	.23*
CONFIDANTS			
Number	.05*	.03	−.02
Proximity[b]	.09*	.03	.05
Frequency[c]	.11*	.04	.06*
Enough opportunities	.17*	.12*	.15*

Note: Functional health, education, and occupational prestige were controlled.
[a]Coded so that higher scores represent less loneliness.
[b]Proximity of nearest of the up to three confidants.
[c]Frequency with which most frequently seen confidant was seen.
*$p = .05$.

help, and having enough opportunities for expressive support), network characteristics generally have only weak associations with subjective well-being. Before assuming that our task is completed, however, we should investigate the various network dimensions in greater detail, paying attention to possible subgroup variations within the older population.

Family ties. Having living children, proximity and frequency of interaction with children, and involvement with other relatives in the area exhibit weak associations with morale, mastery, and loneliness. Table 4.15 indicates, however, that seeing children "enough" is associated with all three. Numerous subgroup analyses yielded little variation, but there is an interesting pattern for the recently widowed. Among those widowed for five years or less, reduced loneliness is particularly related to both frequency of interaction with children (partial correlation $r = .24$, when we control health and socioeconomic status) and seeing children enough (.28); associations are not significant for those who have been widowed a longer time. Seeing children enough also has stronger associations with morale for rural respondents (.29) and for those who have some functional health impairment (.29). Thus we begin to see some evidence that the contributions of informal networks to well-being depend upon individual circumstances, particularly vulnerability.

On the whole, however, objective indicators of family involvement have little relation to well-being. Associations with seeing children enough suggest that "quality" of ties is more important than "quantity." We can consider the matter in another way. Table 4.16 presents associations between morale and a composite measure of relations with children, combining access and frequency with whether children are named as helpers or confidants. The first column indicates a weak pattern ($p < .10$) whereby morale is lower among those who (1) rely on children for support but see them infrequently, (2) see children frequently but do not use them for instrumental or expressive support, or (3) both see them infrequently and do not indicate supportive ties. These three groups can all be viewed as "deprived" in their relations with children. Table 4.16 indicates that this pattern is more pronounced for certain vulnerable subgroups—those who are widowed, have health impairment, or reside in rural areas. It is noteworthy that morale is generally not lower for those who are childless. Rather, low morale is associated with weak ties to children or less frequent interaction with supportive children.

Friends. Friendships outside the neighborhood have weak positive

Table 4.16   Multiple Classification Analyses of Morale with Quality of Relations with Children

Quality of relations with children	Total sample	Widowed	Some functional impairment	Rural
			Mean morale	
See weekly, named as confidant	52.2 (241)	50.9 (108)	48.4 (65)	53.5 (72)
See weekly, named as instrumental helper	52.6 (255)	51.0 (108)	46.7 (75)	53.4 (75)
See less than weekly but named as helper and/or confidant; or see weekly but named as neither helper nor confidant	50.4 (185)	48.0 (54)	43.6 (56)	49.8 (52)
See less than weekly and named as neither helper nor confidant	51.4 (124)	46.9 (36)	45.3 (28)	51.3 (40)
No living children	52.1 (248)	50.9 (83)	46.7 (72)	51.4 (44)
β	.08	.16*	.17*	.16*

Note: Functional health, education, and occupational prestige were covariates. Parenthetical values are N.
*p = .05.

associations with subjective well-being (see Table 4.15). Patterns are stronger for certain subgroups, however. Morale, for example, is more strongly correlated (when we control health and socioeconomic status) with number of friends for rural (.14) and suburban (.12) residents, for persons who have children but see them only weekly or less often (.20), and for persons with some functional impairment (.19). Thus poor health and limited involvement with children appear to heighten the "value" of friends, whereas such ties appear less influential with city residents.

There was evidence that subjective well-being is associated with the "quality" of relations with children. We have no measure of whether nonneighbor friends are seen "enough," but a composite measure was constructed similar to that for children (in Table 4.16). Interestingly, Table 4.17 indicates that morale and mastery are slightly higher for those who have friends but do not name them as confidants or as

instrumental helpers. We saw earlier that friends who are not neighbors are not preferred sources of such assistance. Although such
friends appear to make a small contribution to well-being, their use as
confidants or helpers may signal an unwelcome deficit elsewhere in
the support network. Golant (1984), for example, found that perceived
availability of assistance was greatest for those who relied on family
and weakest for those who relied on friends and others.

Neighbors. Like involvement with children, objective measures of
ties with neighbors have only weak associations with subjective well-
being, whereas seeing neighbors "enough" has stronger associations;
again see Table 4.15. Here too, however, patterns of association with
neighbors exhibit variation across respondent subgroups. Partial correlations (we control health and socioeconomic status) between morale and frequency of interaction with neighbors, for example, are
stronger for persons with some functional health impairment (.21),
widowed persons (.16), and people who have moved within five years
(.19). These variations suggest that restrictions and disruptions of social activity, such as those associated with health problems, widowhood, and residential mobility, heighten the importance of
proximate contacts such as neighbors.

It remains true, however, that well-being has stronger associations
with the subjective measure of whether neighbors are seen "enough."
This tendency again suggests the importance of the perceived
"quality" of interpersonal ties. As with the measures we used with
children and friends, we created a composite measure of quality of
relations with neighbors by combining frequency of interaction with

Table 4.17   Multiple Classification Analyses of Morale and Mastery with
Quality of Relations with Friends

Quality of relations with friends	Mean		N
	Morale	Mastery	
Has friends and named as confidant or helper	51.1	20.9	136
Has friends but not named as confidant or helper	52.4	21.3	573
Has no friends	50.9	20.9	209
β	.08*	.06*	—

Note: Functional health, education, and occupational prestige were covariates.
*p = .05.

the measures of assistance (expressive and instrumental) received from neighbors. Table 4.18 relates this composite to morale (a similar pattern is evident with mastery). Although morale is somewhat lower for persons having little involvement with neighbors, higher morale also characterizes those who see neighbors frequently but indicate that they receive *no* assistance from them. The pattern is not large (though it is more pronounced for those who are widowed or who have some functional health impairment), and it is relatively unusual to interact regularly with neighbors but receive no assistance from them. This pattern is noteworthy, however, in its similarity to the pattern found for "quality" of friendship ties. As with friends, receiving instrumental and expressive support from neighbors may be indicative of unwanted isolation from sources of aid that appear to be preferred or normative, such as children.

Instrumental assistance. The more objective measures of instrumental support, including number of situations for which helpers are

Table 4.18 Multiple Classification Analyses of Morale with Quality of Relations with Neighbors

Quality of neighbor relations	Mean morale		
	Total sample	Widowed	Some functional impairment
See weekly and expressive help	51.8 (289)	49.9 (123)	46.8 (77)
See weekly and instrumental help	52.6 (201)	51.9 (68)	48.4 (52)
See less than weekly but expressive or instrumental help	51.4 (240)	49.0 (72)	44.5 (63)
See weekly but neither expressive nor instrumental help	53.9 (77)	52.5 (32)	51.1 (20)
See less than weekly and neither expressive nor instrumental help	51.5 (115)	49.2 (50)	44.8 (38)
β	.08*	.13*	.21*

*$p = .05$.
Note: Functional health, education, and occupational prestige were covariates.
Parenthetical values are N.

available, proximity of helpers, and type of person named as helper exhibit little association with subjective well-being. Having helpers in the neighborhood (relatives or neighbors), however, is moderately related to morale (we control health and socioeconomic status) for persons with some functional impairment (partial correlation $r = .16$) and for people who have moved within five years (.14). As with children and neighbors, Table 4.15 indicates that the subjective measure of having "enough" help has stronger associations with morale, mastery, and loneliness.

Confidants. A number of objective variables linked to confidants were investigated, including number, proximity, and frequency of interaction with both first-named confidant and any confidant, and type of person named as a confidant. The results of these analyses are reflected in Table 4.15—at best, weak positive associations with well-being.

We do not mean that no relationships exist. Proximity and frequency of interaction with confidants, for example, are related to morale. Table 4.19 clarifies these relationships. Morale is highest for those with very close proximity and frequent interaction with confidants. Persons with no confidants, however, have higher morale than those who see confidants infrequently and higher morale in particular than the relatively few respondents whose confidants all reside outside the metropolitan area. Less proximity and interaction with confidants is associated with greater use of letters and the telephone for contact, but there is no evidence that these forms of contact are related to well-being. Although the patterns in Table 4.19 are statistically significant, they are not sizable. In general, objective access and involvement with confidants appears to contribute only marginally to well-being, despite the attention given to such ties in the literature. These confidants are restricted to persons outside the respondent's own household. It may be that the value of confidants has been at least partly confounded in previous studies with the value of being married (so that one has a confidant in one's household).

The lower morale of persons who have confidants but reduced access to them would seem to reflect feelings of deprivation and isolation. This aspect is further underscored by the more substantial associations between subjective well-being and whether respondents have "enough" opportunities to "share confidences and feelings with another person" (see Table 4.15). The associations are particularly noteworthy because this question was asked only of persons who had at least one confidant, and 95% of these indicated that they have

Table 4.19 Multiple Classification Analyses of Morale with Proximity and Frequency of Interaction with Any Confidant

	Morale		β
CLOSEST PROXIMITY			
Neighborhood	52.3	477	.09*
SMSA	51.7	329	—
Outside SMSA	47.6	36	—
No confidant	51.9	253	—
MOST FREQUENT			
Daily	52.9	311	.09*
2–6 days a week	51.5	215	—
Weekly	51.1	202	—
Monthly or less	50.6	111	—
No confidant	51.9	253	—

Note: Functional health, education, and occupational prestige were covariates.
*p = .05.

enough opportunities. As with children, neighbors, and instrumental helpers, the subjective network perception has stronger associations with subjective well-being than do more objective network characteristics.

Combined effects. To this point the various components of informal networks have been discussed separately. Multiple regression analyses, combining these components, offer the opportunity to assess their joint contributions to well-being as well as the relative contributions of the different network components. Attention will be restricted to morale because patterns for mastery and loneliness are similar. Models are analyzed first for the more objective network characteristics, with subjective network characteristics then added to the models. Stepwise regression models, comparable to those employed previously for service knowledge, were analyzed. Table 4.20 presents results of the analysis of morale.

Functional health is clearly the dominant factor, with education also having a strong association. As a whole, the network variables make a relatively weak contribution, explaining only an additional 2% of the variance in morale. Number of friends outside the neighborhood makes the only noteworthy contribution, but this variable adds only 1% to the variance explained.

It was apparent in earlier analyses that associations between net-

Table 4.20   Stepwise Multiple Regression Analysis of Morale

Health	.37*	.37*	.37*	.37*
Education	.19*	.20*	.19*	.19*
Occupational prestige	−.08*	−.08*	−.08*	−.08*
Instrumental helpers in neighborhood		.06*	.06*	.05*
Confidants (number)		−.01	−.04	−.03
Confidants (frequency)		.03	.04	.03
Children (frequency)			−.00	.00
Other relatives (number)			.05*	.05*
Nonneighbor friends (number)			.10*	.10*
Neighbors (frequency)				.05
Neighbors (assistance)				−.02
R²	.195	.200	.213	.215
ΔR²	—	.005	.013	.002

Note: N = 775. Cells show standardized regression coefficients.
*p = .05.

work characteristics and well-being often vary across subgroups. Table 4.21 presents results of regression analyses for subgroups defined according to the following variables: functional health, marital status, and the composite measures of "vulnerability" and "competence," described in Chapter 2.

One reason for expecting subgroup variation in the contributions of interpersonal ties to well-being is the potential buffering role of social supports, yielding greater contributions for those who have undergone stressful life events such as health problems or widowhood. The implication is that a *general* heightening of the value of social involvement and support occurs, but Table 4.21 indicates little variation for most of the network measures (i.e., frequency of interaction with children and confidants and number of nonneighbor friends and other relatives). This absence of variation may reflect the fact that our subgroups are defined according to *circumstances* rather than *events*. Kessler and Essex (1982) suggest that social embeddedness, or integration, may be more beneficial in dealing with unexpected, traumatic life *events* rather than ongoing or chronic *strains*. The latter are more characteristic of age-related changes (poor health, retirement, or widowhood).

The environmental-docility hypothesis implies a more specific expectation that *proximate* ties will be particularly influential when

Table 4.21   Multiple Regression Analyses of Morale

	Functional impairment		Marital status	
	None	Any	Married	Widowed
Instrumental helpers				
in neighborhood	.03	.14*	.02	.08
Confidants (number)	−.06	.03	−.03	−.04
Confidants (frequency)	.05	−.01	.06	.09
Children (frequency)	−.01	.02	−.00	−.01
Other relatives (number)	.03	.08	.07*	−.02
Nonneighbor friends (number)	.13*	.09	.11*	.09
Neighbors (frequency)	.01	.15*	−.03	.13
Neighbors (assistance)	−.04	−.01	.01	−.08
N	569	206	421	276

Note: Standardized regression coefficients are italicized when corresponding unstandardized coefficients differ by more than their combined standard errors.
*p = .05.
aVulnerability is defined as follows: low = aged 60–69, married, and no functional impairment; high = aged 70+, widowed, and with some functional impairment.

competence is reduced. The patterns in Table 4.21 are consistent with this finding. In general, availability of proximate helpers and frequency of interaction with neighbors exhibit stronger associations with morale for more vulnerable and less competent older persons. The one anomaly is a negative coefficient for assistance received from neighbors in the "high vulnerability" subgroup (aged 70+, widowed, and with some functional impairment). Knowledge that assistance will be available if it is needed (e.g., helpers in the neighborhood) is particularly comforting for such persons, but actual assistance serves as a demoralizing reminder of one's problems and dependency. In addition we have noted that neighbors are not generally preferred as sources of support. Heavy assistance from neighbors may signal unwelcome deficits elsewhere in the support network.

Table 4.21 indicates that the contributions of network characteristics to well-being vary across subgroups of the older population. Even so, however, these contributions do not appear to be substantial. We have noted that the quality of interpersonal ties may be more important than their quantity. Table 4.22 indicates the results of adding subjective network characteristics—whether children are seen enough, whether neighbors are seen enough, whether there is

Vulnerability[a]		Competence	
Low	High	High	Low
.04	.31*	.14*	.11
−.05	−.11	−.10*	.11
.06	.18	.07	−.06
−.02	−.07	−.01	.02
.01	−.13	−.01	.08
.17*	.03	.08	.09
.01	.24*	−.03	.15*
−.04	−.24*	−.01	−.01
239	83	340	154

enough help for instrumental situations, and whether there are enough opportunities for expressive support—to the regression model of morale, both individually and in combination. Results of these analyses should be viewed with some caution. Subjective questions about children and confidants were not asked of all respondents. As a result, numbers of cases for these analyses are reduced, particularly when the subjective variables are used in combination.

These subjective characteristics appear to have significant associations with well-being even when we control for objective network characteristics. Indeed, the subjective characteristics all have stronger associations than the corresponding objective characteristics, in combination adding 6% to the variance explained in morale. When they are entered in combination, seeing children enough and having enough instrumental help exhibit the strongest associations with morale. Because children are preferred sources of instrumental help, these measures may be tapping similar concerns on the part of respondents. Gubrium (1973) has suggested that older people experience feelings of "precarious flexibility," questioning their ability to cope with problems that may arise. Feeling that one has sufficient help available if it is needed would be valuable in the face of such concerns.

Subjective assessments of network "quality" apparently have stronger associations with morale than do objective indicators of network "quantity." The prominent contribution of seeing children enough is particularly noteworthy in light of the general failure to find

Table 4.22   Multiple Regression Analyses of Morale, with Subjective Network Assessments Added Singly and in Combination

Health	.37*	.35*	.36*	.34*	.32*	.32*
Education	.19*	.22*	.19*	.19*	.19*	.22*
Occupational prestige	−.08*	−.07*	−.09*	−.09*	−.09*	−.11*
Instrumental helpers in neighborhood	.05*	.03	.05	.02	.02	−.03
Confidants (number)	−.03	−.04	−.03	−.03	−.01	−.03
Confidants (frequency)	.03	.07*	.02	.01	.06	.05
Children (frequency)	.00	.00	.00	−.01	.01	−.01
Other relatives (number)	.05*	.02	.04	.03	.02	−.03
Nonneighbor friends (number)	.10*	.10*	.09*	.09*	.08*	.07*
Neighbors (frequency)	.05	.01	.04	.03	.02	−.01
Neighbors (assistance)	−.02	−.03	−.01	−.02	−.01	−.03
Children (see enough)	—	.19*	—	—	—	.16*
Neighbors (see enough)	—	—	.12*	—	—	.05
Helpers (have enough)	—	—	—	.25*	—	.15*
Confidants (have enough)	—	—	—	—	.16*	.05
R^2	.215	.250	.229	.279	.201	.263
ΔR^2	—	.032	.013	.057	.025	.060
N	775	609	744	775	598	454

Note: Cells show standardized regression coefficients.
*$p < .05$.

associations between well-being and actual involvement with children. It is not entirely clear what to make of the apparent importance of perceived social "sufficiency." Whether one sees children "enough," for example, is itself a measure of satisfaction. We should perhaps make little of a relationship between domain satisfaction and overall morale; the former is a component of the latter. Associations between subjective network assessments and well-being are only moderate, however, indicating that they are not simply tapping the same thing. Other patterns also suggest that social deprivation is important. Having children or confidants but little access or involvement with them is associated with lower morale than having no children or confidants at all. The amount of social support thus appears to be less important than perceived adequacy versus deprivation.

Conclusions

Members of this sample exhibit generally robust informal networks in all three types of interpersonal ties (family, nonneighbor friends, and neighbors) and both types of supports (instrumental and expressive). The support networks of most of these older people are thus "adequate" in both objective and subjective terms. There is variation in this network adequacy, of course, related to such characteristics as sex, socioeconomic status, and location. Such patterns often reflect differences that remain stable throughout the life course and extend into old age. Health, retirement, widowhood, and age itself have only weak and scattered relationships with network characteristics. Thus the nature and quality of informal networks appear relatively resistant to the effects of aging and its accompaniments, at least in a sample of noninstitutionalized older persons who are relatively healthy and are long-term residents of their communities.

Perhaps the clearest "lesson" to be drawn from the data presented in this chapter is the value of variety or diversity in the composition of informal networks. Older people clearly prefer to receive assistance, both expressive and instrumental, from informal sources. As suggested by Litwak (1985), they will be best served in this regard by a diverse network of ties. Kin, especially children, are preferred normatively and behaviorally to the extent that they are available, but other interpersonal ties play particular roles and offer compensation and replacement. The value of neighbors, for example, appears to be heightened in later life. Neighbors are often sources of instrumental and expressive support, particularly when children are less accessible, and involvement with neighbors is a good indicator of the extensiveness of social ties more generally. The aged turn to nonlocal friends less frequently for social support, but number of such friends exhibits the most consistent associations with subjective well-being. This link may reflect the consensual, peer-based nature of friendship ties. Friendships may also be important because they represent a wide-ranging network of "weak" ties. Indeed, having few friends may be demoralizing not because friends actually fulfill important functions but because their lack triggers feelings of marginality. We can elaborate on the value of network diversity by considering the patterns of results on service knowledge and subjective well-being.

These data show little evidence that interpersonal ties are major sources for knowledge of services. There is evidence that friends and neighbors may make some contribution to such awareness, but the informal network may also reduce awareness of services, as knowledge is lower among those with higher access to children, confidants, and instrumental helpers. It is thus possible that informal networks may block access to more formal assistance, a problematic notion in two respects. First, although informal assistance is preferred by the elderly, formal services may be more appropriate and of higher quality. Adult children, for example, are seldom trained in providing medical, psychological, or social services. Informal support may thus constitute an unwitting disservice to older persons when the "shared functions" of informal and formal assistance (Litwak, 1985) are not properly coordinated. Provision of assistance may also do a disservice to caregivers, as there is the possibility of physical, emotional, and financial strain (Cantor, 1983). The elderly, then, will apparently be best served by a combination of "strong" ties, which can provide assistance to the extent they are able, and "weak" ties, which can facilitate access to more formal service networks.

The value of network diversity is also suggested by the findings concerning subjective well-being. Objective network characteristics generally have only weak associations with subjective well-being; such personal characteristics as health and socioeconomic status make much more substantial contributions to well-being. There is considerable evidence of subgroup variation in the contributions of informal networks, however, and of different components of those networks, to the well-being of older persons. The larger sample size offers unusual opportunities to make such comparisons. Of particular interest is the pattern of results indicating greater importance of proximate ties (interaction with neighbors and instrumental helpers in the neighborhood) for more vulnerable elderly (reduced health and competence, widowed, recently moved). The particular role played by *localized* ties supports the concept of environmental docility and a view that accessibility of social supports is a critical dimension of person-environment congruence in later life.

We cannot claim to have "closed the door" on understanding the role of informal networks in the lives of older people. Although the informal network may not be a major source of *initial* service awareness, for example, and may in some respects reduce such awareness, such networks may nonetheless have important involvement in the *process* of seeking and receiving formal services. Informal ties play a role in subjective definitions of need for services and of the appropriateness of specific services; for example, family members may convince reluctant older persons of their need for professional assistance. The mediating role noted by Sussman (1976) is also an important one, as kin and other members of informal networks can help oversee and coordinate formal services. We need to understand more fully the complexities of the support role of the informal network and to study the ways in which this role unfolds and changes over time.

Our analyses of subjective well-being also suggest the need for further work. In general, network characteristics did not exhibit substantial associations with the indicators of well-being used in this study. These indicators are quite global, however. A measure of more contemporary and transitory "peaks" in well-being, as in Bradburn's (1969) measure of affect, may be more sensitive to social involvement. There is a need to investigate which elements of well-being, or "quality of life," are most sensitive to the composition and functioning of informal networks (Ward, 1985).

The distinction between "quantity" and "quality" of informal ties and supports is also clearly an important one. Associations with well-being are stronger and more consistent with the subjective network characteristics—seeing children and neighbors enough and having enough instrumental and expressive support. Whether older people have "enough" interpersonal ties in an objective sense appears to be less important to feelings of well-being than whether they *perceive* that they have enough. We have not exhaustively investigated the quality of the informal networks of our respondents. Our subjective measures primarily reflect feelings of deprivation (not having "enough" contact or support). Other dimensions need to be investigated. We were unable to explore in a meaningful way the importance of having "enough" expressive support, for example, because the relevant question was asked only of those who had a confidant. More generally, Thoits's (1982) emphasis on the gratification of social needs (e.g., affection, approval, and security) indicates that one would ideally wish to relate network characteristics directly to the fulfillment (or hindrance) of such needs.

In conclusion, two general observations may be made. The first is that there is value in viewing informal networks as part of the environment within which individuals age. Such networks potentially offer assistance in meeting age-related needs, and their availability represents an aspect of person-environment congruence. Second, the characteristics of informal networks and their contributions to well-being are neither straightforward nor general. We are thus reminded of the need to explore the complexities of aging and diversity within the older population, because age itself is a very weak indicator of individual circumstances and needs.

5 The Social Context of Aging: Orientations to Aging and Age Peers

Thus far we have discussed the role of environmental factors, particularly the neighborhood, in the lives of older people, and the possible contributions of informal networks to well-being. We now turn to a discussion of age-related attitudes, including age identification and aging-group consciousness, and socialization for old age. These topics relate to our earlier discussions in two ways. First, orientations toward age constitute a social-psychological dimension of the environment within which individuals age. These individual orientations arise from and reflect the broader social environment for aging. As indications of the meaning of growing old for the individual, they can also be expected to influence perceived quality of life. In particular, it has been suggested that socialization for old age is a critical aspect of the aging experience.

Second, such attitudes are linked to informal networks in several ways. Personal attitudes about aging and age identity arise at least partly from social interactions, comparisons, and socialization experiences. Age-related attitudes also partly determine who is chosen for the informal network—for example, whether age-homogeneous or age-heterogeneous friends are sought.

Although the gerontological literature has paid some attention to patterns of age identity, aging-group consciousness, and socialization for old age, the sources of age-related orientations and their consequences for well-being are only sketchily understood. In particular, feeling "old" appears to undermine morale, yet it is often proposed that involvement with older persons may bolster well-being. Two general empirical issues suggest themselves. First, what factors shape age identity and feelings of solidarity with other older people? These factors would at least partly reflect what aging symbolizes to the individual. Second, what are the "costs" and "benefits" of age identity and aging-group consciousness for the aging individual? On the one hand, self-identification as "old" would seem detrimental to subjective well-being, given the generally negative imagery of old age. On the other hand, aging-group consciousness may buffer the individual from such imagery, and socialization by age peers may be beneficial to the elderly.

This chapter investigates the nature and sources of a range of age-related orientations that indicate the meaning of old age and access to socializing experiences. We also examine the consequences of such orientations for general feelings of well-being. The specific areas of age-related orientations include attitudes toward aging and age peers, personal age identification, socialization for old age, and aging-group consciousness. After presenting the distributions on these clusters of variables, we study the interrelationships among the variables as well as the personal characteristics with which they are correlated. We examine in depth the predictors of an attitudinal and a behavioral measure—age identification and participation in organizations, respectively. Finally, we study the effect the age orientations have upon morale, mastery, and knowledge of services.

Attitudes toward Aging and Age Peers

Attitudes toward aging have been a frequent concern in gerontology. While some scholars (Seltzer and Atchley, 1971, and Tibbits, 1979) have found reasons to believe that societal images of aging are changing, most research indicates that societal stereotypes of aging and the aged remain largely negative. Indeed, old age may be regarded as a type of stigma that "discredits" its possessor (Goffman, 1963). Such stigma may have two types of detrimental effects. Older people may be excluded from various activities because of their age, so that they are increasingly isolated. More relevant here, however, is the possibility that those who are stigmatized will internalize the stigma. Ward (1977a), for example, found that older persons having more negative attitudes toward old people in general also had lower self-esteem. This finding underscores the importance of understanding the images older people have of aging and the factors that shape those images.

As is true generally in the population, older people tend to overestimate the problems of other older people (National Council on the

Aging, 1975). O'Gorman (1980) refers to this phenomenon as "pluralistic ignorance"; the aged without serious problems assume that they
differ from their age peers, who are presumed to have serious problems. It is thus important to distinguish between attitudes toward
personal aging and *perceptions of the aged*, a distinction that has not
generally been made in the literature. Brubaker and Powers (1976)
conclude that research does not unequivocally support a negative
perception of aging; positive elements are found as well. They explain
this finding in terms of the individual's previous self-concept and
desires for consistency. Individuals who define themselves as old and
have positive self-concepts will also have positive perceptions of old
age.

   In our study, several sets of items were used to describe attitudes
toward both older people and younger people, including adjective
rating scales of each age group, comparison of self to age peers, associational and housing preferences, and perceived sufficiency of interaction with each group.

Adjective Ratings

Respondents were asked to indicate how descriptive 11 adjectives are
of "most older people"; a subset of 4 adjectives was also used for "most
younger people." Table 5.1 indicates the responses for each of these
adjectives. Members of this sample have generally favorable attitudes
toward their age peers. "Most older people," for example, are considered "very" wise, trustworthy, and friendly and are described as at
least "somewhat" flexible, tolerant, effective, and active. Most age
peers, however, were considered to be at least somewhat sick and
dependent, and nearly half considered them somewhat sad. Attitudes
toward other older people are thus generally positive but are colored
with some less favorable attitudes, reflecting presumed illness and
dependency. A sum score over the 11 adjectives was constructed.
Scores could range from 11 (unfavorable) to 33 (favorable), and the
mean was 26.2 (SD = 3.2; Cronbach's α = .72).

   Table 5.1 indicates that attitudes toward "most younger people" are
also generally favorable but somewhat less so than for age peers; for
example, 70% consider older people very trustworthy, but only 41%
say the same of younger people. Similar comparisons are evident for
friendly, selfish, and *tolerant.* These respondents thus hold a generally favorable view of other older people in both absolute terms and
compared with persons in their twenties.

Table 5.1   Responses to Adjectives Describing "Most Older People" and
"Most Younger People" (percent)

	Descriptive of the group		
	Very	Somewhat	Hardly at all
MOST OLDER PEOPLE			
Wise	53	43	4
Trustworthy	70	28	2
Sick	11	62	27
Friendly	74	25	1
Flexible	34	50	16
Tolerant	34	55	11
Selfish	7	32	61
Effective	30	59	11
Active	40	54	6
Sad	7	42	51
Dependent	18	48	34
MOST YOUNGER PEOPLE			
Trustworthy	41	46	13
Friendly	54	38	8
Selfish	18	44	38
Tolerant	28	52	20

Note: "Most older people" were people aged 65 and older. "Most younger people"
were people in their twenties.

Peer Comparisons

In comparison with themselves, however, these respondents generally
have somewhat less favorable impressions of age peers. Table 5.2 indicates their comparisons of social ties, health, and finances with "most
other persons your age." Very few respondents consider themselves
worse off, and many consider themselves better off. A sum score over
all four items ranging from 4 to 12, with higher scores indicating
comparisons more favorable to the respondent, had a mean of 9.8 (SD
= 1.7; Cronbach's α = .65). This more negative perception of the
circumstances of age peers may partly reflect the somewhat advantaged characteristics of this sample noted in Chapter 2, but it may also
reflect the "pluralistic ignorance" discussed above, in this case the
greater likelihood that other older people would be viewed as sick,
dependent, and sad.

Table 5.2 Comparisons with "Most Older Persons Your Age" (percent)

	Better off	About the same	Worse off
Relationships with family	66	32	2
Social contacts other than family	48	45	7
Health	54	35	11
Financial situation	33	57	10

Age Preferences

Results from the adjective ratings might suggest that these older people would prefer to associate with their age peers. This is not generally the case, however. When asked with whom they would prefer to spend most of their time, only 16% indicated "people your own age"; 10% indicated a preference for younger people, whereas 63% preferred people of different ages (a group that could, presumably, include some age peers), and an additional 11% volunteered that age does not matter. These findings are similar to those of a national survey, which found that only 23% of older people preferred to spend most of their time with people their own age (National Council on the Aging, 1975). A somewhat greater percentage (25%) indicated that they would prefer to live in housing limited to people their own age, but even this figure is not a large preference for associating with age peers. Age integration represents the clear preference of these older persons.

Table 5.3 lists reasons given by respondents for their associational preferences. Those who prefer to associate with age peers generally cite similarity of interests and, secondarily, similarity of needs and experiences. The peership represented by shared age and cohort is thus salient for such persons, whereas more negative attitudes toward the young are seldom mentioned. Such persons are very much in the minority, however. Although for some people the sense of self is enhanced by being "mirrored"—mechanical solidarity is life giving—others prefer complementarity or organic solidarity. In general, respondents in the latter category prefer the variety represented by exposure to different age groups, and many cite the perceived enthusiasm and fresh ideas of younger people.

Sufficiency of Involvement with Age Groups

Respondents were also asked whether they see enough of age peers and of younger people ("younger families, people under 40") as they

Table 5.3   Reasons Given for Preferring to Spend Time with Various Age Groups (percent)

	Associational preference			
Reason	Own age	Younger people	Different ages	Age does not matter
Contact with old people is depressing	0	24	8	2
Young people are cheerful, enthusiastic	0	61	32	15
Like exposure to fresh ideas	2	40	43	18
Like to keep up with the times	0	21	25	10
Like variety	0	22	58	62
People own age have same interests	78	0	6	12
People own age have same needs	34	0	3	3
People own age have same experiences	37	0	4	5
Hard to keep up with younger people	7	0	1	1
Younger people not very friendly	6	0	0	1
N	179	111	721	122

Note: Multiple responses permitted.

would like. Respondents generally expressed satisfaction with their involvement with both age groups—80% see age peers enough (and 3% would like to see them less), and 77% see younger people enough (2% would like to see them less).

Age Identification

These respondents appear to have generally favorable attitudes toward other older people, but they also wish to "distance" themselves from any overly exclusive association with age peers. This tendency may reflect their apparent perception that other older people are in somewhat disadvantaged situations. Possibly reflecting negative stereotypes about the aged and resistance to a personal perception of aging, studies have found that a substantial portion of the older population does not consider itself "elderly" (Ward, 1977a; Bultena and Powers, 1978). Bultena and Powers, for example, found that three-fourths of a sample of persons aged 60 and over defined themselves as "middle-aged"; 10 years later, when the median age was 76, 32% continued to identify themselves as middle-aged.

It has been claimed that an older age identity is associated with reduced feelings of happiness or well-being. We will discuss this point further below. Age identity is an important consideration from another standpoint. To the extent that persons resist identifying themselves *individually* as elderly or old, one would not expect to find a great deal of *group* consciousness or political activism on the basis of age.

Like their counterparts in previous research, our respondents resist identifying themselves as "elderly" or "old." Table 5.4 indicates that, when asked whether they consider themselves as young, middle-aged, elderly, or old, nearly two-thirds of the sample responded with "middle-aged" or "young." Although age is clearly related to age identity, 39% of even those respondents aged 80 and over identify themselves as young or middle-aged. Such self-perceptions help account for the preference for associating with a variety of age groups. Respondents do not view themselves as "old," nor do they wish to associate primarily with "old people" in presumably dependent circumstances. Perhaps having age peers who socialize others to the role of old age and provide more positive definitions of aging makes it easier to identify oneself as "old."

Socialization to Old Age

The allocation by society of roles according to age has been described by Riley et al. (1972), Schrank and Waring (1983), and others. Socialization plays an important role within this system of age stratification, as socialization "serves to teach individuals at each stage of the life course how to perform new roles, how to adjust to changing roles, and how to relinquish old ones" (Riley et al., 1972:11). In particular, Riley et al. cite the importance of preparation for age-related role transitions. Socialization occurs throughout the life course as individuals change roles and situations. Socializing experiences contribute to well-being by providing continuity and structure to the transitions that individuals encounter. Such contributions might be viewed as analogous to a "buffering" view of social support (Dean and

Table 5.4   Age Identification, for the Total Sample and by Age (percent)

Age identification	All	Age 60–69	Age 70–79	Age 80+
Young	22	26	16	20
Middle-aged	42	54	33	19
Elderly	21	14	30	23
Old	15	6	21	38
Total	100	100	100	100
N	1134	587	387	160

Lin, 1977), whereby age-related experiences (e.g., poor health, widowhood) are less detrimental when age-related socialization is available. George (1980) has cited evidence that socialization experiences have a positive impact on adjustment to a broad range of transitions. Trela and Jackson (1979) posit the ability of community roles to serve as integrating links in the absence of other roles and as functional substitutes for family roles.

Socializing experiences are part of the social environment for aging, and considerable importance has been attached to the presence or absence of socialization for old age. The extent to which such experiences exist for the transition to old age has been an issue in gerontology. Some researchers cite the existence of age-related expectations. Neugarten et al. (1965), for example, found agreement about the appropriate age for persons to marry, have children, and so on, and Wood (1971) reports the existence of certain norms for grandparents and the emergence of norms for leisure behavior in retirement. Offenbacher and Poster (1985) extracted a "baseline normative code" from Thematic Apperception Test responses given by the elderly. This code, shared by the elderly for themselves and others, includes: "Don't be sorry for yourself. Try to be independent. Don't just sit there; do something. Above all, be sociable." Offenbacher and Poster's findings are similar to Perkinson's (1980) findings that adjustment is viewed by peers as accepting aging and participating responsibly in the community. Characteristics of role models included a determination to keep going, being alert and aware, not feeling sorry for oneself, participating in committees, service to the wider community (instrumental and expressive support), congeniality, relaxation, cooperation, and harmoniousness.

Rosow (1974, 1976), however, has argued that old age is a normless, amorphous "roleless role" for which adequate socialization does not exist. According to Rosow, socialization properties operating throughout adulthood break down in old age. Rites of passage are vague or nonexistent, and there is role discontinuity. There is little motivation to prepare for old age, because it is associated with reduced status and responsibilities. Simplistic "act your age" norms provide little structure for an older person's activities and general lifestyle. Little research has investigated the extent to which older persons are socialized for old age or the sources of such socialization. Simpson et al. (1966), however, found that relatively few retirees reported discussing retirement with other retired persons, and the Harris Survey (National Council on the Aging, 1975) found that only 35% of the sample 65 years of age and over had talked to other people about growing old.

Although it seems to be true that there is no general "old age role" to which older people are socialized, it has been noted that informal roles may exist or may be "created" by individuals (Hess, 1976; Ward, 1984a; George, 1980). Aging individuals may negotiate roles within their own particular social worlds, even in the absence of formal or universal socialization for old age. Rosow (1976) notes that informal roles can limit the impact of losing "institutional" roles. Promotion of such roles is one potential function of the social networks discussed in the previous chapter.

Rosow (1974) in particular notes the potential value of the peer group in providing group membership and support, new roles and role models, and insulation from stigma. Age peers may thus be particularly valuable in socializing one another for old age, and such socialization may exist under certain circumstances. Friedman (1975), in a study of nursing home residents, reported that they socialized each other by helping to deal with such issues as family rejection and death. In such situations, age peers may represent a subculture that "provides its participants with adaptive techniques to deal with a set of recurring problems" (Sarbin, 1970:31). Because reference groups mediate culture through the evaluative information that they provide about such categories as "old person" (Woelfel and Haller, 1971), a culture of age peers could circumvent feelings of relative deprivation and self-derogation arising from comparison with middle-aged standards. In so doing, the culture might enhance aging-group consciousness and activism. Visible and supportive age peers can also provide role models to assist in socialization to old age. Such socialization may be an important benefit of age concentration, which we discuss in the next chapter.

We used a number of items to assess the availability of socialization experiences for our respondents. There were three major indicators: having a role model, having a helper with transitions, and knowledge of services. Role models and help from peers represent access to socializing experiences; service knowledge represents a possible outcome of socialization. When asked whether they had a friend, relative, or neighbor whom they considered "a good example of what a person should be like" in old age, over half (54%) reported having such a "role model"; the median age of this role model was 74. Perhaps reflecting their proximity, neighbors were cited most frequently as role models (44%), followed by friends (30%), and relatives (25%). Respondents also cited a number of qualities that they admired in the indicated role model, including: cheerfulness (66%), physical activity (52%), mental alertness (37%), being "young at heart" (31%), having many interests (31%), community activity and helping others (17%), still being able to work (16%), adjusting well to retirement (10%), overcoming illness (5%), and adjusting well to widowhood (5%). Role models thus appear to exemplify upbeat ("youthful") attitudes, activity, and ability to overcome age-related deficits. The category of person named as a role model was not related to the qualities which were admired.

Although half the respondents had a role model, only 30% of the sample indicated that they had found age peers helpful in offering advice and support about their age-related life changes. Among those receiving such help, a variety of concerns are represented: occupying leisure time (26%), changes in health (23%), adjustment to retirement (21%) and widowhood (15%), financial concerns (12%), family relations (9%), and feelings about death and dying (4%). On the whole, however, these respondents have experienced relatively little socialization from age peers.

In contrast to persons named as role models, neighbors are infrequently named as age-peer helpers (8% of all such helpers); relatives are cited most often (51%), followed by friends (39%). A role model may reflect proximity because of its implied observational content, whereas advice and support require the long-term intimacy of family and old friends. Assistance varies by type of helper. Relatives are cited more often for help with family relationships, widowhood, and feelings about death; friends are most helpful with regard to financial concerns, leisure, and retirement; and neighbors are most helpful with regard to health problems.

Knowledge of services also represents an aspect of socialization for old age. We noted in Chapter 2 that knowledge of five area services for the elderly (telephone or visiting, group or home-delivered meals, legal services, visiting nurses or home health aides, and transportation) was moderate; 31% know of all five services, whereas 20% know of none of them ($M = 2.9$). We also noted in Chapter 4, however, that relatives, friends, and neighbors were very minor sources of information about such services; this therefore seems to be an area for formal rather than informal socialization.

Aging-Group Consciousness

Socialization to old age can both be enhanced by and help to create aging-group consciousness. The existence of age-based social positions within a system of age stratification means that age is a basis of "structured social inequality" (Foner, 1974, 1979). Foner suggests that age inequality is as firmly entrenched as that based on class and sex. Such inequality implies at least the potential for group consciousness and political activism. As noted in Chapter 1, Rose (1965a and b) defined aging-group conscious persons and posited the development of an aging subculture because of the growing number and proportion of older persons, because of an increase in their vigor and educational level, because of common grievances and self-segregating trends, because of an increase in compulsory retirement, and because of a tendency to live apart from their children.

Whether or not such aging-group consciousness exists, and whether there is activism based on it, has been a topic of considerable debate, however (Williamson et al., 1982; Ward, 1984a). Although there is evidence of age homogeneity in social networks (Fischer, 1977), there is little evidence of aging-group consciousness in a political sense. Streib (1976), for example, suggests that the aged have stratum awareness, or a perception of separateness from other age groups, but that they lack a sense of belonging to an age stratum, an identification of interests in conflict with those of other strata, or activism as a stratum. Thus it is often argued that the aged lack an interest in organizing on their own behalf and have not identified common political interests. Binstock (1974) has concluded that "there is no evidence to indicate that aging-based interest appeals can swing a bloc of older persons' votes from one party or candidate to another" (pp. 202–203). Many reasons have been given, including the perceived stigma of old age, lack of age identification, the greater salience of other bases for identification (race, sex, and class), cross-generational contacts, and limitations on mobility (Rosow, 1974; Williamson et al., 1982; Ward, 1984a). To the extent that persons resist identifying themselves *individually* as elderly or old, one would expect to find little *group* solidarity and even less active political participation. A national survey found that only 13% of the older population had attended a senior center or club (National Council on the Aging, 1975).

Furthermore, a sense of identification with age peers is itself unlikely to be sufficient to stimulate political activism. A recent study of subjective group affiliation by older people found that 28% felt "closest" to older people (from a list of social categories) and another 46% felt "close" (Miller et al., 1980). Although racial and ethnic affiliation is typically associated with greater political participation, Miller et al. found a negative relationship between voting and this measure of age-group identification. They attributed this negative relationship to lack of economic resources and feelings of both individual and age-group powerlessness among age-group identifiers.

It appears, then, that aging-group consciousness has not yet coalesced into a political force. Dowd (1980a) suggests that young and old both attach legitimacy to the current age stratification system. He asserts that age inequality does not produce age-group consciousness because cross-age social exchange is governed by a rule of rationality rather than a rule of distributive justice. Aging-group consciousness and political activism on the basis of age may increase in the future, with better-educated older cohorts, the growing size of the older population and visibility of old-age associations, and the existence of such potentially unifying issues as retirement support and health care, but such predictions are fraught with uncertainty (Williamson et al., 1982; Ward, 1984a).

Several writers (e.g., Rose, 1965b; Rosow, 1967; Foner, 1974; Sherman, 1975b; Anderson and Anderson, 1978; Dowd, 1980a) have suggested that age-segregated settings tend to foster aging-group consciousness. In Chapter 6 we will consider the extent to which neighborhood age concentration fosters aging-group consciousness in our sample.

If aging-group consciousness is viewed as a sense of solidarity with other older persons, a solidarity that is likely to be expressed in behavior as well as in attitudes, there seems little evidence of such consciousness in our sample. As noted earlier, most respondents do not consider themselves elderly or old, nor do they wish to associate primarily with age peers. We will also see in the next chapter that there is only moderate age homogeneity in the networks of these respondents.

Nearly three-fourths (74%) of our respondents have never partici-pated in a club or organization for older people. Among those who do, less than half attend more than once a month. In addition, only 11% of the sample have "taken any action on behalf of older people," and 63% of these indicated that they had engaged in only one such ac-tivity. Among those who had done so, activities included: volunteer or charity work (44%); attending informational meetings and hearings (33%); writing letters to politicians, newspapers, or agencies (29%); membership in a committee or organization (21%); having a lead-ership position in a committee or organization (12%); and signing petitions (10%). These respondents thus exhibit very little activism on the basis of age; indeed, only 2 persons out of 1,185 indicated that they had participated in political demonstrations on behalf of older peo-ple.

To summarize our findings pertaining to age-related orientations, we have found that other older persons are generally rated favorably by our sample without being considered as well off as themselves. They prefer to associate with persons of a variety of ages, and the modal identification is "middle-aged." There was only moderate so-cialization to old age, as reflected by the presence of a role model for aging or a helper with age-related transitions. Aging-group con-

Table 5.5   Zero-Order Intercorrelations among Age-Related Orientations

	1	2	3
1. Attitudes toward older people	—		
2. Prefer to associate with age peers	−.01	—	
3. Prefer to live with age peers	−.00	.35*	—
4. Peer comparisons	.17*	−.09*	−.17*
5. See age peers enough	.09*	−.08*	−.11*
6. Age identification	−.08*	.14*	.17*
7. Role model	.12*	−.06*	−.03
8. Advice and support from age peers	.12*	.05*	.08*
9. Attend clubs for older people	−.00	.04	.07*
10. Action on behalf of older people	.04	−.05*	−.02
11. Service knowledge	.05*	−.05	−.01
12. Service use	−.07*	.04	.03

*p = .05.

sciousness as measured by participation in groups for seniors was also moderate, and there was little action on behalf of older persons as a group.

Interrelations among Age-Related Orientations

We turn now to an exploration of the interrelations among the various age-related orientations. There are a number of possible patterns. Resistance to viewing oneself as elderly or old is likely to stem from negative stereotypes of the aged, thereby contributing to reduced aging-group consciousness. It might be suggested that those older persons who do not subscribe to negative stereotypes will be less likely to resist self-identification as "old," though Ward (1977a) and Daum (1978) found that age identification was not related to attitudes about aging. Access to role models and to other socializing experiences could be expected to yield more favorable attitudes toward aging and the aged, greater willingness to identify oneself as old, and heightened aging-group consciousness. Rose (1965b), however, found that those who were in aging-related organizations were less likely to say they preferred to associate with age peers. Ward (1977c) found that associational preference and recommendations for political action were related to age identification but not to attitudes toward old people. Previous research has thus generated inconsistent findings.

Table 5.5 summarizes the relationships among the age-related ori-

4	5	6	7	8	9	10	11	12
—								
.17*	—							
−.23*	−.12*	—						
.12*	.02	−.08*	—					
.03	−.05	−.00	.23*	—				
.07*	.06*	.01	.06*	.06*	—			
.09*	.06*	−.07*	.16*	.14*	.18*	—		
.03	.09*	−.03	.15*	.14*	.12*	.13*	—	
−.07*	−.06*	.10*	.00	.03	.19*	.02	.16*	—

entations. Many of the orientations have little relation to one another, indicating that we are dealing with several distinct dimensions. Within these dimensions, variables are related as one might expect. Preferring to associate primarily with older people is associated with a preference for age-segregated housing, though these preferences are by no means empirically identical. Having a role model is related to receiving advice and support from age peers, and involvement in clubs for older people is related to taking action on their behalf.

Some other patterns are evident in Table 5.5. Not surprisingly, older age identity is related to preferring to associate with and to live with other older people. Among individuals who identify themselves as elderly or old, for example, 22% prefer to spend time with age peers, whereas only 12% of those who identify themselves as young or middle-aged prefer to do so. Similarly, among those who identify themselves as elderly or old, 33% prefer to live with age peers, whereas only 21% of those who identify themselves as young or middle-aged prefer to do so. In addition, feeling better off than age peers is associated with preferring not to associate primarily with them or to live with them. Although persons who feel better off than age peers might be assumed to wish to associate with them in order to retain feelings of "superiority," the evidence indicates that such persons do not prefer to associate with "inferiors."

There is some evidence of the potential benefits of socializing experiences. Naming a role model and having received advice and support from age peers is related to more positive attitudes toward older people in general, to greater knowledge of services for older people, and to taking action on behalf of older people. Involvement in clubs for older people is related to greater knowledge of services; indeed, we noted in Chapter 4 that such organizations are frequently cited as sources of information.

In other respects, however, our expectations were not fulfilled. Contrary to expectations, age identification is negatively related to attitudes toward older people. The association is small, however, suggesting that other factors influence age identity and attitudes. In the next section we explore the influence of health and comparisons with age peers upon age identification. Age identity also has little association with taking action on behalf of older people and is unrelated to involvement in clubs for older people, to having a role model, and to receiving advice from age peers. Subjective age identity does not seem to be a function of generalized attitudes (or "stigma") about old people or of socialization for old age. Rather, it may be a response to circumstances that symbolize aging for the individual, such as ill health.

Attitudes toward older people in general do not appear to be a pivotal dimension in personal orientation to aging. As noted earlier, such attitudes are related to socialization experiences. The concept of pluralistic ignorance might suggest that favorable comparisons with age peers would be related to more negative attitudes toward older people, but Table 5.5 indicates that persons who feel worse off (or no better) than age peers also have more negative attitudes toward older people. It is thus possible that negative impressions of the elderly are perhaps partly reflections of one's own difficulties. Still, these attitudes have little relation to age identity, to associational or housing preferences, to involvement in clubs for older people, or to taking action on behalf of older people.

In general, the absence of relationships among age-related orientations would suggest that we look for other factors in the causal model. One set of factors are personal characteristics of the individual, such as age, gender, and socioeconomic status.

Variations in Age-Related Orientations

The literature suggests that age-related orientations are likely to vary by personal characteristics. Health, for example, is likely to be an important determinant of age identity, and poor health may account for low age-based activity. We will now explore such correlates and sources of age-related attitudes and socialization experiences.

Age

We have already seen (in Table 5.4) that age is related to age identity ($r = .37$). We will see in Chapter 6 that older respondents have somewhat older networks (e.g., older friends and confidants). Otherwise, age has relatively weak associations with age-related orientations and behaviors. Age, for example, is unrelated to attitudes toward older and younger people that are reflected in the adjective rating scales. Table 5.6 also indicates that age has little relation to preference for associating with or living exclusively with age peers, participating in clubs for older people, or taking action on behalf of older people. Perhaps surprisingly, older respondents are less likely to have a role model or to receive advice and support from age peers. It is possible that role model and age changes are more salient for the "young-old" who are

Table 5.6   Age Differences in Age-Related Orientations

	Age (%)			
	60–69	70–79	80+	p
Prefer to associate with age peers	15	16	20	.55
Prefer to live with age peers	24	26	30	.31
Has role model	54	44	30	.0001
Received advice and support from age peers	32	27	18	.005
Know of all 5 services	34	30	23	.05
Used any of the 5 services	12	18	23	.001
Has attended club for older persons	23	30	26	.05
Taken action on behalf of older people	11	12	9	.50

in the process of transition than for the "old-old." Older respondents are also less knowledgeable about senior services, though use of such services rises with age.

Sex

There are only scattered and very slight sex differences in age-related orientations. Men and women, for example, do not differ in preference for associating with age peers or comparisons with age peers. No sex difference was found in age identification for the first two age categories, but 69% of the 97 women aged 80 and over consider themselves elderly or old, whereas only 49% of the 63 oldest men consider themselves elderly or old. Males are somewhat more likely to know of none of the five services (24% vs. 17%), and females are more likely to have attended a club or organization for older persons (29% vs. 21%), but on the whole, men and women exhibit few differences in age-related orientations.

We noted in Chapter 4 that women appear to be more active in support networks, and men are more likely to name women as instrumental helpers and confidants than the reverse. A similar pattern is evident in terms of socializing experiences. Although 35% of males cited a female as their role model, only 17% of females cite a male; similarly, most men and women who cite a friend or neighbor as the primary source of information about senior services indicate that this person is a woman (75% of males, 92% of females). Among persons indicating that they have received advice or support about aging from age peers, 59% of women indicate that most of those who have helped are the same sex, compared with only 36% of the men. This difference further underscores the centrality of women in the support networks of older people.

Socioeconomic Status

Table 5.7 indicates associations between age-related orientations and socioeconomic status. Attitudes toward older people do not vary significantly by education, income, or occupational status. Higher-status respondents, however, are less likely to prefer to associate with or to live primarily with age peers and are more likely to say they see enough of age peers. Such persons also have younger age identities, though these associations are reduced by controls for age (partial correlation for age identity with education and income $r = -.11$). Higher-status persons are more likely to indicate a role model, however. Such people are also more knowledgeable about services while using them less. Finally, higher-status respondents are not more likely to participate in clubs or organizations for the elderly, but they are more likely to have taken some action in their behalf. These patterns suggest that higher socioeconomic status is related to greater resistance to identifying with the elderly but that there is perhaps somewhat greater access to socialization for old age.

Table 5.7 also indicates that higher-status respondents compare their own circumstances more favorably with those of age peers. This is particularly true for "financial situation," but such persons also feel better off with regard to social ties and health.

Health

Table 5.8 summarizes associations of age-related orientations with functional health and subjective health. These are similar to the associations with socioeconomic status. Better health, for example, is associated with more favorable attitudes toward older people but less preference for associating or living with age peers and to more favorable comparisons with age peers. Better health is also positively related to having a role model, to receiving advice from age peers, and to knowledge of services, though health is negatively related to service use. Patterns for both health and socioeconomic status thus indicate that socializing experiences and service knowledge are greater for those who perhaps need them less.

Both functional and subjective health exhibit strong associations

Table 5.7   Zero-Order Correlations between Socioeconomic Status Variables and Age-Related Orientations

	Education	Income	Occupational prestige
Attitudes toward older people	.00	.06	−.03
Prefer to associate with age peers	−.11*	−.10*	−.03
Prefer to live with age peers	−.15*	−.18*	−.09*
See age peers enough	.10*	.10*	.04
Age identification	−.16*	−.22*	−.05*
Role model	.17*	.12*	.07*
Advice and support from age peers	.03	.01	−.04
Service knowledge	.15*	.08*	.10*
Service use	−.08*	−.15*	−.03
Attend clubs for older people	.03	−.04	.02
Action on behalf of older people	.19*	.12*	.10*
Age-peer comparisons			
Family relations	.07*	.10*	.03
Other social contacts	.12*	.09*	.02
Health	.16*	.18*	.07*
Financial situation	.22*	.31*	.13*

*$p = .05$.

with age identity. Only 28% of those with no functional health impairment consider themselves "elderly" or "old," compared with 58% of those with any impairment. Similarly, only 17% of those who perceive their health as excellent consider themselves elderly or old, compared with 70% of those who view their health as poor or very poor. These relationships hold when age is controlled (partial correlations are −.27 for functional health and for subjective health). These patterns suggest that health problems are symbolic of being "old" for

Table 5.8   Zero-Order Correlations between Health and Age-Related Orientations

	Functional health	Subjective health
Attitudes toward older people	.06*	.15*
Prefer to associate with age peers	− .06*	− .16*
Prefer to live with age peers	− .05*	− .14*
See age peers enough	.16*	.16*
Age identification	− .34*	− .32*
Role model	.13*	.08*
Advice and support from age peers	.07*	.03
Service knowledge	.08*	.09*
Service use	− .12*	− .14*
Attend clubs for older people	.07*	.01
Action on behalf of older people	.06*	.07*
Age-peer comparisons		
Family relations	.14*	.19*
Other social contacts	.15*	.19*
Health	.45*	.57*
Financial situation	.16*	.26*

*$p = .05$.

these respondents. A later section of this chapter combines several measures of health with other predictors in a multiple regression model of age identification.

Role Loss

Retirement and widowhood are two age-symbolic events that might be expected to affect age-related orientations. Retirement exhibits some weak associations. Retirees, for example, are more likely to prefer to associate with older people (17% vs. 7%) and to participate in senior clubs (27% vs. 18%); these associations hold when age is controlled. Retired persons are also more likely to consider themselves elderly or old (36% vs. 14%), but the association is weak when age is controlled (partial correlation $r = .07$). Retirement is otherwise unassociated with age-related orientations, including comparisons with age peers.

Being widowed is unrelated to preferring to associate or live with age peers, having a role model, receiving advice and support from age peers, comparisons with age peers, or knowledge of services. Widowed persons are more likely to identify themselves as elderly or old than are married persons (47% vs. 30%), but this relationship is not significant when age is controlled. Widowed persons are somewhat more likely to participate in clubs for older people (31% vs. 23%). On the whole, however, widowhood and retirement exhibit little association with the age-related orientations.

Location

City residents are more likely to categorize themselves as "elderly" or "old" (40%) than are suburbanites (38%) or rural residents (29%) and are least likely to have received advice and support from age peers (27%, 31%, and 37%, respectively). These associations remain when age and functional health are controlled, but they are rather small. On the whole, residential location has little relation to age-related orientations. It was noted in Chapter 4, however, that city residents are most knowledgeable about services for older people, followed by suburban residents, with rural residents least knowledgeable.

Informal Networks

It could be expected that age-related orientations reflect characteristics of informal support networks. A preference for associating or living primarily with age peers, for example, may result from deficits in the social network. We can use some of the variables analyzed in Chapter 4 to explore such possibilities.

Not surprisingly, network characteristics are related to peer comparisons. Table 5.9 indicates that the robustness of networks is generally related to feeling better off than age peers in terms of family and other social ties. Those who have children and see them more frequently, for example, rate their family relations as better than those of age peers. This is particularly true for persons with some functional impairment (partial correlation $r = .29$) or living alone (.23). Those who feel that they have enough instrumental help also compare themselves favorably with other older persons. These associations are not large, however. It is thus possible that such comparisons are a product of more generalized stereotypes (and "pluralistic ignorance") about

Table 5.9   Partial Correlations of Network Characteristics with Peer Comparisons

| | Peer comparisons | | | |
	Family	Other social	Health	Financial
Frequency of interaction with children	.11*	.06*	.07*	.07*
Number of nonneighbor friends	.04	.11*	.02	.04
Frequency of interaction with neighbors	.08*	.13*	.04	.03
Number of confidants	.10*	.04	.02	.01
Frequency of interaction with a confidant	.05	.08*	.00	.05
Enough instrumental help	.11*	.16*	.09*	.14*

Note: Functional health, socioeconomic status, and age were controlled.
*p = .05.

the circumstances of the elderly rather than a more objectively based comparison between one's own situation and that of other older persons.

Interestingly, naming a neighbor as an instrumental helper is associated with feeling worse off in regard to family ties (partial correlation r = −.14). We noted in Chapter 4 that children are preferred sources of such assistance. Although neighbors are often used as substitutes because of their proximity, their use is apparently also experienced as a social deficit.

Network characteristics are generally unrelated to whether the respondent has a role model. Neighbors are often named as role models, however, and having a role model is related to number of neighbors known (partial correlation r = .16 when we control functional health and socioeconomic status), frequency of interaction with neighbors (.12), and assistance received from neighbors (.27). Involvement in a neighborhood support network thus appears to make some contribution to socialization.

There is also some evidence that preference for associating and living with age peers is partly a response to social deficits, particularly when an individual has physical problems. Persons who feel that they do not have enough instrumental help, for example, are more likely to prefer to associate primarily with older people (25% vs. 15%) and to live in housing limited to older people (40% vs. 24%). Similarly, a preference for age-segregated housing is greater among respondents who find it hard to make friends in their neighborhoods (36% vs. 25%) and who feel they do not have much in common with their neighbors (31% vs. 23%). Finally, there are indications that lack of access to children and friends, in combination with physical impairments, is related to a preference for age-segregated housing. Among persons with some functional impairment, 43% of those who see their children only weekly or less and 37% of those with no friends in the area would prefer to live in age-segregated housing; only about 25% of all other respondent subgroups wish to do so. The attractiveness of age-segregated housing thus appears to derive from the combination of physical and social deficits. It should be recalled that at the time of the interviews only 14 respondents (1.2% of the sample) were residing in housing they described as "especially for older people."

Multiple Determinants of Age-Related Attitudes and Behaviors

Previous sections have indicated that the various forms of age-related attitudes and behaviors have different correlates and sources. These attitudes and behaviors are by no means unidimensional, and several are orthogonal to each other. In turn, they are related to different personal characteristics. Older subjective age identity, for example, is associated with worse health, whereas knowledge of service and availability of a role model are related to better health and higher socioeconomic status.

In the present section we combine personal characteristics, age-related characteristics, and age-related orientations to determine the best predictors of two age-related orientations: age identification and club participation. Age identity reflects a more personal and internal orientation to age, and participation in clubs or organizations for older people represents a behavioral dimension. Multiple regression analysis was employed to explore these dimensions in greater detail. The variables entered in the models were those that had been reported in the literature as relating to age identification or organizational participation or those that we have found to be related in our bivariate analyses.

Although most previous research has considered bivariate rela-

tionships rather than multivariate relationships, considerable attention has been given to the factors that determine age identification.
Age is an important determinant, of course, but the correspondence
between chronological age and self-identification is far from perfect
(Brubaker and Powers, 1976). Peters (1971) categorized influences
upon age identification as cultural, physiological, and social and suggested that we study these sets of variables in combination. Although
age identity might be seen as representing age denial, it also does not
appear that age identity is related to attitudes about aging and old
people (Ward, 1977a; Daum, 1978). Age identity reflects events and
changes that symbolize loss for the individual rather than simply
chronological age or denial of age. The losses can include declines in
health, changes in roles, such as retirement and widowhood, and
income decline. Many studies (Ward, 1977a; Bultena and Powers,
1978; Linn and Hunter, 1979; Mutran and Burke, 1979a and b; George
and Bearon, 1980; Carp and Carp, 1981; Mutran and Reitzes, 1981;
and Baum and Boxley, 1983) have found that age identification was
related to health. Markides and Boldt (1983) found that not only
health but decline in health were related to change in subjective age
from young or middle-aged to old.

Several investigators have considered the effects of the major status
losses of retirement and widowhood as they affect age identification,
with somewhat inconsistent results. Ward (1977a) found that retirement was strongly related to age identity. Other studies have found
that widows and retirees were more likely to identify as old (Phillips,
1957; Guptill, 1969; Peters, 1971). Mutran and Reitzes (1981) found
that widowhood but not retirement was associated with an older age
identity; Blau (1956) found the opposite. Blau suggested that retirement socially connotes lack of fitness, whereas widowhood is a natural event that does not have such meaning. Mutran and Burke (1979b)
found that for white and black men, and for black women, identification was associated with retirement and only indirectly with health,
whereas for white women, identification was associated with health
and not with retirement.

Some research has indicated that social class is negatively related to
older age identity (Peters, 1971; Mutran and Burke, 1979b; Baum and
Boxley, 1983; Markides and Boldt, 1983). Ward (1977a) found that
financial decline was strongly related to age identity.

A sense of mastery, perhaps emanating not from age-related losses
but from lifelong patterns of coping, might influence age identification. Carp and Carp (1981) found an inverse association between mas-

tery and old age identification. Linn and Hunter (1979) found that older age identification was associated with external locus of control, even when social class, disability, and impairment were controlled. On the other hand, Baum and Boxley (1983) found that, although the bivariate relationship between locus of control and age identification was significant, the relationship disappeared when health, psychological health, income, and interviewer effects were partialed out.

In addition to such "age-related deprivation" as health change, retirement, widowhood, and income decline, comparisons with age peers are important. Bultena and Powers (1978), using a reference-group framework, found that peer comparisons of health, finances, social contacts, and dependence are strongly linked to age identity; those who feel "better off" than others their age are much more likely to consider themselves middle-aged.

Our model, then, to predict age identification included age, attitudes, functional health, retirement and marital status, income and education, feelings of mastery, and comparisons with age peers, as well as age concentration of census tract, having a role model, and having help with life's changes. The results of a stepwise multiple regression analysis using age identification as the dependent variable appear in Table 5.10. The results indicate that the primary determinants of subjective age identification, in addition to age, are: comparisons of own health with that of age peers; functional health; and feelings of mastery. These four variables accounted for 21% of the variance in age identification. Contrary to prediction, marital status, retirement status, education, income, attitude toward older people, concentration of age peers in tract, having a role model, or receiving help in aging from age peers were not related to age identification. It is of note that only comparisons with peers with respect to health were related, not comparisons with respect to family and other contacts or with respect to finances.

The role losses of retirement and widowhood, in contrast to earlier research, did not influence age identification. It is possible that, since health is a major cause of retirement, retirement may have served as a proxy for poor health in other studies. In fact, in Streib and Schneider's (1971) longitudinal study, retirement and age identification were not correlated. Mutran and Burke (1979a) and Mutran and Reitzes (1981) found that employment was important for identity only as it influenced loneliness and community activities. It is also possible that both retirement and widowhood are sufficiently normative that they do not independently engage one's age identity.

Table 5.10   Stepwise Regression Analysis of Age Identification

Age	.33*
Peer comparisons: health	−.12*
Mastery	−.10*
Functional health	−.11*
Peer comparisons: social contacts	−.03
Retired[a]	−.04
Role model	.04
Attitudes toward older people	−.03
Advice and support from age peers	.03
Peer comparisons: family	−.03
Tract: percentage aged 60 +	.03
Financial status	.03
Education	−.03
Widowed[b]	−.01
R^2	.22
N	912

Note: Old = 4. Elderly = 3. Middle-aged = 2. Young = 1. Cells show standardized regression coefficients.
*p = .01.
[a]Retired = 1. All others = 0.
[b]Widowed = 1. All others = 0.

Furthermore, rather than using composite measures of peer comparisons, the present study, using a multivariate approach, was able to separate those aspects of comparisons with one's peers that make a difference from those that do not. In contrast to Bultena and Powers's (1978) findings, comparisons with age peers on the basis of family and social contacts did not influence age identification. These patterns suggest that "being old" is symbolized by a very specific decrement in health, which itself reflects a type of stigma associated with old age. It is of interest that comparison of one's own health with that of one's peers was as strongly related to identification as was objective health. In the present study, health (both absolutely and relatively) seems to have the primary effect on age identification.

Subjective age identification, contrary to prediction, seems to be a function neither of generalized attitudes or stigma about old people nor of having been socialized to the status of old age. The concentration of age peers in the census tract also does not affect age identification. Age identification is a response to personal circumstances rather than to generalized attitudes about aging or to social supports for aging.

The second age-related orientation of concern was a more be havioral one. Using frequency of participation in a club or organization for older people as the dependent variable, we entered the following independent variables in stages: (1) functional health, education, and occupational prestige; (2) age, sex, marital status, and work status; and (3) age-related orientations—attitudes, preferred associations, age identification, having a role model, and socializer for age-related changes. The results in Table 5.11 indicate a tendency for such participation to be greater among persons who are in good health, widowed, retired, and female, though none of these associations is substantial. The general lack of association with the age-orientation variables, which in combination explain only 0.6% of the variance in associational participation, is noteworthy. Involvement in such groups does not appear to be affected by, or indeed to affect, generalized orientations to aging and older people or socialization experiences.

Table 5.11   Multiple Regression Analysis of Frequency of Participation in a Club or Organization for Older People

Functional health	.05*	.09*	.09*
Education	−.00	.01	.01
Occupational prestige	.03	.02	.02
Age		.05	.06
Sex[a]		−.09*	−.09*
Widowed[b]		.10*	.10*
Retired[c]		.09*	.09*
Attitudes toward older people			.00
Prefer to associate with age peers			.05
Age identification			.01
Role model			.04
Advice and support from age peers			.03
R^2	.003	.034	.040

Note: N = 942. Cells show standardized regression coefficients.
*p = .05.
[a]Male = 1. Female = 0.
[b]Widow = 1. All others = 0.
[c]Retired = 1. All others = 0.

Consequences of Age-Related Orientations

The literature suggests a number of ways in which age-related orientations may affect overall well-being. Negative attitudes toward older
people and self-identification as elderly or old, for example, may
reduce subjective well-being, reflecting a stigma attached to being old.
Age identification is important for several reasons. It is an indicator of
the events and processes that symbolize aging from the perception of
the individual and of society. To the extent that "middle age" or "old
age" is a categorization that is central to the self-concept, the social
and personal meanings of aging might be expected to be central to
feelings of well-being. The generally negative imagery attached to old
age in modern societies makes this possibility particularly likely. Several studies have found a negative relationship between age identity
and a battery of mental health measures, including life satisfaction,
positive affect, morale, and well-being (George and Bearon, 1980;
Carp and Carp, 1981; Mutran and Reitzes, 1981). There is some uncertainty about the extent to which age identity per se is responsible for
these patterns. Linn and Hunter (1979), for example, found that older
age identification was negatively related to life satisfaction but that the
relationship disappeared when disability or impairment were
covaried. Hoyt et al. (1980) and Phillips (1957), however, found that
self-identification as old or elderly was associated with lower life
satisfaction or maladjustment, even when they controlled for age,
health, socioeconomic status, marital status, retirement, and social
activity.

Socialization for old age, on the other hand, could be expected to
enhance well-being. Aging-group consciousness, defined as a
positive sense of identification with age peers and a perception of the
elderly as a group, not merely as a category, can be seen as having
social-psychological benefits for older persons. Ward (1977c) found
evidence that such attitudes are positively associated with subjective
well-being. Such patterns may stem from the potential benefits of a
"subculture" of older people: (1) allowing older persons to pursue
their own interests (such as leisure) without concern for society's
expectations, (2) reducing the isolation and marginality potentially
associated with exclusion from other groups, and (3) providing meaningful roles and a more positive definition of "old person" (Ward,
1984a).

This section explores the relationship between age-related orientations and the two general measures of subjective well-being, morale

and mastery. The composite measure of comparisons with age peers is also used here as an indicator of perceived quality of life; indeed, peer comparisons are related to both morale (partial correlation $r = .27$, when we control functional health and socioeconomic status) and mastery (.28). Finally, knowledge of services is used as a more objective measure that is related to well-being. Such knowledge is only weakly related to overall morale (partial correlation $r = .06$), but the association is somewhat stronger for disadvantaged groups—for example, widows and widowers (.10) or people who have some functional impairment (.11). Such knowledge is also important in its own right, however. This section will focus on the following age-related orientations: (1) attitudes toward older people and age preference for association and housing, which represent generalized orientations to age peers; (2) age identification; (3) having a role model and receiving advice from peers on age-related changes, which indicate socialization experiences; and (4) frequency of participation in clubs for older people and taking action on their behalf, which are behavioral indicators of age-group affiliation.

Table 5.12 summarizes the bivariate associations between age-related orientations and well-being. Respondents with more positive attitudes toward older people exhibit higher levels of subjective well-being, even in comparing themselves with age peers. The relationship was not dependent on self-categorization as "old," as other analyses indicated that attitudes toward older people are positively related to subjective well-being regardless of age identity. The relationship between attitudes and well-being may reflect the attachment of a generalized positive view of aging to oneself. Alternatively, ratings of older people may reflect a projection of generalized well-being rather than a personalized response to older persons. Subjective well-being is also negatively related to preferring to associate with or to live primarily with age peers.

The negative association between age and identification and subjective well-being is particularly noteworthy, and more detail appears in Table 5.13, which indicates that each successively "older" age identity is associated with lower morale. (In fact, an older age identification is related to lower morale, regardless of attitudes toward older people.)

As Table 5.12 indicates, age identification is related to the overall morale scale (though the relationship dropped substantially from the zero-order correlation of $-.28$ when controls were introduced). Furthermore, although the zero-order correlation between age and morale was $-.12$, when health was controlled, the partial correlation be-

Table 5.12   Partial Correlations of Age-Related Orientations with Morale, Mastery, Peer Comparisons, and Service Knowledge

	Morale	Mastery	Peer comparisons	Knowledge
ATTITUDES				
Attitudes toward older people	.21*	.18*	.17*	.05
Prefer to associate with age peers	−.09*	−.08*	−.06*	−.03
Prefer to live with age peers	−.13*	−.11*	−.11*	.02
Age identification	−.15*	−.15*	−.09*	.04
SOCIALIZATION EXPERIENCES				
Role model	−.01	−.05	.03	.12*
Advice and support from age peers	−.07*	−.09*	−.01	.13*
AGE-GROUP AFFILIATION				
Attend clubs for older people	−.01	.01	.04	.12*
Action	.02	.03	.04	.10*

Note: Functional health, education, and occupational prestige were controlled.
*$p = .05$.

Table 5.13   Multiple Classification Analysis of Morale by Age Identification

Age identification	Mean morale		N
	No covariates	With covariates	
Young	54.8	53.7	226
Middle-aged	53.0	52.5	452
Elderly	50.0	50.4	226
Old	47.2	49.5	158
η/β	.28	.16	—
p	—	.001	—

Note: Functional health, education, occupational prestige, and age were covariates.

tween age and morale dropped to −.02. In other words, "feeling" old (age identification) is important for morale rather than "being" old (chronological age)—a finding similar to those reported by Mutran and Burke (1979b).

The morale scale used in this study, the Philadelphia Geriatric scale, has three subscales. They are Agitation (e.g., I sometimes worry so much that I can't sleep), Lonely-dissatisfaction (e.g., Life is hard for me much of the time), and Aging attitude (e.g., I have as much pep as I had last year). When each of these subscales was run separately by age identification, a most interesting pattern appeared. Although the partial correlation, when we controlled for age and functional health, was −.17 with the total scale, the partial correlation between age identification and Agitation was −.05; with Lonely-dissatisfaction it was −.17 (p = .000), and with Aging attitude it was −.24 (p = .000). This set of findings accords with Lowenthal and Robinson's (1976) notion of the former self as the referent other. Direction of causality cannot be definitely determined with these correlational data. The fact that there is no correlation between age identification and the subscale Agitation, however, suggests that feelings of subjective well-being in the dimensions of Attitude toward own aging and Lonely-dissatisfaction may influence age identification rather than being influenced by age identification.

It appears that age identification reflects a more generalized sense of well-being. Again demonstrating the utility of a multivariate approach, the specificity of the relationship to two of the three subscales of the Philadelphia Geriatric Center Morale Scale suggests that these domains help to define one's age identity (similar to Baum and Boxley's finding [1983] with respect to "purpose in life" and to Mutran and Burke's findings [1979a] regarding loneliness), but age identity does not have a more generalized effect upon feelings of satisfaction. If one is lonely and dissatisfied with respect to one's own aging, one will tend to identify as older rather than the opposite. Similarly, it may be that reduced subjective well-being leads one to prefer associating with age peers. Perhaps higher morale and perceived mastery, and favorable comparisons with peers, result in greater confidence for engaging in age-integrated exchange relationships. As suggested by Dowd (1980a, 1980b), persons low on these dimensions may fear unbalanced exchanges when interacting with younger persons. They may desire the "shelter" of associations with age peers, seeking a form of person-environment congruence.

Table 5.12 shows no evidence, however, that feelings of age-group solidarity contribute in a positive fashion to feelings of well-being. Indeed, there is little relation between subjective well-being and either socialization experiences or age-group affiliations. Subgroup analyses indicated no significant variation in these patterns by age, health, marital status, or socioeconomic status. There is one interesting pattern. Respondents who have both participated in an organization for older persons *and* taken some action on behalf of older people have higher morale than those who have done only one of the two or neither of them (morale $M = 53.9, 51.2$, and 52.0, respectively, when we control health, socioeconomic status, and age). Such persons represent only 5% of the sample, however, and as we noted earlier, socialization experiences and age-group affiliations are associated with greater knowledge of services. In this sense, involvement with age peers may contribute indirectly to well-being. The potential value of age homogeneity will be investigated in greater detail in Chapter 6.

As in Chapter 4, regression analysis was used to investigate the consequences of age-related orientations in combination to assess their relative and joint contributions to well-being.

Subjective Well-being

Measures of subjective well-being used as dependent variables include morale, mastery, and comparisons with peers. Variables were added to the models for each in the following stages: (1) functional health and socioeconomic status (education and occupational prestige); (2) age and age-linked events (widowhood and retirement); and (3) measures of age-related orientations—age identification, attitudes toward older people, availability of a role model, advice and support from age peers, and frequency of participation in a club or organization for older people. Comparisons with peers and service knowledge were also added as a last stage for morale and mastery. The results of the last stages of these analyses are indicated in Table 5.14.

The models account for 28% of the variance in morale and 27% of that in mastery. Functional health and socioeconomic status have significant associations with both morale and mastery, whereas age per se has little bearing on either (though it is negatively related to perceived mastery). Work status is unrelated to morale and mastery, whereas widowhood is related to lower morale but not to lower mastery. These sets of variables together account for 18% of the variance in morale and 17% of that in mastery.

Of primary interest here, however, are the associations with age-related orientations, which account for an additional 10% of the variance in morale and mastery. As in the bivariate relationships, positive attitudes toward older people continue to be related to personal feelings of morale and mastery. Again, this relationship may indicate generalized attitudes toward aging that come to affect self-perceptions, or it may be that feelings about one's own life and capabilities

Table 5.14   Multiple Regression Analyses of Morale, Mastery, and Comparison with Peers

	Morale	Mastery	Peer comparisons
Functional health	.27*	.24*	.27*
Education	.12*	.10*	.16*
Occupational prestige	− .07*	− .06*	.01
Age	.03	− .07*	.11*
Widowed[a]	− .08*	− .03	.08*
Retired[b]	.01	.01	.02
Age identification	− .09*	− .09*	− .13*
Attitudes toward older people	.15*	.13*	.12*
Role model	− .02	− .02	.05
Advice and support from age peers	− .09*	− .07*	− .03
Attend clubs for older people	− .01	.02	.03
Peer comparisons	.21*	.25*	—
Service knowledge	.08*	.04	—
R^2	.277	.269	.167
N	903	889	923

Note: Cells show standardized regression coefficients.
*p = .05.
[a]Widowed = 1. All others = 0.
[b]Retired = 1. All others = 0.

are projected onto age peers. These analyses cannot clearly distinguish the causal ordering involved.

Table 5.14 also indicates that older age identity is associated with lower morale (as in Table 5.13) and perceived mastery, even controlling for the other variables in the models. Perhaps "feeling old" is demoralizing (or perhaps feeling demoralized leads to feeling old). There is no evidence that socializing experiences (having a role model or receiving advice from age peers) contribute to subjective well-being; indeed, there is a small negative association between receiving help from peers and both morale and mastery, perhaps indicating that advice is sought in response to dissatisfaction and reduced competence or that receiving help emphasizes one's frailty. Participation in clubs for older people is also unrelated to morale and mastery.

Knowledge of services is weakly related to morale and is unrelated to mastery. Favorable comparisons with age peers, however, are associated with significantly greater morale and mastery, even controlling for the indicators of personal circumstances included in the model. This reference-group orientation thus appears to be a significant component of subjective well-being in later life.

The third column in Table 5.14 indicates, not surprisingly, that better health and education are associated with more favorable comparisons with age peers. Interestingly, older respondents and those who are widowed have somewhat more favorable peer comparisons. This difference may reflect the basis of peer comparisons by such persons; that is, age peers are *older* and *widowed*. Favorable comparisons with peers are also related to more positive attitudes about older people. This finding seems counterintuitive and again suggests that attitudes toward older people are perhaps partly a projection of one's own circumstances.

Younger age identity is associated with feeling better off than other older people, although age is positively related to peer comparisons. This pattern suggests that it is not a problem to be old as long as you do not *feel* old. Indeed, the highest peer comparison score is for persons aged 70 and over who identify themselves as young or middle-aged (M = 10.2), whereas the lowest score is for those who are younger than 70 but identify as elderly or old (M = 9.2). Rather than age identity affecting peer comparisons, however, it is likely, as shown earlier, that peer comparisons are a factor in shaping subjective age identity (Bultena and Powers, 1978). Table 5.15 indicates that the combination of age and age-peer comparisons has a powerful association with age identity. Respondents aged 60–69 who score above the mean on comparisons with age peers are least likely to consider themselves "elderly" or "old," whereas persons aged 70 and above who score below the mean on peer comparisons are most likely to do so. Peer-based comparisons appear to have their greatest influence on younger persons (age 60–69) with health problems.

Table 5.14 also indicates that having a role model, receiving advice from age peers, and participating in clubs for older people are not related to peer comparisons. There is thus no evidence in Table 5.14 that age-related socialization experiences or age-group affiliations contribute to generalized feelings of well-being.

Knowledge of Services

Using service knowledge as the dependent variable, we added the following independent variables in stages: (1) functional health, education, and occupational prestige; (2) age, sex, marital status, and

Table 5.15 Percentage Categorizing Themselves as "Elderly" or "Old" by Combinations of Age and Age-Peer Comparisons

	Total sample		No health impairment		Some health impairment	
	%	N	%	N	%	N
Age 60–69, above mean on peer comparison	13	314	13	283	13	30
Age 60–69, below mean on peer comparison	26	253	21	182	39	67
Age 70+, above mean on peer comparison	44	273	38	190	57	82
Age 70+, below mean on peer comparison	66	241	57	111	76	123
p	.001		.001		.001	

work status; and (3) age-related orientations—age identification, having a role model, advice and support from age peers, and frequency of participation in a club or organization for older people. The results of this analysis are indicated in Table 5.16. As in Chapter 4, service knowledge is not well predicted by the variables measured in this study (the model accounts for only 8% of the variance), but some patterns are evident.

There is a tendency for younger persons and those with better health and higher socioeconomic status to be more knowledgeable about services. The coefficients are not large, but it is clear that those most likely to be in need are *not* more aware of the services that exist.

Socialization experiences and age-group affiliations appear to be most influential with regard to service knowledge. Although such variables did not appear to contribute to subjective well-being, knowledge of services is positively related to having a role model, receiving advice from age peers, and participating in clubs and organizations for older people. These measures of age-related orientations account for nearly 3% of the variance in service knowledge. Age peers may thus serve as a type of "lay referral" network. Subgroup analyses were performed to explore variations in this contribution to service knowledge. Variations across sample subgroups were generally not substantial, but one is noteworthy. Among rural respondents, service knowledge has particularly strong associations with help from age

Table 5.16   Multiple Regression Analysis of Service Knowledge

Functional health	.08*	.07*	.05*
Education	.13*	.11*	.10*
Occupational prestige	.06*	.07*	.07*
Age		−.10*	−.09*
Sex[a]		−.05	−.04
Widowed[b]		.04	.02
Retired[c]		−.04	−.04
Age identification			.01
Role model			.08*
Advice and support from age peers			.09*
Attend clubs for older people			.11*
R^2	.035	.051	.080

Note: N = 1026. Cells show standardized regression coefficients.
*p = .05.
[a]Male = 1. Female = 0.
[b]Widowed = 1. All others = 0.
[c]Retired = 1. All others = 0.

peers (β = .20) and club participation (β = .23), and these variables account for 12% of the variance in knowledge. Such age-group affiliations may thus be especially valuable referral sources in rural areas, where older persons are likely to be most isolated from services and formal informational sources. Among city residents, however, having a role model is the strongest predictor of service knowledge (β = .17), whereas coefficients for help from peers and club participation are not significant.

Conclusions

This chapter has analyzed patterns and consequences of a variety of age-related attitudes and behaviors, which can be regarded as the social context within which the individual ages. We raised two general issues concerning these age-related orientations. First, what factors shape age identification and age-group solidarity? Second, what are the consequences of these orientations in light of the possible stigma attached to being old? The data presented in this chapter bear on both issues.

Research reviewed suggested the existence of somewhat negative images of old age and old people. By contrast, the older respondents in this study have generally favorable views of other older people, at least in terms of their being "nice" people (e.g., very trustworthy and friendly). In other respects, however, their impressions are less favorable. They are more likely to consider most older people to be sick and dependent, for example, and respondents generally consider themselves better off than age peers. "Pluralistic ignorance" may account for such findings.

The images held of other older people are not very influential, however. Holding positive or negative attitudes about the aged has only weak associations with age identification, preferences for associating with age peers, or organizational involvement. Persons with more favorable images of older people do exhibit somewhat greater subjective well-being. Similarly, favorable personal comparisons with age peers are related to greater subjective well-being, indicating the importance of such reference-group comparisons.

Neither age-related socialization experiences nor age-group solidarity are much in evidence in this sample. Feelings of peership with other old persons do not appear to be very salient, as relatively few respondents prefer to associate with or to live primarily with age peers or to participate in senior clubs. There is some evidence that a desire for age-segregated housing is partly a response to physical and social deficits, representing a type of "shelter." This possibility may account for the negative associations between subjective well-being and preferring to associate with or to live with older persons. Most older community residents appear neither to need nor to desire the shelter of age homogeneity.

Half the sample could indicate a role model for aging—persons exemplifying such traits as youthful attitudes, high activity, and ability to overcome age-related deficits—but only about one-third had received advice or support from age peers concerning age-related difficulties and concerns. Perhaps the role models are primarily passive and observational rather than active sources of socialization for old age. Our indicators of socialization and age-group affiliation do not appear to make direct contributions to subjective well-being. There is some evidence of indirect contributions, however, as having role models, advice from age peers, and participation in senior clubs were related (though not strongly) to more positive attitudes toward older people and greater knowledge of senior services. Future research needs to expand the measures of socialization. In particular, it would be useful to have more details about both the process and the content of socialization (e.g., how and when it is initiated, whether it involves a generalized role of older person or more specific roles and values, and the extent to which it counteracts stigma).

As much of the research literature indicates, these respondents do not tend to identify themselves as "elderly" or "old." Chronological age is an important factor in determining age identification, but the two are by no means identical; an older age identity is also a response to health problems and less favorable peer comparisons. These patterns suggest that "being old" is symbolized by decrement, which itself reflects a type of stigma associated with old age. Preference for age-segregated associations and housing are linked to older age identification, suggesting again a desire for "shelter" by withdrawal from age-integrated involvements, but age identity is only weakly (and negatively) related to attitudes toward older people or to socialization experiences. Age identity is a response to one's own circumstances rather than to general images of aging and old people.

Older age identification is associated with lower subjective well-being. It is noteworthy that age has little association with well-being, whereas age identification, attitudes toward older people, and peer comparisons all exhibit significant relations. It is not age per se that is important but personal orientations concerning age; that is, whether one "is" old is less important than whether one "feels" old. Cause and effect are difficult to determine here, of course. It may be that low morale partly leads one to feel "old" as well as the reverse.

Whichever direction the causal flow may take, there is little evidence here that age-group affiliations or socialization experiences contribute to well-being or buffer the effects of feeling old. We have not exhaustively investigated the socialization experiences of these respondents. The experiences we have studied, such as having a role model, may be too "incidental" to have much demonstrable impact. Rosow (1974) cites the need for group membership and support and for roles and values that insulate the individual from stigma. We lack indications of these "subcultural" elements, which may be more characteristic of the age-segregated housing to be discussed in Chapter 6. We have noted that preferences for age-segregated association and housing may represent a desire for "shelter" in the face of physical and social deficits. Indeed, this is a benefit attributed to age homogeneity by the literature to be reviewed in Chapter 6. Whether such benefits are evident in this sample constitutes the focus of the next chapter.

6 Age Patterns for Residential Places and Social Spaces and Their Consequences

In our earlier discussions we have seen the heightened effect of environmental factors in the lives of older persons. We have also noted the importance of social networks and particularly the localized support represented by neighbors. In this chapter we turn our attention to the age structure of the environment of older people, focusing on the age composition of both their neighborhoods and their informal networks. There is reason to believe that access to age peers yields benefits at any age but particularly in later life. Indeed, the possible benefits represent an intersection of issues related to spatial, interpersonal, and social dimensions of the environment for aging.

The concerns of this chapter relate quite directly to two of the components of the human ecosystem described by Lawton (1980). The age composition of residential neighborhoods is an aspect of the "suprapersonal" environment of spatially clustered individuals. The age composition of informal networks is also an aspect of the interpersonal environment or network of significant others. Several aspects of these environmental dimensions are addressed in this chapter. We begin with a discussion of patterns of residential age "segregation" (i.e., the tendency for older persons to be distributed unevenly throughout metropolitan areas) and present an ecological model to account for these patterns. We then discuss the age composition of informal networks (e.g., ages of friends and confidants), with analysis of the sources of network age homogeneity. As we will see, neighborhood age concentration is often reflected in the age composition of social networks. Finally, the chapter concludes with analyses of the consequences of neighborhood and network age composition.

Patterns and Causes of Residential Age Segregation

The cities of modern industrial societies are characterized by a distinct pattern of residential segregation according to social class, family cycle, and ethnicity (Shevky and Bell, 1955; Timms, 1971). Of particular relevance to our discussion here, residential mobility models stress the importance of life cycle factors in the decision to move, encouraging mobility at some ages while constraining it at others. The cumulative effect of life cycle residential decisions results in patterns of residential age segregation, as people at similar stages in the life cycle cluster together within metropolitan areas.

As part of his model examining the effects of modernization on the status of the aged, Cowgill (1974) argues that urbanization results in spatial separation of young and old, as the young migrate to cities, leaving the old "behind" in rural areas. Age-related spatial patterns, however, are not restricted to rural/urban differences associated with modernization. Recent evidence indicates that residential age segregation is substantial and growing within metropolitan areas in the United States (Kennedy and DeJong, 1977; Cowgill, 1978; Pampel and Choldin, 1978; La Gory et al., 1980). This pattern is not restricted to the United States; Schutz (1982), for example, has indicated that residential age segregation is present in Hamburg, West Germany. These patterns were explored in detail in a sample of 70 standard metropolitan statistical areas (La Gory et al., 1980; La Gory et al., 1981).

The extent of age segregation in SMSAs was measured using an "index of dissimilarity," a method utilized by Taueber and Taueber (1965) to measure racial segregation. The index ranges from 0 to 100, indicating the percentage of older population (aged 65 and over) who would have to be shifted residentially to yield a completely proportional distribution across all census tracts in a SMSA. Table 6.1 indicates values of this index in 1970 for the 70 SMSAs in the sample. Age segregation is clearly not as pronounced as racial segregation. The mean age segregation is 24.2, whereas Taueber and Taueber (1965), using 1960 data for 207 cities, found a mean racial segregation of 86.2. Nevertheless, the level of residential age segregation appears to be substantial, and there are indications that it has been growing since 1940 (Cowgill, 1978). Table 6.1 also indicates that there is considerable variation in the degree of age segregation across metropolitan areas, as the index ranges from 11.9 to 46.4.

What accounts for this pattern of residential age segregation and for variation in the extent of the segregation? The literature on the process

Table 6.1   Index of Age Segregation for 70 Standard Metropolitan Statistical
Areas

SMSA	Age segregation index	SMSA	Age segregation index
Washington, D.C.	46.4	Cincinnati, Ohio–Ky.–Ind.	22.3
Fayetteville, N.C.	44.4	Lorain-Elyria, Ohio	21.9
Miami, Fla	36.6	Springfield, Ohio	21.7
Columbus, Ga.–Ala.	36.4	Flint, Mich.	21.1
San Diego, Cal.	34.2	Buffalo, N.Y.	20.8
San Bernadino–Riverside–		Evansville, Ind.–Ky.	20.7
Ontario, Cal.	34.0	Odessa, Tex.	20.7
West Palm Beach, Fla.	33.1	Cleveland, Ohio	20.5
Dallas, Tex.	33.0	Mansfield, Ohio	20.4
Grand Rapids, Mich.	32.7	South Bend, Ind.	20.4
Newport News–		Green Bay, Wis.	20.2
Hampton, Va.	32.6	Syracuse, N.Y.	20.0
Sacramento, Cal	32.6	Kalamazoo, Mich.	19.6
Fort Lauderdale–		Roanoke, Va.	19.2
Hollywood, Fla.	32.5	Kenosha, Wis.	19.1
San Jose, Cal.	31.6	Lawrence-Haverhill,	
Oklahoma City, Okla.	31.6	Mass.–N.H.	18.8
Ogden, Utah	31.5	Duluth-Superior,	
Omaha, Nebr.–Iowa	30.3	Minn.–Wisc.	18.7
Fort Worth, Tex.	30.0	Anderson, Ind.	18.6
Charleston, S.C.	30.0	Monroe, La.	18.4
Madison, Wis.	28.7	Canton, Ohio	18.1
Louisville, Ky.–Ind.	28.6	Modesto, Cal.	17.8
Rochester, Minn.	28.3	Albany-Schenectady-Troy,	
Gainesville, Fla.	28.3	N.Y.	16.8
Lafayette, La.	28.2	Greensboro–Winston-	
New Orleans, La.	28.0	Salem–High Point, N.C.	16.7
Columbus, Ohio	27.9	Lancaster, Pa.	16.6
Midland, Tex.	27.9	York, Pa.	15.8
Houston, Tex.	27.0	McAllen-Pharr-Edinburg,	
Lubbock, Tex.	26.0	Tex.	15.7
Baltimore, Md.	25.2	Bay City, Mich.	15.2
Jackson, Miss.	25.1	Racine, Wis.	14.5
New London–Groton–		Asheville, N.C.	13.5
Norwich, Conn.	24.8	Pittsfield, Mass.	13.3
San Angelo, Tex.	24.8	Wheeling, W. Va.–Ohio	13.2
Atlanta, Ga.	24.6	Gadsden, Ala.	12.6
Atlantic City, N.J.	24.6	Bristol, Conn.	12.0
Fort Wayne, Ind.	23.2	Wilkes-Barre–Hazleton,	
Lowell, Mass.	23.0	Pa.	11.9

of residential location contains three theories of spatial segregation, explaining it as a result of political processes (Ford, 1950; Taueber and Taueber, 1965), cultural processes (Wirth, 1938; Firey, 1945; Milgram, 1970; Michelson, 1976), and ecological processes (Park and Burgess, 1925; Hawley, 1950).

A "political" model of residential segregation recognizes that housing and the competition for space represent less than a pure market situation; rather, it is a process controlled by the cultural majority. Ford (1950), for example, argues that the spatial segregation of ethnic groups varies with their degree of assimilation into the larger culture, at least partly as a result of discrimination. Although such political factors are clearly important for ethnic and social class segregation, age discrimination is unlikely to account for the patterns in Table 6.1. A stigmatized status attached to old age may result in scattered opposition to the location of nursing homes or old-age apartments but not the general patterns of age concentration found throughout metropolitan areas.

The "cultural" model portrays segregation as a response to the heterogeneity and complexity of urban life. As cities increase in size and density, urbanites experience "overload," an inability to process all the stimuli emanating from the urban environment (Milgram, 1970). One adaptation is to reduce the range of stimuli likely to be experienced by creating homogeneous cultural settings that make "undesirable" situations unlikely. People with similar life-styles and values thus choose to live together in order to reduce the complexity created by large size and density. Firey (1945) would add that because neighborhoods are imbued with sentiment and symbolism, certain segments of the population may resist movement even when it is "profitable" for them to leave. Such resistance may enhance existing segregation patterns.

This cultural model may play some role in accounting for movement into such age-segregated settings as retirement communities and old-age apartments, as these reflect life-style similarities and a desire for association with age peers. It is unlikely, however, that cultural processes produce more general patterns of age segregation, given the lack of residential mobility in the older population. "Attachment to place" may accentuate such patterns, but choice on the basis of age is not their source. Chevan (1982), using national data for individuals, found that characteristics of housing were most important in determining choice of neighborhood. Older persons thus often reside in age-segregated neighborhoods because they live in an older house and because families reside in larger homes longer than in smaller apartments. Chevan concludes, "Age segregation exists primarily because people of similar social and economic backgrounds make parallel location and housing decisions, and only secondarily because of any desire to live near one age group or away from another" (pp. 1147–1148).

It seems likely, then, that normal residential age segregation is neither chosen as such nor forced but rather represents an "incidental" result of ecological processes. The ecological model of segregation views it as emerging from competition among groups for scarce and valuable locations. People with comparable incomes are able to acquire similarly valued sites. "Ability to pay" is thus an important selective factor in the process of residential location. This factor becomes particularly important under conditions of urban growth and urbanization.

An Ecological Model

The Park and Burgess (1925) zonal model of the city was perhaps the first attempt to link residential segregation to the growth of cities. It argued that, as urban areas grow, the competition for inner-city land increases, producing a selective outward expansion of population groups. This decentralization process produces periodic change in the residential character of urban neighborhoods, as established areas are "invaded" by new population groups. One by-product is a pattern of age segregation. Because the elderly have relatively low residential mobility, neighborhood change through invasion processes most typically represents youthful, upwardly mobile residents moving out and leaving the aged behind (Birch, 1971). Residential stability of the aged is thus one reason for their segregation.

This relationship can be fully understood, however, only by considering the impact of urban growth on the economic competition for space. Growing urban areas experience keener competition for space as location becomes a more highly valued commodity. Because "ability to pay" becomes a more critical factor in location, older people with reduced financial resources will experience greater locational constraints, contributing to patterns of age segregation. This occurs when population is growing rapidly and the urban community is expanding spatially.

The general form of this ecological model can be diagrammed as follows:

Community
background   Competition   Age
variables $\longrightarrow$ for space $\longrightarrow$ segregation

This model was used to explain the variation in age segregation among
the 70 SMSAs in Table 6.1. (For a more complete discussion of these
analyses, see La Gory et al., 1980, and La Gory et al., 1981.) A number
of variables reflect stage of growth in a metropolitan area—housing
age, population size and growth, region, and extent of suburbanization. These were all expected to affect age segregation indirectly
through a measure of housing competition (median value of renter-
occupied housing units). Age of housing and suburbanization were
also expected to affect age segregation directly. If the housing market
consists substantially of older homes, younger residents will be more
likely to choose older homes than they normally would. Because the
elderly are also more likely to reside in older neighborhoods, there is
likely to be less age segregation. Degree of suburbanization indexes
the processes of invasion-succession that are central to explanations
of neighborhood change. Invasion occurs primarily in central cities,
with populations experiencing these invasions generally "succeeding
to" suburbs. The more suburban a metropolis, the greater the extent of
recent successions and thus the greater the age segregation as the
elderly remain behind in the older areas of cities.

Figure 6.1 presents a path model that summarizes the results of this
analysis. The ecological model outlined above performs quite well,
explaining 60% of the variance in age segregation in the sample of 70
SMSAs. The cost of housing has the most significant direct influence
on age segregation. As expected, SMSAs that are larger and growing
and have newer housing have tighter (more expensive) housing mar-
kets and therefore greater age segregation. Housing age also has a
direct negative effect on age segregation, and suburbanization has a
direct positive effect.

These results highlight two general ecological sources of residential
age segregation. The first concerns competition in the housing market.
Because of the reduced financial resources of older people, a tight
housing market restricts their residential options. The second factor,
stage in the urban growth process, produces age segregation in two
ways. First, tightness in the housing market is itself a function of
urban growth. Second, urban growth is linked to the process of invasion and succession, producing age segregation independent of com-
petitiveness in the housing market. Older people are thus residen-

Figure 6.1   Path Model of Variables Affecting Level of Age Segregation

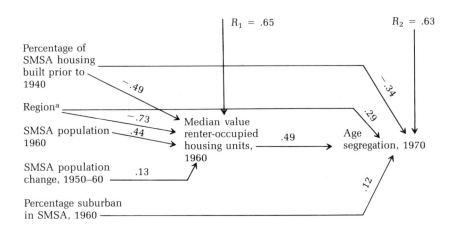

Note: Path coefficients are standardized regression coefficients.
[a]South and West = 1; Northeast and North Central = 0.

tially segregated because they are relatively immobile (aging along with their neighborhoods) and because they are disadvantaged in the competition for space when they are mobile.

The processes that produce age segregation imply that older people will be concentrated in certain types of neighborhoods. A factorial ecology was conducted on a sample of 612 census tracts from the 70 SMSAs (La Gory et al., 1981). The results indicated that the elderly reside disproportionately in areas with a high concentration of unattached persons and of housing that is older, rented, and multiunit. These patterns indicate that older people are concentrated near the city center in neighborhoods characterized by a nonfamilistic lifestyle. The factor containing percentage aged 65 + was quite distinct from two other area factors, (1) a "suburban" dimension, with intact families residing in larger, owner-occupied housing and (2) an "inner-city" dimension, with low-income nonwhites residing in crowded housing.

Age segregation appears to be a regionally variable process, however. Figure 6.1 indicates that the region has opposing direct and indirect effects on age segregation. SMSAs in the Northeastern and

North Central regions have higher segregation to the extent that housing costs are higher. Even apart from housing competition, however,
SMSAs in the South and West have a greater age segregation.

When models of segregation were analyzed separately for the two
regions, different ecological processes were highlighted. The cost of
housing explains a disproportionate amount of the variance in age
segregation in the South and West. In the Northeastern and North
Central regions, age segregation is explained primarily by the age of
housing, though housing competition is still a significant factor. The
South and West are characterized by greater mobility in their older
populations. Because these older migrants are more actively engaged
in residential decision making, the tightness of the local market has
greater influence on where they will live. The elderly in the Northeastern and North Central regions may be characterized as "resisters"
of the competition process, with segregation resulting from their relative immobility. Persons who cannot afford long-distance migration
(e.g., to the Sunbelt) may also not be able to afford residential change
within their current area; residential "inertia" and age of housing thus
account for patterns of age segregation.

The factorial ecology differs in the two areas as well. In the Sunbelt
the elderly are less likely to be concentrated in one type of housing.
Although they generally occupy older housing, as in the North, they
are not concentrated in high-density apartment housing. The Sunbelt
elderly thus appear to be less highly centralized. They are also not
typically found in lower-income areas or in areas populated by divorced or separated persons. Their housing patterns appear to reflect
choices associated with retirement life-styles rather than aging in
place within older neighborhoods.

Age Concentration in the Survey Area

The research that we have summarized involved an investigation of
patterns of residential age segregation across a national sample of
metropolitan areas. Let us turn now to a consideration of these patterns within the Albany-Schenectady-Troy SMSA, the site for the survey reported in this monograph. As noted in Chapter 2, we have two
measures of neighborhood age concentration that reflect different levels of aggregation and "objectivity": (1) the percentage of tract residents aged 60+ reported in the 1980 census and (2) respondent
estimates of the percentage aged 60+ in "your neighborhood." These
two indicators of neighborhood age concentrations are moderately

Table 6.2   Zero-Order Correlations of Neighborhood Age Composition with Tract and Neighborhood Characteristics and Factor Analysis of Tract and Neighborhood Characteristics

	Correlation	
	Percentage aged 60 + in the tract	Estimate of percentage aged 60 + in the neighborhood
NEIGHBORHOOD AGE STRUCTURE		
Percentage aged 60 + in tract	—	—
Estimate of percentage aged 60 + in neighborhood	—	—
POPULATION CHARACTERISTICS		
Median family income	−.21*	−.13*
Median education	−.27*	−.18*
Percentage families below poverty	.21*	.12*
Percentage husband-wife families	−.48*	−.26*
Percentage males work	−.48*	−.22*
Percentage widowed	.64*	.26*
Percentage native-born	−.54*	−.22*
Sex ratio (M/F)	−.48*	−.25*
Percentage take bus to work	.36*	.18*
Percentage married	−.45*	−.21*
Percentage same house, 1965–1970	.24*	.05
Percentage black	.19*	.18*
HOUSING CHARACTERISTICS		
Median contract rent	−.21*	−.12*
Median gross rent	−.24*	−.15*
Median value owner-occupied units	−.25*	−.17*
Percentage built before 1940	.53*	.22*
Percentage 1 person/room or less	.37*	.16*
Percentage housing units vacant	.02	.01
Housing type[b]	.36*	.18*
URBANISM[c]	.60*	.25*
Eigenvalue	—	—
Percentage variance	—	—

Note: The factor analysis was principal factors technique with varimax rotation. N = 1,18
*p = .05.
[a]Only factor loadings greater than ±30 and factors with eigenvalues greater than 1.0 are reported.
[b]Interviewer rating of type of housing on respondent's block. 1 = mostly single family houses. 2 = mostly apartment houses or garden apartments (one or two stories). 3 = mostly high-rise apartments (four stories or more).
[c]1 = rural. 2 = suburban. 3 = city.

	Factors[a]	
1	2	3
—	.73	—
—	.33	—
.84	—	−.33
.78	—	−.34
−.59	—	.58
.45	−.52	−.52
.37	−.47	—
−.37	.71	.30
—	−.75	—
—	−.57	—
—	.43	—
—	−.43	—
—	−.53	—
—	—	.66
—	.93	—
—	.89	—
—	.89	—
—	.58	.60
—	.47	.64
−.31	—	.53
—	.45	—
—	.78	—
9.7	3.5	1.7
58	21	10

correlated ($r = .31$), indicating that they are related but somewhat distinct measures, the estimate of the percentage aged 60+ in the neighborhood being a more localized and subjective measure.

How can we characterize the pattern of residential age concentration in this SMSA? Inspection of Table 6.1 reveals that this metropolitan area is below the average level of age segregation (age segregation index = 16.8 vs. $M = 24.2$); this is within one standard deviation of the mean, however, and so this area cannot be viewed as atypical. To investigate these patterns in more detail, Table 6.2 presents associations of the two measures of neighborhood age composition with tract characteristics (of both population and housing) and an interviewer assessment of the nature of housing on each respondent's block. Table 6.2 also presents results of a factor analysis of these variables.

The correlational analysis in Table 6.2 indicates that both measures of age composition exhibit similar patterns of association with other locational characteristics, though associations with these objective locational characteristics are generally weaker for the neighborhood estimates. These patterns reinforce our conclusion that the two measures are related but somewhat distinct measures. More specifically, older people tend to be concentrated in residential areas with fewer intact families; larger minority and immigrant populations; lower socioeconomic status; older and cheaper housing; and more central (urban) location. These patterns are similar to the national patterns described previously.

The factor analysis reported in Table 6.2 also reflects a factorial ecology that is typical of the Northeast. Factor 1 is a "suburban" factor, including intact families with newer, more valuable housing. Factor 3 is an "inner-city" factor, including low-income and nonwhite populations with more crowded housing. Both measures of local area age composition load on a factor (Factor 2) that includes widowed and immigrant populations, older and rental housing, and more centralized location. These results indicate that patterns of neighborhood age concentration within this metropolitan area are quite typical of those found more generally in metropolitan areas.

Patterns and Causes of Network Age Composition

A related issue, but one distinct from residential age segregation, concerns the age composition of informal networks. A "homophily principle" appears to operate in the selection of reference groups and friends, as individuals seek homogeneity in roles, life-styles, attitudes and values, personality traits, and so on (Homans, 1950; Laumann, 1966; Blau, 1977; Verbrugge, 1977; Singer, 1981). There is a pervasive bias toward homogeneity with regard to virtually all social categories, and particular efforts are made to find similar persons for very close friends. The relative importance of bases of similarity is less clear, however. Jackson (1977), for example, suggests that neighborhood friendships tend to exhibit *age* homogeneity, reflecting leisure pursuits and residential location; kin tend to be *ethnically* similar, but structural similarity is otherwise of little importance; and work friends are similar *economically* but not in terms of age or ethnicity. More generally, the social structure plays a role in determining the relative salience of categories and the normative standards defining groups as more or less appropriate and rewarding (Singer, 1981).

Our interest here is in the salience of age as a source of similarity. Age has long been considered a focal point for the development of social networks. In Blau's (1977) terms, age is a nominal parameter that differentiates among groups of people and increases the likelihood of ingroup over intergroup associations. Friendships are highly voluntary, with peership a critical quality, and cohort membership (shared historical events and socializing experiences) and position in the life course (and in the age stratification system) create shared interests and needs (Hess, 1972). Peership, cohort membership, and shared position combine with the tendency of daily settings (school, work, neighborhood) to be segregated by age. There is evidence that people tend to choose friends their own age (Lowenthal et al., 1975; Stueve and Gibson, 1977; Verbrugge, 1977). In a study of males aged 21–64, for example, Stueve and Gibson found that 38% of friends had an age difference of 2 years or less, and 72% were within 8 years. Same-age friendships were also found to be more intimate. Age dissimilarity in friendships increased with age, however, and friendships formed later in adulthood were more age dissimilar. Age-based friendships may be least important in middle age, when roles cut across age boundaries (Hess, 1972).

It has also been suggested, however, that age-homogeneous friendships are more pronounced in both youth and old age, when roles are more restricted and age-linked (Hess, 1972; Lowenthal and Robinson, 1976); in old age, for example, ties to age-integrated networks may be loosened by retirement and widowhood. There is evidence that the friendships of older people exhibit age homogeneity (Lowenthal et al., 1975; Powers and Bultena, 1976). Powers and Bultena, for example, found that 60% of the intimate friendships of older persons were within the same 10-year age group.

Age homogeneity is not necessarily or universally a characteristic of the networks of older people, however. There are a number of barriers to a perception of similarity with age peers—a perceived stigma attached to old age, cross-cutting social characteristics (such as sex, race, or social class) that may be more salient, and interaction barriers such as poor health. Many older people neither need nor desire access to networks of age peers, as they do not wish to identify themselves as "old" or to identify with persons who are "old." A national survey found that only 23% of the older population wished to spend most of their time with age peers (National Council on the Aging, 1975).

The Extent of Homogeneity

It is clear that some degree of age homogeneity is likely to be found in the networks of older people, but its extent is uncertain. Indeed, the respondents in our survey do not generally express a desire to associate primarily with age peers. (See the earlier discussion of interaction preferences in Chapter 5.) Their networks do exhibit some age homogeneity, however. Measures of network age are available for friends and new friends, neighbors with whom the respondent is friendliest and neighbors to whom the respondent could turn in emergencies, instrumental helpers, and confidants.

Among persons who have nonneighbor friends in the metropolitan area, nearly half (45%) say that most or all of their friends are 60 or over (25% indicate that all are). Half are older and half younger for 35%, and 20% indicate that most or all of their friends are younger than 60. Among those with new friends, 37% indicate that most or all of them are 60 or over. These patterns reflect a moderate but not pronounced degree of age homogeneity in friendships.

There is a similarly moderate degree of age homogeneity for neighbors with whom respondents are friendliest. The mean age of all neighbors named is 57, with 50% aged 60 and over. Two-thirds of those who name any neighbors with whom they are friendly name at least one who is 60 or older, and one-third name only age peers. Neighbors to whom respondents could turn in emergencies tend to be somewhat younger, however; 36% indicate that most or all such neighbors are 60 or older, whereas 41% indicate that most or all are younger than 60.

Among all persons named as instrumental helpers, only 27% are aged 60 and over; 35% of the respondents name at least one age peer as a helper, and 16% name only age peers. This group includes children and other relatives, however, and such ties are likely to involve less "choice" on the basis of age similarity. Among nonkin helpers, 45% are aged 60 and over. Only 18% name an age-peer neighbor as an instrumental helper, but 46% of neighbors named as helpers are aged 60 or over (age $M = 54$).

Nearly half (44%) of all confidants are aged 60 and over, and 62% of the respondents name at least one age peer as a confidant. As with instrumental helpers, nonkin confidants exhibit greater age homogeneity; 62% are aged 60 or over. Only 24% of those with confidants name an age-peer neighbor as a confidant, but 68% of all neighbors named as confidants are aged 60 and over (age $M = 60$).

In sum, age homogeneity appears to be moderate in the social networks of these respondents despite the lack of stated preference. The choice of age peers is more evident among nonkin ties, for whom peership on the basis of status similarity could be expected to be more salient. Age homogeneity is also more apparent for more intimate (confidant) relationships, as suggested by Verbrugge (1977).

Table 6.3 indicates intercorrelations among measures of network age. The ages of different network components tend to be moderately associated with one another. Age of friends and age of new friends have weaker associations with other measures. The ages of close

Table 6.3 Zero-Order Intercorrelation of Indicators of Network Age Composition

	F	NF	N	H	NH	C	NC
FRIENDS							
All friends (F)	—	.32*	.10*	.16*	.15*	.14*	.04
New friends (NF)		—	.18*	.12*	.19*	.12*	.19
CLOSE NEIGHBORS (N)			—	.37*	.56*	.27*	.67*
HELPERS							
All helpers (H)				—	.87*	.38*	.34*
Neighbor helpers (NH)					—	.24*	.52*
CONFIDANTS							
All confidants (C)						—	.81*
Neighbor confidants (NC)							—

*$p = .05$.

neighbors, instrumental helpers, and confidants are more strongly related, partly because in at least some instances they refer to the same person. There is thus a moderate degree of consistency in the age composition of respondent networks, indicating that respondents can be characterized as having generally homogeneous or non-homogeneous networks.

Variation in Composition

Although network age homogeneity is not pronounced among our respondents, it is present to a noticeable degree. In this section we turn to a related question: What determines the extent of age homogeneity? In particular, to what extent are age-homogeneous networks a function of personal characteristics and preferences, and to what extent do they reflect ecological factors such as neighborhood age concentration?

Personal characteristics generally have weak associations with network age composition. Not surprisingly, older respondents have older networks. Age is associated with friends' age ($r = .22$), for example; 57% of persons aged 70 and over indicate that most or all of their friends are aged 60 and over, compared with 36% of persons aged 60–69. Age is also correlated with age of new friends (.09), age of neighbors with whom the respondent is friendliest (.14), age of neighbor helpers (.16), and age of neighbor confidants (.18). Table 6.4 indicates that men also have somewhat younger networks than women; these differences remain when age is controlled. Interestingly, frequency of participation in groups for older persons has little relation to the age of friends or to having an age-peer confidant, but it is more strongly associated with the age of new friends (.28). Such involvements apparently represent one source of new friends. Other respondent characteristics, such as functional health, socioeconomic status, and marital or employment status, bear little relation to network age composition once respondent age is controlled. Patterns of age homogeneity in informal social networks thus appear to be quite general across subgroups of the older population.

There is a gap between the moderate degree of network age homogeneity and the small stated preference for associating primarily with other older persons. Indeed, measures of age-group orientation have little relationship to the age of persons in the network. Although age of nonneighbor friends is related to both associational preference (63% of those who prefer associating with older people indicate mostly age-

Table 6.4   Sex Differences in Age of Network Ties (percent)

	Males	Females
Most friends aged 60+	36	51
Any 60+ neighbor named as confidant		
If any confidant	16	28
If any neighbor named as confidant	55	73

Note: All differences significant at p = .05.

peer friends, compared with 42% of those who do not) and age identity (54% of those who identify themselves as elderly or old indicate mostly age-peer friends, compared with 40% of those who identify as young or middle-aged), for example, neither associational preference nor age identity is related to the age of neighbor friends, the age of neighbor helpers, or the age of neighbors who are confidants. The age of nonneighbor friends, a more "voluntary," less ecologically constrained network, is thus related to preferences, but the age of neighbors in the support network is not.

These findings, combined with the generally weak associations for personal background characteristics, suggest that the age composition of informal networks is a function more of structural and ecological factors than of preference. That is, access is more influential than preference in shaping network age homogeneity. Of particular interest here, of course, is the influence of neighborhood age composition. We noted earlier that patterns of neighborhood age concentration reflect ecological processes rather than "cultural" processes (such as associational preferences). This point is further substantiated by the relatively weak attitudinal preferences expressed for age-homogeneous associations or housing.

Table 6.5 indicates patterns of association between the age of neighbors in the social network and both measures of age composition in the local area. Results of contingency table and multiple classification analyses are presented to indicate the naming of age-peer neighbors as neighbors with whom one is friendliest, instrumental helpers (for all respondents with helpers and for those who name neighbors), and confidants (for all respondents with confidants and for those who name neighbors).

Both measures of local age density are significantly related to having a person aged 60 or over among the neighbors with whom one is

Table 6.5   Associations between Network and Neighborhood Age Composition

| | Percentage aged 60 + in the tract | | | |
	0–14	15–22	23 +	p
CLOSE NEIGHBORS				
Any 60 +	61	65	82	.000
Age M	55	56	61	.001
Percentage aged 60 + M	43	50	66	.001
INSTRUMENTAL HELPERS				
Of all with helpers				
Any 60 + neighbor	14	17	23	.05
Of all with neighbors				
Any 60 +	29	43	55	.005
Age M	52	55	57	.001
Percentage aged 60 + M	32	46	61	.001
CONFIDANTS				
Of all with confidants				
Any 60 + neighbor	24	24	24	.96
Of all with neighbors				
Any 60 +	59	72	77	.05
Age M	59	60	63	.001
Percentage aged 60 + M	52	64	71	.001

Note: Percentages mentioned in the table are from cross-tabulations. Mean values are from multiple classification analyses, with functional health, socioeconomic status, and age as covariates. Statistical significance (p) is reported on the basis of the corresponding analysi

friendliest and to the mean age (partial correlation r = .18 and .31, respectively) and percentage aged 60 + (.21 and .33, respectively) of those named as closest neighbors. Neighborhood age composition is also related to naming an age-peer neighbor as an instrumental helper and more strongly to the age of neighbors named as helpers (e.g., partial correlations with the mean age of neighbor helpers are .12 for percentage aged 60 + in the tract and .29 for percentage aged 60 + in the neighborhood). The objective tract measure is not related to naming an age-peer neighbor as a confidant, and the subjective neighborhood measure is only weakly related. Among respondents naming a neighbor as a confidant, however, both measures are related to the age of neighbor confidants (e.g., partial correlations with the mean age of neighbor confidants are .11 for percentage aged 60 + in the tract and .28 for percentage aged 60 + in the neighborhood).

In sum, it appears that age-dense neighborhoods make it more prob-

| Estimate of percentage aged 60 + in the neighborhood | | | |
0–10	11–29	30 +	p
54	69	81	.0001
53	56	61	.001
37	48	63	.001
10	19	27	.0001
27	35	56	.0001
50	51	58	.001
26	35	60	.001
18	29	29	.05
54	72	77	.005
56	61	63	.001
48	65	68	.01

able that older persons will be involved in the social networks of these respondents. Though this is a matter of simple arithmetic, it is arithmetic with social consequences in that local age density simultaneously promotes more age-homogeneous patterns of social interaction. (We shall explore these consequences shortly.) This pattern is somewhat stronger and more consistent for the subjective neighborhood measure than for the tract measure. Because the neighborhood measure is a more delimited indicator of neighborhood age structure, in this sense it may be viewed as a more valid measure of the neighborhood context experienced by individuals. This is also a subjective estimate, however, and such estimates may at least partly reflect involvement with older neighbors rather than cause them. The empirical patterns for the tract age density index, a broader but more objective measure, nonetheless lend confidence to a conclusion that neighborhood age composition stimulates the operation of a homophily principle relative to age in the social networks of older people.

We noted in Chapter 2 that neighborhood age composition is strongly associated with type of tract, such that older people tend to be concentrated in central-city tracts. This tendency indicates that there is a danger of confounding the effects of neighborhood age composition with those of urbanism. Table 6.6 indicates associations between neighborhood age composition and the presence of age-peer neighbors in the social network for the total sample and separately for residents of central-city, suburban, and rural tracts. The associations for neighborhood age density are generally consistent across tract type, but patterns for tract age density exhibit variation.

Associations of tract age density with the age of neighbor helpers and confidants are relatively weak for the total sample and are no longer significant within tract type. Patterns for the age of neighbors with whom respondents are friendliest are more interesting, however. Tract age density is related to the age of close neighbors among city residents, whereas the association is weaker or nonexistent for suburban and rural residents. This pattern appears to reflect a threshold effect. Table 6.5 indicates that only the highest category of age density

Table 6.6   Partial Correlation of Tract and Neighborhood Age Density with Age of Neighbors in Network

| | Percentage aged 60+ in the tract | | | |
	Total	City	Suburb	Rur
CLOSE NEIGHBORS[a]				
Name any 60+ [b]	.17*	.23*	.08	.
Age M	.18*	.24*	.03	.
INSTRUMENTAL HELPERS[a]				
Name any 60+ neighbor[b]	.07*	.03	.01	.
Age M of neighbors named	.12*	.05	.11	.
CONFIDANTS[a]				
Name any 60+ neighbor[b]	.01	.04	.07	−.
Age M of neighbors named	.11*	.10	.13	−

Note: Functional health, socioeconomic status, and age were controlled.
*p = .05.
[a]Includes only respondents who have close neighbors, helpers, and confidants, respectiv
[b]Coded 1 if respondent names any neighbor aged 60+, 0 if not.

for the tract (23% or more) is associated with having older close neighbors. The highest value of age density in rural tracts is only 22%, however, and only 9% of suburban residents are in tracts containing more than 22% aged 60+, whereas 49% of city residents are in such tracts. Indeed, city residents of tracts at or above this 23% threshold are substantially more likely to name a close neighbor who is an age peer (83% vs. 59%). The effect of neighborhood age concentration is thus not smoothly linear but apparently requires a "critical mass" of local age-peer representation (roughly one in four). The neighborhood age density measure would not necessarily exhibit this pattern, because it is a more localized measure to which individuals would respond more sensitively.

The effects of residential age composition may also vary by orientation to aging and age peers. Two orientations seem particularly relevant—preference for associating with older people and age identity. Table 6.7 indicates associations between neighborhood age composition and the age of close neighbors and neighbor confidants according to these orientations.

In general, patterns of association for tract age density are unaffected by associational preference or age density. The broader and more objective ecological measure of neighborhood age composition thus has consistent effects on network age that do not appear to depend on personal orientations. The more localized and subjective

Estimate of percentage aged 60+ in the neighborhood			
Total	City	Suburb	Rural
.27*	.31*	.24*	.25*
.31*	.35*	.27*	.29*
.21*	.12*	.20*	.27*
.29*	.23*	.23*	.37*
.07*	.00	.15*	.15*
.28*	.22*	.25*	.34*

Table 6.7 Partial Correlations of Tract and Neighborhood Age Density with Naming Age Peers as Close Neighbors and Confidants

| | Percentage aged 60+ in tract | | | |
| | Prefer older people | | Age identity | |
	Yes	No	Older	Younger
CLOSE NEIGHBORS[a]				
Name any 60+	.28	.13*	.16*	.16*
Age M	.20*	.16*	.19*	.16*
CONFIDANTS				
Name 60+ neighbor[b]	.10	−.01	−.01	.01
Name 60+ neighbor among neighbors[c]	.20	.10	.14	.16*

Note: Associational preference: yes = prefer to spend most of time with people own age; no = do not prefer to spend most of time with older people own age. Age identity: older = elderly or old; younger = young or middle-aged. Functional health, socioeconomic status, and age were controlled.

measure of neighborhood age density, however, has generally stronger associations with network age for respondents who prefer to associate with older people or who identify themselves as old, despite the fact that these orientations are not themselves related to the age of close neighbors or confidants. These patterns lend some support to a view that localized age concentration stimulates operation of a homophily principle based on age more among persons who are receptive to involvement with age peers. The patterns should be viewed cautiously, however, because some of the sample subgroups in Table 6.7 are quite small (70 or 80 respondents).

In summary, the presence of age peers in informal networks is related to residential age concentration. Indeed, the moderate age homogeneity found in the networks of our respondents seems less a reflection of the homophily principle, which implies preference and choice, and more a function of ecological arrangements. Age homogeneity within social networks may thus be to an important degree attributable to the ecology of interaction settings (neighborhoods, workplaces, schools, etc.) rather than to a desire for age homogeneity.

| | Estimate of percentage aged 60 + in neighborhood | | |
| Prefer older people | | Age identity | |
Yes	No	Older	Younger
.36*	.27*	.40*	.23*
.33*	.31*	.50*	.21*
.25*	.05	.13*	.05
.44*	.18*	.44*	.12*

*p = .05.
aIncludes only respondents who have close neighbors.
bIncludes only respondents who have confidants.
cIncludes only respondents who name a neighbor as a confidant.

Consequences of Neighborhood and Network Age Composition

To this point we have seen that older people tend to be concentrated in certain types of residential areas, yielding patterns of age segregation, and that their informal networks are characterized by a moderate degree of age homogeneity. We have not yet discussed, however, whether any of this concentration matters. Are there benefits associated with neighborhood and/or network age concentration? Benefits have been suggested for both, and we will discuss each in turn.

Benefits of Neighborhood Age Concentration

Is residential age segregation harmful or beneficial to older persons? A continuing concern in gerontology has been the extent to which older persons are socially integrated into local communities and the larger society. Cowgill (1974) has argued that modernization reduces the status of the elderly partly by increasing the physical and social distance between older and younger cohorts. This reasoning would seem to imply that retirement communities and other age-segregated settings would reduce status and well-being by heightening feelings of marginality and alienation. Mumford (1956), for example, has argued that the marginality of older people makes them feel unwanted and that there is a need to restore them to a position of dignity and usefulness. According to Mumford, age segregation is unfortunate because "to normalize old age, we must restore the old to the community" (p. 192).

It is also true, however, that residential segregation often reflects elements of choice, and it is not unnatural to find similar people living together (Johnston, 1971; Peach, 1975). The functions of racial and ethnic segregation that have been cited include promotion of assimilation and acculturation (Peach, 1975) and provision of subcultural support in the midst of a "foreign" environment (Suttles, 1972). Thus although segregation is typically decried, urban sociologists have also argued that socially homogeneous neighborhoods may have important positive functions (La Gory and Pipkin, 1981). The boundaries represented by residential segregation may be functional if the support and services available within those boundaries are superior to those available outside them. Similarly, it may be that age segregation or concentration offers important benefits for older people.

The impact of environment, particularly the localized environment, on "environmentally docile" older people suggests a similar conclusion. Given the environmental constraints faced by the elderly, access to localized peers may be of particular value, whereas residing in a dissonant context populated by other age groups may only heighten feelings of marginality and isolation. The potential costs and benefits of neighborhood context can thus be viewed in terms of environmental constraint or enhancement of individual choice in social relations, as was noted in the "choice perspective" discussed in Chapter 1.

Studies have been conducted in a variety of specifically age-segregated living arrangements for older people, including old-age apartment complexes (Sherman, 1971, 1975a and b, 1979; Hochschild, 1973; Carp, 1975; Ross, 1977; Osgood, 1982); mobile home parks (Hoyt, 1954; Johnson, 1971; Osgood, 1982); and retirement communities (Messer, 1967; Bultena and Wood, 1969; Sherman, 1971, 1975a and b, 1979; Mangum, 1973; Marshall, 1975; Osgood, 1982). Older people are drawn to such settings by various amenities and specialized services (health care, housing maintenance), a desire for a better environment (cleaner, safer, warmer, fewer children), and the availability of a wide range of leisure activities. These settings would thus seem to heighten the "choice densities" within the localized environment, engendering the positive functions of segregational boundaries. Sherman (1979), in a study of six age-segregated housing sites, found that perceived support and security were greatest when good on-site service availability was combined with low permeability between the site and the surrounding community.

Studies suggest that age-segregated housing is beneficial in a number of ways, as its residents typically exhibit high morale. These are studies of *intentionally* and relatively enclosed age-segregated settings, however, such as retirement communities and old-age apartment complexes. Relatively few older people reside in such housing, and the extent to which patterns in planned age-segregated settings can be generalized is uncertain. Carp (1976), for example, suggests that the effects of age segregation may be confounded with those of moving to newer, service-rich housing.

There has been less study of age segregation within the larger community, though scattered studies suggest some benefits of age concentration. Studies of public housing tenants have found age concentration to be associated with higher morale, housing satisfaction, and activity (Lawton and Nahemow, 1973; Teaff et al., 1978). Rosenberg (1970), using the city block face as the level of aggregation, found an association between age concentration and social interaction, though Lawton (1983a), in an analysis of national survey data, found that subjective estimates of neighborhood age mix were associated only very weakly with morale. It is not clear how far we may generalize from these studies. Lawton has concluded:

> These findings give tentative support to the idea that there are gains for the older person consequent to living in a neighborhood where many age peers live. . . . they seem to show that a case is accumulating in favor of some degree of age concentration. However, the social-area findings, though very significant, indicated a relatively small-sized effect of neighborhood age concentration; in addition, they were obtained on a very special subject group (senior-housing tenants). It is worth emphasizing at this point that the advantages of high age concentration are by no means established. The strength of the favorable effect is relatively small. [1980:45]

This caution notwithstanding, it is possible that neighborhood age concentration may benefit more older people than the more unusual and isolated segregation represented by planned, enclosed retirement settings. Sherman (1972), for example, found that more urban, less isolated retirement settings were experienced more favorably. Neighborhood age concentration combines access to the larger community with access to age peers. We have already seen that neighborhood age concentration is associated with network age homogeneity. Thus even in the absence of "communal" patterns associated with specifically age-segregated settings, neighborhood age concentration may yield benefits associated more generally with involvement with informal networks of age peers.

Benefits of Network Age Homogeneity

A number of potential benefits may be derived from networks composed of age peers. Age homogeneity may arise from a desire to select an "audience" to facilitate identity maintenance (George, 1980). Matthews (1979), for example, argues that the overriding source of uncertainty in the social worlds of older women is related to self-identity and the "weak stigma" of old age. Thus they will attempt to organize their lives to avoid people who question their self-images. Similarly, Berghorn et al. (1978) suggest that age heterogeneity may be too "burdensome," yielding dissonance between self-expectations and the expectations of others.

Dowd (1980a and b) places the issue of age homogeneity more explicitly within the framework of exchange theory. Social interaction is the principal medium through which activities and sentiments are exchanged and the means by which most rewards are obtained. The quality of social exchange reflects the location of exchange partners in the social structure, highlighting the importance of power resources. There is less concern with deference and greater mutual understanding of exchange roles among status equals, and exchange relations will be more satisfying and stable among partners of similar power. Dowd argues that older people in modern societies are in a weak negotiating position for exchange because they are disadvantaged in both material resources and personal and relational resources. Age is a "master status" that accompanies an individual and is used to evaluate the legitimacy of claims for certain levels of rewards. Negative stereotypes about old age and status generalization place a "burden of proof" on older individuals.

This argument implies that it is costly for the elderly to cross age boundaries because the middle-aged will dominate interactions by virtue of their resource advantage. Age homogeneity minimizes the costs of social exchange, bringing together actors with similar interests and resources, and makes it easier to determine routine expectations and rules for exchange. One strategy available to older people in the face of unbalanced and unsatisfying exchanges, apart from outright disengagement, is thus a shift to age-homogeneous interactions. This suggested strategy is similar to Goffman's (1963) discussion of the "discrediting" nature of stigma and the unease felt in interactions with "normals." To the extent that being old carries a stigma in modern society, older persons may be more "comfortable" and satisfied in more balanced exchange relationships with age peers. Indeed, this notion of balanced exchanges suggests that age homogeneity in social networks represents a type of person-environment congruence.

To summarize, the literature we have reviewed suggests that neighborhood age concentration, and associated network age homogeneity, may be beneficial for older persons. In the sections that follow, we investigate this possibility with regard to neighborhood quality, social support, age-related orientations and socialization experiences, knowledge of age-related services, and subjective well-being. In addition to looking at general patterns, we will attend to subgroup variations in the implications of neighborhood and network age composition. The concept of environmental docility suggests the need for such detailed investigation. Similarly, Gubrium (1973) has suggested that age segregation works best for those with low "activity resources" (health, income, and social supports), who are most handicapped in living up to "active middle-aged adult" norms of activity or in "escaping" the local environment.

Neighborhood Quality

Older persons tend to be concentrated in older, more centralized areas, so neighborhood age concentration is likely to be associated with the problems of such areas. Nonetheless, it might be expected that neighborhood age composition would be associated with *perceived* quality of the neighborhood. This is generally not the case, however. Indeed, volunteered responses to open-ended questions indicate little salience of neighborhood age composition: only 44 respondents (4% of the sample) refer to age-peer neighbors as among the "best things about living in this neighborhood," and only 11% mention young people (children and teenagers) as among the "worst" things about the neighborhood.

Several of the findings reported in Chapter 3 are relevant here. Happiness with neighbors and perceived commonality with neighbors are dimensions of neighborhood satisfaction, but neighborhood age composition does not seem salient in this regard. Indeed, the age density of the tract is negatively associated with indicators of neighborhood satisfaction, though this is attributable to the relationship between age segregation and urbanism. Negative associations between neighborhood satisfaction and both local age composition measures disappear when the urbanism of the tract is controlled, and city residents exhibit a moderate positive association between percentage aged 60 + in the tract and general neighborhood satisfaction and happiness with neighbors (partial correlation r = .16 and .19 respectively). Persons residing in age-concentrated neighborhoods have more efficient service areas, but this is again largely attributable to central-city location. Age concentration per se thus has little impact on the quality of neighborhoods; the mix of benefits and costs associated with neighborhood age concentration depends upon the characteristics of the areas in which older people congregate.

Tract age density is also not related to number of neighbors known, frequency of interaction with neighbors, or neighborhood assistance patterns, but it is moderately related to frequency of interaction with neighbors for respondents who are widowed (.13) or have some functional health impairment (.17) and for city residents (.14). The presence of age peers may thus be viewed as more beneficial by residents of more socially complex central-city environments and by more vulnerable elderly. The respondent's estimate of neighborhood age composition is unrelated to number of neighbors known and assistance from neighbors, but it is related to frequency of interaction with neighbors (partial correlation r = .17).

On the whole, neighborhood age concentration appears to make some small contributions to neighborhood quality. These are more evident for more vulnerable elements of the older population.

Social Support

A particular potential benefit of neighborhood age concentration is the availability of more viable social networks when embedded in a pool of locally available age peers. Rosow (1967) found that, as the age density of apartment buildings increased, older residents had more local friends and greater interaction with neighbors and that even those in age-integrated buildings chose friends from age peers. Sherman (1975a) also found that residents of six California retirement sites reported more new friends and greater visiting with neighbors than matched community respondents. It can thus be suggested that older persons will have more friends, and will experience less isolation and loneliness, when they reside in neighborhoods containing more age peers.

The implication is that networks of age peers in age-concentrated neighborhoods may yield "service" benefits through mutual assistance similar to those found in age-segregated housing, such as checking up on one another's well-being, care during illness, shopping, rides, etc. (Rosow, 1967; Hochschild, 1973; Sherman, 1975b; Ross, 1977). A related finding is that age segregation in apartment buildings was associated with less criminal victimization and less fear of crime (Sherman et al., 1976), apparently because of feelings of territoriality and shared surveillance.

It should not be inferred that localized age peers would replace the family as a source of socioemotional support. Assistance from children and from neighbors in age-concentrated settings tends to be cumulative rather than compensatory (Hochschild, 1973; Rosow, 1967; Sherman, 1975b). Although family assistance and interaction can span distances (Adams, 1986), however, age concentration may result in more viable *localized* social networks that can be approached more readily for support. Age-homogeneous settings may also be more satisfying than family networks because of the spontaneity in assuming responsibility for one another, so that more meaningful relationships occur (Lowenthal and Robinson, 1976).

We saw in the previous section that neighborhood age composition has some association with frequency of interaction with neighbors. Neither measure of age concentration is related to neighborhood assistance patterns, however, nor are they related to the general availability of instrumental and expressive support or to naming neighbors as helpers. Similarly, neither measure is related to having a confidant, number of confidants, proximity or frequency of interaction with confidants, or naming a neighbor as a confidant. Neighborhood age concentration thus affects the presence of age peers in support networks but does not affect whether social support is available or accessible. This finding reinforces Adams' (1986) observation that physically close friends are often not the closest friends emotionally.

Age-Related Orientations and Socialization

Age concentration provides a potential source of socializing experiences for assisting in adjustment to the new status of "old person." Throughout the life course, age peers provide emotional support during role transitions, information about new and future roles, and opportunities for role rehearsal (Hess, 1972). Retirement communities appear to help the aged become less active without the guilt associated with middle-aged norms (Messer, 1967) and facilitate less fearful attitudes toward death and dying (Marshall, 1975). Hochschild (1973), for example, found that residents of old-age apartments felt freer with each other to improvise new roles, to reminisce, to joke about old age, and to discuss death. Studies have also found the emergence of internal bases of social status that buffer the effects of role loss, declining health, or lower income (Hochschild, 1973; Seguin, 1973; Ross, 1977). New norms develop with role models and sanctions for conformity to role expectations. Seguin, for example, found that residents of a retirement community generated both formal and informal structures, with both worklike and familylike roles. Old roles such as worker or homemaker can thus be carried over and modified as part of new roles. Interaction with others in similar situations also shields older people from acknowledgment of status loss and may raise morale by making old age a more attractive period of life (Streib, 1976).

It is therefore possible that localized social networks of age peers may circumvent feelings of relative deprivation arising from comparison with middle-aged standards. To the extent that older people interact largely with other older people, they may be insulated from the stigma attached to old age and therefore find it easier to identify as old. Streib (1976), for example, suggests that retirement communities may mitigate negative attitudes toward aging by shielding the older person from acknowledgment of downward mobility or status loss; here there is no need to envy workers or to feel self-pity when one slows down. Age peers can also be role models for the transitions and issues associated with aging, and their availability may alter the meaning of "old age" and "old person." A culture of age peers could provide more positive definitions of aging and meaningful roles within which self-worth could be validated. The combination of interaction with age peers and more favorable attitudes toward aging appears to bolster self-esteem (Ward, 1977a).

A concomitant may be heightened aging-group consciousness and activism based on age. Age concentration provides opportunities to learn of interests and concerns shared with age peers because of the treatment of the aged as a group. Dowd (1980b) suggests that age segregation may reduce age conflict by yielding more satisfying interactions and reducing the conflict and dissatisfaction inherent in cross-age interactions, but cross-generational ties represent "bonds of pluralism" that can also reduce age conflict (Foner, 1974), and Riley (1976) suggests that "solidarity can be promoted where age-peers are in a position to communicate about their similar tasks, needs, and problems" (p. 210). Finally, feelings of personal efficacy could be expected to rise with the availability of socioemotional peer support, and lower feelings of efficacy accompanying aging tend to reduce political activism (Ragan and Dowd, 1974). The effects of age concentration are possibly cyclical; that is, age density may yield more positive attitudes toward aging and greater willingness to identify as old, resulting in greater age consciousness and activism, which in turn make age density more salient.

There is mixed evidence on the political implications of age concentration. Longino et al. (1980), comparing residents of retirement communities with a national sample, found that some cohesiveness and positive regard of the aged emerged in the retirement settings, but this led to a "retreatist" subculture rather than an activist one. This finding seems to support Dowd's argument that age segregation will reduce age conflict by yielding satisfying exchange relationships. Anderson and Anderson (1978), however, found that residence in retirement communities heightened involvement in an "old-age" activist group in Arizona. Similarly, participation in age-graded voluntary associations may foster greater activist self-interest based on age (Trela, 1972).

Table 6.8 summarizes associations of neighborhood age composition and the age of network members with several age-related orientations described in Chapters 2 and 5: attitudes toward older people, comparisons between one's own situation and that of age peers, having a role model for aging, receiving advice from age peers about age-related issues, and age identity (e.g., as "middle-aged" or "elderly").

There is little evidence that neighborhood age concentration or access to age peers within informal networks yields more positive attitudes toward old people. The age of network members, including friends, close neighbors, and confidants, is not related to the adjective ratings of "most older people." A similar pattern is evident for neighborhood age concentration: the estimate of the percentage aged 60 + in the neighborhood is positively related to such attitudes, but the percentage aged 60 + in the tract is negatively related, and both associations are quite small. The age of network members and neighborhood age concentration also have little association with feeling better or worse off than age peers, though persons with age-integrated friendships rate themselves slightly better off compared with age peers. These patterns did not vary significantly across sample sub-groups. On the whole, there is little evidence here that either network or neighborhood age composition has much influence on attitudes toward older people.

There is some indication that access to age peers contributes to socialization for old age. Neighborhood age concentration has very weak associations with having a role model and receiving advice from age peers, but Table 6.9 indicates that neighbors are more likely to be named as role models and age-peer helpers when neighborhood age density is higher. Neighborhood age density is also more strongly related to having a role model and advice from age peers for widowed respondents (partial correlations r = .15 and .14, respectively) and for those who live alone (.15 and .13). Having access to age peers may thus make more of a difference in socialization experiences for older persons who are more isolated. The age of network members has stronger associations with these socialization indicators, however. Indeed, the measures of mean age used in Table 6.8 understate the case. Friends' age is unrelated to having a role model or age-peer advice, but having a close neighbor aged 60 + is related to both; among those who know an age-peer neighbor well, 71% indicate a role model (compared with 43% among those who do not) and 39% have received advice and support from an age peer (25% among those who do not). A similar pattern is evident for having a confidant aged 60 + ; among such per-

Table 6.8   Partial Correlations of Age-Related Orientations with Network and Neighborhood Age Composition

	Neighborhood	
	Percentage aged 60 + in tract	Estimate of percentage aged 60 + in neighborhood
Attitudes toward older people	−.07*	.07*
Peer comparisons	.04	.01
Role model	−.10*	.07*
Advice and support from age peers	−.06*	.06
Age identification	.02	.01

Note: Functional health, education, occupational prestige, and age were controlled.
*p = .05.
aMean age of confidants and neighbors with whom respondent is friendliest.

sons, 64% have a role model (vs. 45%) and 38% have received advice from an age peer (vs. 24%).

Although access to age peers within informal networks apparently makes a contribution to socialization for old age, a more critical issue is whether involvement with other older people makes it "easier" to identify as old, insulating the aging individual from feelings of deprivation and stigma. This does not appear to be the case. Table 6.8 indicates, for example, that age identity is unrelated to both neighborhood and network age composition. We saw in Chapter 5 that self-identification as "elderly" or "old" is associated with lower subjective well-being. This relationship was investigated within categories of neighborhood and network age composition, and there is no evidence that access to age peers alters the pattern. Older age identity, for example, is associated with lower morale regardless of neighborhood age composition, the age of neighbors with whom respondents are friendly, or the age of friends. Age-concentrated contexts thus do not appear to make aging "easier" in these terms.

Knowledge of Services

We noted in Chapter 4 that social networks may serve a "lay referral" function regarding formal services. Results presented in that chapter indicated little association between network characteristics and knowledge of age-related services, but localized networks of age peers may serve a particular role as funnels for service information and referral. Older persons are often unaware of the availability of particular services, partly reflecting inadequate access to information.

	Network age	
Friends	Close neighbors[a]	Confidants[a]
.03	−.05	.02
−.07*	.01	−.01
−.03	.13*	.11*
−.01	.03	.08*
.03	−.01	−.01

Table 6.9 Associations between Estimate of Neighborhood Age Concentration and Naming a Neighbor as a Role Model and as a Peer Helper

Designation of neighbor	Estimate of percentage aged 60+ in neighborhood			
	0–10	11–29	30+	p
Role model	38	40	56	.05
Peer helper	5	2	12	.05

Knowledge can be gained directly or by word-of-mouth, but older residents of more complex urban areas are more dependent upon secondary sources (Taietz, 1975). Urban age concentration might lessen this dependence upon formal paths of information and referral, increasing knowledge about services and social programs.

Neighborhood age concentration is associated with greater knowledge of services (partial correlations are .14 with percentage aged 60+ in the tract and .12 with percentage aged 60+ in the neighborhood). The tract measure of age concentration is not related to service knowledge within categories of tract type (city, suburb, and rural), however, indicating that this association is a reflection of the greater knowledge exhibited by city residents (and greater service accessibility in cities). The estimate of neighborhood age concentration, on the other hand, is related to knowledge of services only among city residents (partial correlation $r = .13$). There are other indications that age-peer neighbors may make some modest contribution to service knowledge. Respondents who have a close age-peer neighbor know about more services ($M = 3.2$) than both those who know no neighbors well (2.7) and those who know neighbors well but none aged 60+ (2.8), but service knowledge is unrelated to the age of friends, instrumental helpers, and confidants. Access to age peers, then, may bolster awareness of services to some degree, but this tendency appears to be restricted to quite localized ties.

Subjective Well-being

Our earlier review suggests that access to age peers (localized or otherwise) may contribute generally to well-being. Because of similarity and equality, relationships with age peers may simply be more intimate, satisfying, and stable. Proximate age peers may represent a supportive context to bolster individual coping efforts. We have already investigated associations between neighborhood and network age composition and several specific indicators of well-being or quality of life (neighborhood quality, social support, age-related orientations and socialization, and service knowledge); these associations are modest at best. In this section we turn our attention to two more global indicators of subjective well-being: morale and perceived mastery.

Table 6.10 summarizes the associations of neighborhood and net-

Table 6.10 Partial Correlations of Neighborhood and Network Age Composition with Morale and Mastery

	Morale	Mastery
NEIGHBORHOOD AGE STRUCTURE		
Percentage aged 60+ in tract	.01	.00
Estimates of percentage aged 60+ in neighborhood	−.03	−.05
FRIENDS		
Age of friends	−.14*	−.16*
Age of new friends	−.17*	−.14*
CLOSE NEIGHBORS		
Any 60+	.04	.04
Age M	.02	−.01
INSTRUMENTAL HELPERS		
All with helpers		
Any 60+	−.07*	−.05
Age M	−.05	−.05
Any 60+ neighbor	−.05	−.06*
All with neighbors		
Any 60+	−.02	−.06
Age M	.01	−.05
CONFIDANTS		
All with confidants		
Any 60+	−.06*	−.04
Age M	−.04	−.00
Any 60+ neighbor	−.02	−.03
All with neighbors		
Any 60+	−.03	−.00
Age M	−.04	−.01

Note: Functional health, socioeconomic status, and age were controlled.
*$p = .05$.

work age composition with morale and mastery. The most notable aspect of Table 6.10 is the dearth of noteworthy associations. Neighborhood age structure and involvement with age peers, generally or as neighbors, have little relation to well-being.

One issue of particular interest was the effect of access to an age-peer neighbor. Regression analyses were conducted with morale that parallel those presented in Chapter 4, adding as the last step a dummy variable for having a close neighbor aged 60 and over. Having a close age-peer neighbor did not make a significant contribution to morale (β = .02). Inclusion of variables indicating whether age-peer neighbors were named as instrumental helpers or confidants also made no significant contributions to morale. Numerous subgroup analyses yielded little variation. In particular, the apparent effects of having a close age-peer neighbor did not vary by age-related orientation (associational preference and age identity) or competence.

It appears that age concentration makes little contribution to subjective well-being. Indeed, Table 6.10 indicates that having older friends and new friends is related to lower morale and mastery. These relationships are noteworthy because they run counter to arguments in the literature. Table 6.11 clarifies the relationship between friends' age and morale. Age-integrated friendship networks are associated with higher morale than those in which age peers predominate. Those who have older friends also have fewer friends, but the relationship with lower subjective well-being remains when number of friends is also controlled (partial correlation r = -.10 with morale and -.13 with mastery). It is noteworthy that having mostly older friends is related to lower morale even among respondents who indicate they prefer to associate with older people (-.08) and who identify themselves as elderly or old (-.12). The negative relationship with mastery is also stronger for persons with some functional impairment (-.22) and those who are widowed (-.21), suggesting that "old" friendship networks may be especially problematic to the perceived coping ability of more vulnerable older persons. Age-homogeneous networks may thus contribute to feelings of marginality and insecurity.

As in other analyses, we investigated variation related to "competence." Having mostly older friends is related to lower morale for the high-competence group but not for the low-competence group (partial correlations r = -.16 and .00, respectively). Persons with higher competence are better able to meet the greater exchange demands of age-integrated networks and may be dissatisfied with the implied marginality of an age-concentrated network, but there is no evidence

Table 6.11   Multiple Classification Analysis of Morale by Friends' Age

		Morale M	
FRIENDS' AGE	N	No covariates	With covariates
All 60+	181	50.4	50.7
Most 60+	149	51.6	52.2
Half 60+, half younger	256	53.9	53.6
Most or all younger	146	54.1	53.6
η/β	—	.17	.13
p	—	.001	.001

Note: Functional health, socioeconomic status, and age were covariates.

that age-homogeneous networks contribute *positively* to the morale of older persons with reduced competence. On the whole, there is little evidence here that either neighborhood age concentration or network age homogeneity makes much difference to the well-being of older persons.

Conclusions

Although there is little expressed preference for associating or living primarily with age peers, there is moderate age homogeneity in the social networks of these respondents. As the gap with stated preferences suggests, network age homogeneity is a function more of structural/ecological factors than of personal factors. In particular, neighborhood age concentration stimulates network age homogeneity, regardless of associational preference or age identity.

The contributions of either neighborhood or network age concentration to well-being are quite limited, however. The age of neighbors has little bearing on perceptions of neighborhood quality, and age concentration is unrelated to social support. Age peers in the network appear to make some contribution to socialization, but neighborhood and network age concentration do not appear to make aging "easier" in a social-psychological sense. Finally, network age homogeneity makes a small contribution to service knowledge but does not bolster morale or mastery. There are some associations and some subgroup variations, but even those associations of which we have taken note are not substantial. These minimal patterns contradict expectations derived from several strands of literature in sociology and gerontology. In particular, two issues need to be addressed. First, why does age homogeneity within informal networks apparently have little bearing on well-being? Second, why are patterns associated with neighborhood age concentration not consistent with those evident in age-segregated housing?

The first issue bears on the homophily principle and on the significance of age for affiliation and exchange. Age represents a salient similarity that structures close relationships, but age homogeneity has little bearing on subjective well-being. Indeed, having mostly older friends is associated with lower morale. Many older people prefer not to associate or identify with "old" people, who reflect stigma and lowered status (Ward, 1977a; Bultena and Powers, 1978). Heavy involvement with age peers may stimulate unwelcome feelings of marginality with regard to the larger social world.

Expectations of the value of age homogeneity are partly derived from exchange theory. The patterns in these data call into question the relevance of age in determining exchange "balance." Dowd (1980a, b) has argued that older people have a subordinate status in the modern age stratification system, yielding a generalized stigma and associated reduction in exchange resources, but this devaluation may not be experienced in informal ties, as we tend not to devalue the *particular* old people we know and interact with (Branco and Williamson, 1982). Propositions derived from exchange theory about the value of homogeneity may rely on overly universalistic categories, overlooking the fact that individuals live and interact within particularistic worlds. Rejection of the aged as a group does not necessarily imply rejection of older people within their normal, ongoing exchange relationships. It appears that age homogeneity matters little to the quality of exchanges with friends and neighbors.

The neighborhood age concentration studied here is also apparently much less influential than that found in retirement communities, old-age apartments, and the like. Neighborhood age concentration differs quantitatively and qualitatively from age-segregated housing. Rosow (1974) suggests that the formulation of a distinctive new role, expectations and norms appropriate to it, and a set of eligible role models, will be promoted by large concentrations of socially homogeneous elderly (i.e., homogeneous with regard to social class, race, marital status, etc.). Neighborhood age concentration may represent insufficiently large concentrations of age peers compared with the more complete segregation of retirement communities. A neighborhood can be considered age concentrated if 25% of its members are older persons; this may be an insufficient "critical mass." Retirement communities and old-age apartments are also typically quite homogeneous on social characteristics other than age, perhaps more so than age-concentrated neighborhoods. The fact that such neighborhoods are also embedded in more heterogeneous, age-integrated surroundings may further limit the emergence of age-group solidarity, because heterogeneity in the social and physical environment increases the probability of intergroup relations (Blau, 1977).

These community residents also have not chosen to be age segregated; rather, their neighborhoods are age concentrated by "ecological accident." Indeed, a preference for age concentration per se may not be a primary motivation for choosing specifically age-segregated housing; rather, the availability of amenities and services appears to be a more salient reason (Sherman, 1971). Sherman, for example, found that only one-fifth of a sample of older persons in Los Angeles County expressed any desire to move to retirement housing. Furthermore, of those who already lived in such housing, only one-third indicated that they chose to do so from a desire to be with age peers. Neighborhood age concentration, of course, does not represent a self-contained "package" of services.

The lack of such services also implies a lack of structural facilitators for the emergence of "community" in age-concentrated neighborhoods. Status similarity alone is not sufficient for the emergence of social solidarity. Feld (1981) suggests that the relevant aspect of the social environment is "foci" around which individuals organize their social relations. Activities, and therefore interactions and sentiments, are organized around foci. If individuals share many foci, they are also likely to have multifaceted exchange relationships. Joint activities are a characteristic of planned age-segregated housing (e.g., congregate meals, shared social and recreational programs), but are not evident in age-concentrated neighborhoods of dispersed housing.

As a final point, it can be noted that most older people are not in need of the potential benefits of age segregation. Rosow (1967) has suggested that age-integrated settings work well for long-term residents of stable neighborhoods whose local ties are relatively intact. This is a good description of our sample and indeed of most older community residents. They are not in need of the "shelter" represented by age segregation or concentration.

In conclusion, the findings reported in this chapter warn against too facile generalization about the consequences or benefits of age concentration. Age mix may appear to be a significant variable in specialized housing because it is planned and chosen as such; relocation to a special setting triggers selectivity processes that heighten person-environment congruence. The "aging in place" that produces patterns of neighborhood age concentration does not involve these selectivity processes.

The functions or dysfunctions of age concentration are dependent on the qualities of the residential context as well as of the categories of people residing in the place. The boundaries represented by residential segregation may be functional if support and services available within the area are superior to those available outside, but age-concentrated community neighborhoods lack the design features that give age-segregated housing its supportive advantages. Indeed, neighborhood age concentration tends to occur in lower-quality areas (e.g., older and cheaper housing), and older people tend to be concentrated in areas with environmental problems associated with low-income populations and deteriorating housing (Struyk and Soldo, 1980). Although the more centralized location of age-concentrated neighborhoods may heighten access to many services, it may also increase exposure to "urban distress" (crime, deteriorating housing, cultural diversity). Solidarity with localized age peers may also weaken ties to more general networks outside the localized setting, increasing isolation and marginality.

We do not mean that age-segregated living arrangements are not beneficial when they are chosen and when they include appropriate design features. Policy should continue to facilitate voluntary age segregation as one option for the older population. It is also clear, however, that age concentration cannot be embraced as a general guide for policy. In particular, patterns of residential age concentration found within American metropolitan areas cannot be viewed as a vehicle for informal support of the elderly. We can assume neither that older people residing in age-concentrated neighborhoods have greater access to support nor that those in age-integrated neighborhoods have less access. Neighborhood age concentration, and network age homogeneity more generally, do not appear to be important dimensions of person-environment congruence for most older people.

7 Implications and Conclusions

The general theme of this book is that aging is a contextual process; the nature and consequences of aging depend on the environment within which it occurs. This is not to say that the elderly are at the "mercy" of their environment. Elder (1981) has described the life course as both contextual and transactional, the latter term recognizing that individuals do exercise choice in shaping their own lives. The findings described in this book reflect both the contextual and the transactional quality of aging. Before turning in greater detail to these general themes, let us briefly summarize our findings.

Several aspects of the environment for aging have received attention here. These include the neighborhood, the interpersonal environment of informal networks and supports, the social environment reflected in individual orientations toward aging and the aged, and the age composition of neighborhoods and informal networks and supports. Such interests capture at least some aspects of each of the components of the human ecosystem discussed at length in Chapter 1.

The Neighborhood Environment

Space is an elemental property of all social structures, reflecting a complex interplay of physical, social, and cultural forces. The neighborhood space in particular represents a resource system that potentially constrains or enhances behavior through the "choice densities" it presents to individuals. The neighborhood is likely to represent a particularly important context for older persons, given their reduced mobility and heightened local dependence. The concept of environmental docility, for example, emphasizes the importance of person-environment congruence to the well-being of the elderly.

We have found that the neighborhood territories of these older respondents are delimited, as one would expect, but not strikingly so. The extent to which older persons are "environmentally docile" depends upon their competence. The older people in this sample have relatively high levels of competence, as would generally be true of community samples of the older population. There are actually two types of neighborhoods: (1) a "social" neighborhood, defined by social ties and knowledge of residents, and (2) a "service" neighborhood, defined by patterns of use of community facilities. The latter ranges more widely. Indeed, relatively competent community residents exhibit high mobility in using services and appear to be able to reach services that extend beyond the usual definitions of "critical distances" (Regnier, 1976; Newcomer, 1976).

There are, nevertheless, indications that the environmental experience is affected by age-related processes. Despite the fact that older people are often clustered in areas that are of lower quality in objective terms, our data (as well as those from other studies) indicate high levels of neighborhood satisfaction. This satisfaction is partly attributable to investment in familiar places and the experience of cognitive dissonance in response to a perception of limited options. Older people also experience the environment more passively and vicariously; in Rowles's (1978) terms, their mode of spatial experience involves less action and greater fantasy. The importance of neighborhood maintenance as a dimension of neighborhood satisfaction, for example, reflects a vicarious, observational mode of neighborhood involvement. In this respect, older people respond to a "neighborhood of the mind."

The environmental experience in later life also has complexity. Different residential situations are associated with different mixes of advantages and disadvantages for different types of people. Urbanism and environmental docility have received particular attention here. Residents of cities, for example, express lower neighborhood satisfaction, but their location has advantages of convenience. Persons with reduced competence appear to be more sensitive to environmental context, supporting the environmental docility hypothesis and indicating the importance of person-environment congruence. Such persons, however, seem to be less directly affected by the objective conditions of city residence—both the advantages of convenience and the disadvantages of generalized urban distress. Persons with reduced competence may respond to a subjectively defined neighborhood and may have less direct experience with the neighborhood.

The Interpersonal Environment

Informal networks represent a contextual dimension of aging that is less locally based. Such networks are sources of gratification and support throughout life, and their value may be heightened in old age because of role loss and reduced mobility. As has been indicated in previous research, older persons have relatively robust informal networks; they are not isolated. In objective terms, they typically interact regularly with relatives, friends, and neighbors and have access to both instrumental and expressive support. In subjective terms, they generally feel that they have enough interpersonal contacts and support.

Children and neighbors hold the most prominent positions in the support networks of the elderly. Interestingly, however, nonlocal friends play minor roles as helpers or confidants, but such friendships have the most consistent associations with morale. This finding may reflect the voluntary and peership qualities of such ties, and lack of friends may carry implications of marginality and age-related status loss. Children are typically favored as sources of assistance, yet involvement with children has little relation to perceived well-being. This may reflect the problematic quality of parent-child relations in later life.

The patterns of findings indicate that age has little bearing on the characteristics of informal networks. Age and age-related changes (health, retirement, and widowhood) have only weak and scattered associations. Apparent variations—socioeconomic status, urbanism, and sex—most likely represent patterns that are relatively stable throughout life. Women, for example, appear to occupy a central position in the support networks of older people. This position may be partly attributable to a sex-ratio in old age that favors women, but the pattern is not eliminated by controls for age, suggesting that it endures from earlier in the life cycle.

Although the informal networks of older people are relatively strong, there has been debate and uncertainty concerning the contributions of interpersonal ties to well-being. Our findings offer some clarification. The "quality" of such ties is more salient to subjective well-being than is the "quantity"; whether older people perceive that they have enough contacts and assistance is more important than

actual frequency or proximity of interpersonal ties. Perceived availability of instrumental support plays a particularly important role,
reflecting a somewhat precarious present and future situation experienced by the elderly. The relative importance of different dimensions
of informal networks also varies across subgroups of the older population. Vulnerability and competence are of particular interest. Supporting the environmental-docility hypothesis, neighbors and proximate
instrumental help are of particular value to persons with reduced
resources and competence.

The Social Environment

Age-related orientations to aging and the aged represent a social-psychological dimension of the aging environment that reflects the
broader social environment. There has been considerable interest in
such orientations, but their sources and consequences are not well
understood. It is not clear, for example, how individual attitudes
toward aging affect well-being. Age stratification also creates some of
the conditions for age-group solidarity, but aging-group consciousness does not appear to be widespread. Lack of socialization for
old age has been cited as a particular problem, but relatively little is
known about patterns and consequences of socializing influences.
The findings that have been presented here address each of these
issues.

Our respondents express generally favorable views of the older population, though their attitudes have some negative dimensions. They
tend to see sickness and dependency as problems of older people, for
example, and also typically view themselves as better off than their
age peers. Favorable attitudes toward older people and favorable comparisons with age peers both contribute to higher morale.

A negative orientation to old age is perhaps most clearly evident in
the findings on age identity. As in previous research, these respondents resist identifying themselves as "elderly" or "old." Age identity
does not appear to be a function of general images of aging and the
aged, however, but rather represents a response to one's personal situation. The major predictors of age identity, in addition to age itself, are
comparisons with other older people and health. "Feeling old" is a
response to personal decrement, indicating that aging is symbolized
in terms of loss. Indeed, older age identity appears to be demoralizing.
It is not age that is important but perceptions of aging relative to peers
and to one's former self.

Socializing experiences and age-group solidarity might be expected to counteract negative perceptions of old age, bolstering the morale of those who "feel" old. In our work as in previous research, however, there is little evidence of aging-group consciousness; for example, relatively few respondents prefer to associate with or to live primarily with age peers, and there is little activism on the basis of age. Approximately half of the respondents can name an age-related role model, and about one-third indicate that they have received helpful advice and support on age-related concerns from other older people. Still, such experiences exhibit little direct contribution to morale. On the whole, age-related socialization and involvement with age peers do not appear very salient in the lives of these older people.

Neighborhood and Network Age Composition

In undertaking the research reported here, we were particularly interested in the consequences of residential age concentration. Age patterns emerge from ecological processes: the reduced residential mobility of the elderly and their disadvantage in the competition for space. It has been argued that age concentration would be beneficial. In the context of a "choice perspective," such spatial arrangements provide improved sets of opportunities. This is particularly relevant for older persons, who manifest greater environmental constraint. Most generally, social differentiation is felt to pose barriers to interaction, whereas homogeneity encourages it (Blau, 1977). An exchange theory perspective emphasizes the value of age homogeneity, as this presumably yields more satisfying relationships and insulation from the stigma associated with old age.

Research on specifically age-segregated housing has appeared to support such expectations, but these do not appear to transfer to the less marked and more typical neighborhood age concentration studied here. It is apparent that the effects of age concentration (or, indeed, of any form of segregation) depend on qualities of the context within which it occurs. Neighborhood age concentration lacks the beneficial features of planned, age-segregated housing—specialized services and amenities, and joint activities that encourage and support social integration. Indeed, such features, rather than age concentration per se, more likely account for the heightened morale often found in retirement communities and old-age apartments.

This conclusion is bolstered by the finding that there are limited benefits associated with network age homogeneity. Despite minimal feelings of age-group solidarity, these respondents exhibit a moderate degree of age homogeneity in their social networks. Age structures social relationships, and neighborhood age concentration contributes to network age homogeneity, but involvement with age peers makes only limited contributions to well-being. Although it has some influence on age-related socialization, it does not appear to make aging "easier." Age peers also make a small contribution to service awareness but not to morale or mastery. Indeed, age-concentrated friendship networks are associated with lower morale, perhaps reflecting an implied marginality of old age. On the whole, age homogeneity does not appear to be salient in the lives of these older people.

Conclusions

In the concluding section for each chapter we have discussed themes that are relevant to the issues addressed there and have pointed to directions for future work. Clearly we have not said the last word in any of these areas. A number of research needs remain; for example, there is a need to (1) assess the nature, determinants, and effects of the quality (both objective and perceived) of neighborhood services, (2) investigate the quality of interpersonal ties in greater detail, assessing the fulfillment of social needs, and (3) study the full complexity of the elements and experiences of age-related socialization. It is appropriate here to consider more general themes and implications of this study. Three related themes suggest themselves: (1) the relative unimportance of age per se, (2) the considerable variability and diversity within the older population, and (3) the value of a transactional view of the aging experience.

The Relative Unimportance of Age

Age itself has little bearing on neighborhood perceptions and ratings, characteristics of informal networks, and age-related orientations and behaviors. Indeed, age is unrelated to overall morale, a finding echoed in other research (e.g., Herzog and Rodgers, 1981). Such age-related changes as retirement and widowhood also exhibit weak patterns of association. This result emphasizes the degree of continuity and stability in people's lives. It also underscores the need to avoid "myths" about aging, as people (including the elderly themselves) tend to exaggerate the changes and problems associated with aging (National Council on the Aging, 1975). We have seen, for example, that our respondents exhibit a high degree of satisfaction with their neighborhoods and informal networks.

These patterns suggest a rather restricted salience of age (Ward, 1984b). Age represents only one among many personal characteristics, and it does not appear to "loom large" in the lives of these older persons. There is little evidence of age-group solidarity, for example, and the age structure of personal and neighborhood situations seems of little importance. We should consequently beware of simplistic theoretical or policy statements about "the elderly." In particular, we have found that the apparent benefits of age-segregated housing cannot be generalized to a community sample.

Although old age may in fact carry a stigma in modern societies (Cowgill, 1974; Dowd, 1980a), older people are at least partly insulated from the larger social structure. Emphasis on the importance of age as a differentiating characteristic derives from a view of age as a universalistic category (Blau, 1977; Dowd, 1980a). Older people do not live in universalistic worlds, however; rather, their lives are lived within particularistic worlds of family and friends. Family and friends interact with older people on the basis of their knowledge of the individual, not in terms of general stereotypes about "old people."

We do not mean to imply, however, that age entirely lacks significance. As acknowledged by the model of age stratification (Riley et al., 1972), age is a "social fact" endowed with more than simple chronological meaning. Age becomes important when its social meaning is made salient. Three examples suggest themselves from our findings. First, people with older age identities have lower morale, although age itself is not related to morale. Second, people who feel that they do not have enough interpersonal contacts and support have lower morale; these feelings may symbolize the implied marginality of old age. Third, age-concentrated informal networks that lack the subcultural elements found in age-segregated housing appear to undermine morale, perhaps again contributing to perceptions of age-related marginality and status loss. Thus "being" old does not matter, but "feeling" old does.

The Diversity of Aging

The relative unimportance of chronological age is also a reflection of the diversity within the older population. This diversity is seen throughout our findings. Patterns and consequences of the environmental contexts we have discussed vary by sex, socioeconomic status, residential location, and many other factors. In particular, two sources of variation have received particular attention. Different residential situations represent complex mixes of advantages and disadvantages; city residence, for example, combines "urban distress" with service convenience. The environmental-docility hypothesis has also proven very useful in shedding light on the diversity of aging. Our composite measures of "vulnerability" and "competence," for example, have yielded patterns of interaction between personal and contextual factors.

The diversity of aging and the aged must be kept in mind for planning and policy. There is no "typical" older person. Older people have diverse environmental needs, preferences, and responses. We have most clearly indicated this in our analysis of the consequences of neighborhood age concentration. The implications of age concentration are not general or straightforward; rather, some forms of age concentration are beneficial for some subgroups of the older population.

A Transactional View of Aging

As we noted at the beginning of this chapter, older persons are not simply shaped or pushed around by environmental factors. A transactional view recognizes that negotiations take place between individuals and their environments. The myriad choices and accommodations arising from such negotiations are reflected in the complexity and diversity of contextual effects. One reason that age per se has little importance is that older persons seek what they want from the environment; they create informal networks to meet their needs, they avoid age peers if doing so protects them from feelings of deprivation, and so on.

Age-related processes may reduce behavioral options, limiting flexibility in the transactions between individuals and the environment. We have referred throughout the book to environmental docility. Persons with reduced competence are less able to act upon and create their environment, hence the greater influence of environmental factors. Choices and transactions with the environment are not necessarily behavioral, however; they are also perceptual and subjective. High levels of neighborhood satisfaction in the face of limited residential options illustrate the subjective transactions between individuals and the environment. We have seen that the most influential aspects of neighborhoods, informal networks, and age-related orientations are subjective. The environment for aging is a "symbolically constructed phenomenon" (Karp and Yoels, 1982). Similarly, Golant (1984) has noted that "the reality of the environment is in large part the reality of the 'knower'" (p. 105).

In this sense, individuals create their own environments for aging, perceptually if not actively. This statement reminds us of Rowles's (1978) distinction between "action" and "fantasy" as modalities of spatial experience. The vicarious or subjective world is likely to have heightened salience for the elderly to the extent that they experience reduced environmental mobility and competence. One writer, reflecting on his own aging, has noted, "More and more the older person is driven back into himself; more and more he is occupied with what goes on in his mind" (Cowley, 1982:55). This is not disengagement but rather a different form or modality of engagement with the world.

We must avoid a "machine-based" model of the older social actor that deals only with "inputs" and "outputs." Subjective meaning and definition of situation are crucial to an understanding of the behaviors and feelings of older persons (Marshall, 1978; Karp and Yoels, 1982).

We do not deny the importance of the physical and social context in which the older person is embedded. Golant (1984) has noted that views of the "purposively behaving individual" must be combined with an understanding of contextual boundaries and constraints. Context matters. Although individuals play an active role in "creating" their own experiences, this does not necessarily occur under conditions of their own choosing. Neighborhood satisfaction offers an example of efforts to adapt within the constraints represented by limited options and environmental docility. Elder (1981) recognizes, for example, that "individuals are both products and producers of their history" (p. 78). We need to understand both processes, attending to lives as they are lived and experienced, in order to understand the complexities of the aging experience.

Appendix A Interview

1. INTERVIEWER: FROM YOUR PERSONAL OBSERVATION,
   INDICATE THE TYPE OF DWELLING RESPONDENT LIVES
   IN. IF YOU ARE NOT SURE OF THE PROPER RESIDENCE,
   CLARIFY WITH RESPONDENT.
   1 APARTMENT BUILDING/CO-OP APARTMENT (5 UNITS
       OR MORE)
   2 MULTIPLE FAMILY DWELLING (2-4 UNITS)
       (garden apts., condominiums, double story
       rows, or homes in which more than one family
       lives)
   3 ROW HOMES or DOUBLE HOMES
       (with separate entrances)
   4 SINGLE FAMILY HOME
       (detached homes only)
   5 MOBILE HOME
   6 OTHER (Specify):_____
   IF APARTMENT BUILDING, ASK Qs. 2 and 3.

2. About how many apartment units are
   in this building?
   (RECORD NUMBER)

3. Is this housing especially for older people?
   2 YES
   1 NO

4. (Now) (First of all) I'd like to ask you some
    questions about your family. Are you now
    married, divorced, separated, widowed, or have
    you never been married?
    1 MARRIED
    2 DIVORCED
    3 SEPARATED
    4 WIDOWED
    5 NEVER MARRIED
    IF CURRENTLY MARRIED, ASK Qs. 5a
    THROUGH 5c.
    IF CURRENTLY DIVORCED, SEPARATED,
    OR WIDOWED, ASK Qs. 6a and 6b.

5a. How many years have you been married? If you
    have been married more than once please answer in
    terms of your current marriage only.
    (PROBE FOR ACTUAL NUMBER OF YEARS.)

5b. Is your husband/wife currently working full-time,
    part-time, retired, keeping house, or just what?
    1 WORKING FULL-TIME
    2 WORKING PART-TIME
    3 HAS JOB BUT NOT WORKING DUE TO TEMPORARY
         ILLNESS, VACATION, STRIKE, ETC.
    4 UNEMPLOYED, LAID OFF, LOOKING FOR WORK
    5 RETIRED
    6 KEEPING HOUSE
    7 IN SCHOOL
    ASK Q. 5c ONLY OF FEMALE RESPONDENTS. IF MALE,
    SKIP TO Q. 7.

5c. What kind of work has/did your husband done/do
    most of his working life? That is, what is/was
    the job called?
    What kind of business is that? What do/did they
    make or do?

6a. For how many years have you been (divorced),
    (separated), (widowed)?
    (PROBE FOR ACTUAL NUMBER OF YEARS.)
    ASK Q. 6b ONLY OF FEMALE RESPONDENTS. IF MALE,
    SKIP TO Q. 7.

6b.   What kind of work did your husband do during most
      of your married life? That is, what was the job
      called?
      What kind of business was that? What did they
      make or do?

 7.   Are you currently working full-time, part-time,
      retired, keeping house, or just what?
      1   WORKING FULL-TIME
      2   WORKING PART-TIME
      3   HAS JOB, BUT NOT WORKING DUE TO TEMPORARY
              ILLNESS, STRIKE, VACATION, ETC.
      4   UNEMPLOYED, LAID OFF, LOOKING FOR WORK
      5   RETIRED
      6   KEEPING HOUSE
      7   IN SCHOOL
      IF "6" OR "7", ASK Q. 8a.

8a.   Have you ever worked full-time for as long as one
      year?
      2   YES
      1   NO
      IF "YES," ASK:

8b.   How many years did you work full-time?
      (PROBE FOR ACTUAL NUMBER OF YEARS.)

 9.   What kind of work have you done most of your
      working life? That is, what is/was the job
      called?
      What kind of business is that? What did/do they
      make or do?
      IF EVER MARRIED (CATEGORIES 1, 2, 3, OR 4 ON Q.
      4), ASK Q. 10, OTHERWISE, SKIP TO Q. 17.

10.   Do you have any living children?
      2   YES
      1   NO
      IF "NO," SKIP TO Q. 17.

11.   How many living children do you have? (RECORD
      NUMBER)

12. How many of your children live:
    (RECORD NUMBER)
    (a) in the same house or building as you
    (b) within walking distance (but not in the same house or building)
    (c) in the same city, but not within walking distance
    (d) within the Albany-Schenectady-Troy area
    (e) outside the Albany-Schenectady-Troy area

13. How often do you usually spend time with your child(ren): that is, you go to see them or they come to see you, or you go out to do things together? (READ CATEGORIES)
    6 once a day or more
    5 2-6 days a week
    4 once a week
    3 at least once a month
    2 several times a year
    1 once a year or less

14. How often do you usually talk to your children on the telephone?
    (READ CATEGORIES)
    6 once a day or more
    5 2-6 days a week
    4 once a week
    3 at least once a month
    2 several times a year
    1 once a year or less
    IF RESPONDENT HAS CONTACT ONCE A MONTH OR LESS OFTEN TO BOTH Q. 13 AND Q. 14, ASK Q. 15. OTHERWISE, SKIP TO Q. 16.

15. How often do you write to each other? This would include letters as well as notes and cards.
    (READ CATEGORIES)
    4 at least once a week
    3 at least once a month
    2 several times a year
    1 once a year or less

16.   Do you see your children about as often as you
      would like to, or would you like to see them more
      often or less often?
      3   SEE AS OFTEN AS WOULD LIKE TO
      1   WOULD LIKE TO SEE THEM MORE OFTEN
      2   WOULD LIKE TO SEE THEM LESS OFTEN
      4   SEE SOME OFTEN ENOUGH BUT OTHERS NOT ENOUGH
      5   SEE SOME OFTEN ENOUGH BUT OTHERS TOO MUCH
      6   SEE SOME NOT ENOUGH BUT OTHERS TOO MUCH

17.   Do you have any relatives, other than children,
      living in the Albany-Schenectady-Troy area?
      2   YES
      1   NO
      IF "YES," ASK Qs. 18a and 18b.

18a. How many? (RECORD NUMBER)

18b. How many do you see or hear from regularly?
      (RECORD NUMBER)

19a. NOT including yourself, how many people live in
      your household with you? (RECORD NUMBER)
      IF SOMEONE LIVES WITH R, ASK 19b.

19b. What (is their) (are their) relationship(s) to
      you? (RECORD NUMBER)
      1   SPOUSE (OR PARTNER)
      2   SIBLING (BROTHER OR SISTER)
      3   PARENT
      4   CHILD
      5   OTHER RELATIVE
      6   NON-FAMILY

20.   How long have you lived at this address?
      1   LESS THAN ONE YEAR
      2   1 YEAR OR MORE BUT LESS THAN 2 YEARS
      3   2 YEARS OR MORE BUT LESS THAN 5 YEARS
      4   5 YEARS OR MORE BUT LESS THAN 10 YEARS
      5   10 YEARS OR MORE BUT LESS THAN 20 YEARS
      6   20 YEARS OR MORE
      IF 10 YEARS OR MORE AT SAME ADDRESS, SKIP TO
      Q. 22.

21a. How long have you lived <u>in this neighborhood?</u>
1 LESS THAN ONE YEAR
2 1 YEAR OR MORE BUT LESS THAN 2 YEARS
3 2 YEARS OR MORE BUT LESS THAN 5 YEARS
4 5 YEARS OR MORE BUT LESS THAN 10 YEARS
5 10 YEARS OR MORE BUT LESS THAN 20 YEARS
6 20 YEARS OR MORE
IF 20 YEARS OR MORE IN SAME NEIGHBORHOOD SKIP TO
Q. 22.

21b. How long have you lived in the
Albany-Schenectady-Troy area?
1 LESS THAN ONE YEAR
2 1 YEAR OR MORE BUT LESS THAN 2 YEARS
3 2 YEARS OR MORE BUT LESS THAN 5 YEARS
4 5 YEARS OR MORE BUT LESS THAN 10 YEARS
5 10 YEARS OR MORE BUT LESS THAN 20 YEARS
6 20 YEARS OR MORE

21c. What kind of dwelling did you live in before this
one?
1 APARTMENT BUILDING/CO-OP APARTMENT (5 UNITS OR
     MORE)
2 MULTIPLE FAMILY DWELLING (2-4 UNITS)
     (garden apts., condominiums, double story
     rows, or homes in which more than one family
     lives)
3 ROW HOMES OR DOUBLE HOMES
     (with separate entrances)
4 SINGLE FAMILY HOME
     (detached homes only)
5 MOBILE HOME
6 OTHER (Specify)

22. In which of these types of places would you say
you have spent most of your adult life?
4 WITHIN A MODERATE TO LARGE-SIZED CITY (SUCH AS
     ALBANY, BUFFALO, OR NEW YORK CITY)
3 IN A SUBURB (SUCH AS GUILDERLAND OR COLONIE)
2 IN A SMALL CITY, TOWN, OR VILLAGE (SUCH AS
     SARATOGA SPRINGS OR GLENS FALLS)
1 IN A RURAL AREA

23. We are interested in your judgement of just how large your neighborhood is. Could you try to imagine where the center of your neighborhood is? If you were at the center, how many <u>blocks</u> would you have to walk in any one direction before the people there would not be considered your neighbors? (RECORD NUMBER OF BLOCKS)

24. How many minutes would it take you to walk this far? (RECORD NUMBER OF MINUTES)

25. Of all the people who live in your neighborhood, what proportion (percentage) would you say are about 60 years or older? (PROBE: Just give me your best estimate.) (RECORD PERCENTAGE)

26. How would you rate this (house) (building) as a place to live--would you say it is excellent, good, fair, or poor?
    4 EXCELLENT
    3 GOOD
    2 FAIR
    1 POOR

27. How satisfied are you with the state of repairs or maintenance of the interior and exterior of your (house) (apartment) -- very satisfied, fairly satisfied, or not very satisfied?
    3 VERY SATISFIED
    2 FAIRLY SATISFIED
    1 NOT VERY SATISFIED

28. How would you rate the space you have in this (house) (apartment)--would you say it is much too large, a little too large, just about right for what you need, a little too small, or much too small?
    5 MUCH TOO LARGE
    4 A LITTLE TOO LARGE
    3 JUST ABOUT RIGHT
    2 A LITTLE TOO SMALL
    1 MUCH TOO SMALL

29. In general, how would you rate this neighborhood
    as a place to live--would you say it is
    excellent, good, fair or poor?
    4 EXCELLENT
    3 GOOD
    2 FAIR
    1 POOR

30. In general, how convenient is your neighborhood
    for getting to shopping, medical care, and other
    things you need? Is it very convenient, fairly
    convenient, or not very convenient?
    3 VERY CONVENIENT
    2 FAIRLY CONVENIENT
    1 NOT VERY CONVENIENT

31. How convenient is your neighborhood for getting
    out to visit friends or to do things together
    with them? Is it very convenient, fairly
    convenient, or not very convenient?
    3 VERY CONVENIENT
    2 FAIRLY CONVENIENT
    1 NOT VERY CONVENIENT

32. What about the condition of the other houses in
    this neighborhood--would you say they are well
    kept up, fairly well kept up, not very well kept
    up, or not kept up at all?
    4 WELL KEPT UP
    3 FAIRLY WELL KEPT UP
    2 NOT VERY WELL KEPT UP
    1 NOT KEPT UP AT ALL

33. If for some reason you had to move away from this
    neighborhood, how would you feel about
    leaving--would you be very sorry to leave, sorry,
    pleased, or very pleased?
    4 VERY SORRY
    3 SORRY
    2 PLEASED
    1 VERY PLEASED

34. How happy are you about the <u>kind</u> of people who
    live in your neighborhood--are you very happy,
    somewhat happy, somewhat unhappy, or not happy at
    all?
    4   VERY HAPPY
    3   SOMEWHAT HAPPY
    2   SOMEWHAT UNHAPPY
    1   NOT HAPPY AT ALL

35. What do you think are the <u>best</u> things about
    living in this neighborhood?   (PROBE: Is there
    anything else?)

36. What do you think are the <u>worst</u> things about
    living in this neighborhood?   (PROBE: Is there
    anything else?)

37a. Has the neighborhood been changing in the past
     few years?
     2   YES
     1   NO
     IF "YES," ASK Q. 37b.

37b. In what ways?   (PROBE FOR A COMPLETE RESPONSE.)

38. How safe do you feel being out alone in your
    neighborhood?   Do you feel safe <u>all</u> of the time,
    safe <u>most</u> of the time, <u>unsafe</u> <u>most</u> of the time,
    or unsafe <u>all</u> of the time?
    4   SAFE ALL OF THE TIME
    3   SAFE MOST OF THE TIME
    2   UNSAFE MOST OF THE TIME
    1   UNSAFE ALL OF THE TIME
    5   SAFE DURING THE DAY BUT NOT SAFE AT NIGHT
        (VOLUNTEERED RESPONSE)

39. Are you thinking seriously of moving from this
    neighborhood in the next year or so?
    2   YES
    1   NO

40. Suppose that you had to move from the place that
    you are living at now.   Do you think it would be

very easy, fairly easy, fairly difficult, or very
difficult to find a new place?
1 VERY EASY
2 FAIRLY EASY
3 FAIRLY DIFFICULT
4 VERY DIFFICULT

41. Now, please tell me if you ever go to any of the
following places.
ASK Q. 41a THROUGH 41e TO ESTABLISH ALL PLACES R
GOES. THEN ASK Qs 42 THROUGH 46 FOR ALL PLACES
MENTIONED.)
a. Grocery or food store
b. Church or synagogue
c. Drug store or pharmacy
d. Doctor or clinic
e. Bank

42. About how often do you go to _____?
7 ONCE A DAY OR MORE
6 2-6 TIMES A WEEK
5 ONCE A WEEK
4 2-3 TIMES A MONTH
3 ONCE A MONTH
2 SEVERAL TIMES A YEAR
1 ONCE A YEAR OR LESS
(IF R GOES TO MORE THAN ONE GROCERY, CHURCH, ETC.
ASK Qs. 43-46 FOR THE ONE THEY GO TO MOST OFTEN.)

43. About how many blocks is the _____
from your home?
1 1-3 BLOCKS
2 4-6 BLOCKS
3 7-10 BLOCKS
4 11-20 BLOCKS
5 MORE THAN 20 BLOCKS
(IF ANSWER IS IN MILES, SPECIFY EXACT NUMBER)

44. About how long does it take you to get
    to _____?
    1 5 MINUTES OR LESS
    2 6-15 MINUTES
    3 16-30 MINUTES
    4 31-60 MINUTES
    5 MORE THAN ONE HOUR

45. How do you usually get
    to _____?
    1 WALK
    2 BUS
    3 DRIVE MYSELF IN A CAR
    4 DRIVEN BY SOMEONE ELSE (FRIEND, RELATIVE,
         NEIGHBOR, ETC.)
    5 TAXICAB
    6 OTHER (Specify)

46. Do you consider this _____ to be
    in your neighborhood?
    2 YES
    1 NO

47. About how many blocks is the nearest bus stop
    from your home?
    1 LESS THAN 1 BLOCK
    2 1-3 BLOCKS
    3 4-6 BLOCKS
    4 7-10 BLOCKS
    5 11-20 BLOCKS
    6 MORE THAN 20 BLOCKS

48. Do you consider this bus stop to be in your
    neighborhood?
    2 YES
    1 NO

49. How often do you use the bus?
    7 ONCE A DAY OR MORE
    6 2-6 TIMES A WEEK
    5 ONCE A WEEK

4   2-3 TIMES A MONTH
3   ONCE A MONTH
2   SEVERAL TIMES A YEAR
1   ONCE A YEAR OR LESS
0   NEVER

50. From time to time all of us are faced with
     situations in which we might need help. For each
     of the situations I describe, please tell me who,
     if anyone, you would be <u>most</u> <u>likely</u> to turn to if
     you needed help.
     (ASK Qs 50 THROUGH 54 FOR SITUATION a, THEN GO
     BACK AND ASK Qs 50 THROUGH 54 FOR b; THEN c AND d
     IN TURN.)
     a.   If you need someone to look in on you and
          see how you are doing.
     b.   If you need a ride to go shopping or to see
          the doctor.
     c.   If you need someone to get you something
          from the store.
     d.   If you need someone to look after the
          house/apartment while you are
          away.
          1   NO ONE
          2   SPOUSE
          3   SON/DAUGHTER
          4   OTHER RELATIVE
          5   FRIEND/NEIGHBOR
          6   CHURCH
          7   SOCIAL AGENCY
          8   OTHER (Specify)
     IF "SPOUSE," ASK Q. 51.

51. Suppose your husband/wife were not available.
     Who else, if anyone, would you be <u>most</u> <u>likely</u> to
     turn to in this situation?
     (SAME CATEGORIES AS ABOVE)
     FOR THE "NON-SPOUSE" HELPER IN EACH SITUATION,
     ASK Q. 52.

52. Does this person live (is this church/agency located) in your neighborhood?
    2 YES
    1 NO
    IF HELPER IS A PERSON RATHER THAN AN AGENCY, ASK Qs 53 and 54.

53. About how old is this person?   (RECORD ACTUAL AGE)

54. Is this person a man or woman?
    1 MAN
    2 WOMAN

55. On the whole, do you feel that you have enough people or places to turn to for help in situations like these, or would you be happier if you had more people or places to turn to?
    1 HAVE ENOUGH
    0 WOULD BE HAPPIER IF HAD MORE

56. Now I am going to read you a list of programs and services which some people feel would be helpful to older people. As far as you know, are any of these now available to older persons in your county?
    a. Someone who telephones or visits older persons
    b. Facilities for group meals or delivery of
       meals to the home for older persons
    c. Legal services and advice for older persons
    d. Visiting nurses or home health aides for
       older persons
    e. Special transportation programs, including
       buses or escorts for older persons
       1 PROGRAM/SERVICE AVAILABLE
       0 NOT AVAILABLE
    FOR EACH PROGRAM/SERVICE INDICATED AS AVAILABLE, ASK Q. 57.

57. Have you ever used (PROGRAM/SERVICE)?
    2 YES
    1 NO

58. In general, who or what has been your most
    important source of information about these
    programs and services? (Whether or not you have
    actually used them.)
    (PROBE FOR ONE RESPONSE.)
    1 COUNTY OFFICE FOR THE AGING, OTHER AGENCY FOR
         OLDER PEOPLE
    2 SOCIAL SERVICE AGENCY (OTHER THAN THE ABOVE)
    3 PROFESSIONAL REFERRAL (E.G., DOCTOR, LAWYER,
         ETC.)
    4 RELATIVE
    5 FRIEND/NEIGHBOR
    6 CLERGY (PRIEST, MINISTER, RABBI, ETC.)
    7 SENIOR CITIZENS CLUB
    8 OTHER (Specify)
    9 MEDIA SOURCES (E.G., TV, NEWSPAPER, RADIO)
    IF 1-8, ASK Q. 59.

59. Does this person live (is this agency located) in
    your neighborhood?
    2 YES
    1 NO
    IF SOURCE IS A FRIEND OR NEIGHBOR, ASK Q. 59a AND
    59b.

59a. About how old is this person? (RECORD ACTUAL AGE)

59b. Is this person a man or a woman?
    1 MAN
    2 WOMAN

60. Now I'd like to ask you about people you may feel
    very close to. Is there anyone -- friends,
    neighbors, or relatives -- that you feel very
    close to -- someone you share confidences and
    feelings with?
    2 YES
    1 NO
    IF "YES," ASK Q. 61.

61. Do any of these people with whom you feel very close reside <u>outside of your home</u>?
    2 YES
    1 NO
    IF "YES," ASK Qs 62 THROUGH 77.

62. How many such people are there? (RECORD ACTUAL NUMBER)

63. Of these people, please tell me the <u>first name</u> of the person you feel <u>closest to</u>. Remember, we are speaking about people who reside <u>outside of your home</u>. And who do you feel <u>next</u> closest to? And <u>next</u> closest to? (RECORD A MAXIMUM OF THREE NAMES)
    FIRST PERSON_____
    SECOND PERSON_____
    THIRD PERSON_____
    ASK Qs 64 THROUGH 76 FOR EACH OF THE PERSONS MENTIONED ABOVE.

64. What relationship is _____(PERSON)_____ to you?
    1 BROTHER/SISTER
    2 SON/DAUGHTER
    3 OTHER RELATIVE (Specify)
    4 NEIGHBOR FRIEND
    5 NON-NEIGHBOR FRIEND
    6 CLERGY
    7 PHYSICIAN
    8 OTHER (Specify)

65. About how old is _____(PERSON)_____ ?
    (RECORD ACTUAL AGE)

66. Is this person a man or a woman?
    1 MAN
    2 WOMAN

67. Where does _____(PERSON)_____ live?
    6   SAME BUILDING
    5   SAME NEIGHBORHOOD
    4   SAME CITY/TOWN
    3   ALBANY-SCHENECTADY-TROY METROPOLITAN AREA
    2   BEYOND THE METROPOLITAN AREA
    1   OUTSIDE THE STATE

68. How often do you get together with
    (PERSON)_____?
    6   ONCE A DAY OR MORE
    5   2-6 DAYS A WEEK
    4   ONCE A WEEK
    3   AT LEAST ONCE A MONTH
    2   SEVERAL TIMES A YEAR
    1   ONCE A YEAR OR LESS

69. How often do you talk on the phone with him/her?
    6   ONCE A DAY OR MORE
    5   2-6 DAYS A WEEK
    4   ONCE A WEEK
    3   AT LEAST ONCE A MONTH
    2   SEVERAL TIMES A YEAR
    1   ONCE A YEAR OR LESS
    IF RESPONDENT HAS CONTACT ONCE A MONTH OR LESS
    OFTEN ON BOTH Q. 68 AND Q. 69, ASK Q. 70.

70. How often do you write to each other? This would
    include letters as well as notes and cards.
    4   AT LEAST ONCE A WEEK
    3   AT LEAST ONCE A MONTH
    2   SEVERAL TIMES A YEAR
    1   ONCE A YEAR OR LESS

71. What is _____(PERSON'S)_____ religion?
    1   PROTESTANT
    2   CATHOLIC
    3   JEWISH
    4   OTHER
    5   NO RELIGION

72. Do you happen to know from which country or part
    of the world
    _____(PERSON'S)_____ ancestors come from?
    2 YES
    1 NO
    IF "YES," SHOW CARD AND ASK Q. 73.

73. Looking at this card, from which countries or
    part of the world did _____(PERSON'S)_____
    ancestors come? (RECORD COUNTRY CODE FROM CARD)
    IF "MORE THAN ONE COUNTRY," ASK Q. 74.

74. With which one of these countries would (PERSON)
    be associated most closely? (RECORD COUNTRY CODE
    FROM CARD)

75. How far did (PERSON) go in school?
    1 8 YEARS OR LESS
    2 SOME HIGH SCHOOL
    3 HIGH SCHOOL COMPLETE
    4 POST HIGH SCHOOL BUSINESS OR TRADE SCHOOL
    5 1-3 YEARS OF COLLEGE
    6 4 YEARS OF COLLEGE
    7 POSTGRADUATE SCHOOL

76. About how many years have you known (PERSON)?
    (RECORD NUMBER OF YEARS)

77. On the whole, when you would like to share
    confidences and feelings with another person, do
    you think you have enough opportunities to do so,
    or would you like to have more opportunities?
    2 HAVE ENOUGH OPPORTUNITIES
    1 WOULD LIKE MORE OPPORTUNITIES

78. Now let's talk about your neighbors.
    How many neighbors do you know well enough to
    visit with, either in their homes or yours?
    (RECORD NUMBER)
    IF "NONE," SKIP TO Q. 87.

79. Of these (NUMBER OF NEIGHBORS MENTIONED IN Q. 78)
    neighbors you know well enough to visit with,
    could you please give me just the first name of
    the neighbor your are <u>friendliest</u> with?   And who
    are you <u>next</u> friendliest with?   And <u>next</u>
    friendliest?
    (RECORD A MAXIMUM OF THREE NAMES.)
    FIRST NEIGHBOR _____
    SECOND NEIGHBOR _____
    THIRD NEIGHBOR _____
    ASK Qs 80 THROUGH 86 FOR EACH NEIGHBOR MENTIONED
       ABOVE.

80. About how old is <u>(NEIGHBOR)</u>?   (RECORD ACTUAL AGE)

81. Is <u>(NEIGHBOR)</u> a man or a woman?
    1 MAN
    2 WOMAN

82. What religion is <u>(NEIGHBOR)</u>?
    1 PROTESTANT
    2 CATHOLIC
    3 JEWISH
    4 OTHER RELIGION
    5 NO RELIGION

83. How far did <u>(NEIGHBOR)</u> go in school?
    1 8 YEARS OR LESS
    2 SOME HIGH SCHOOL
    3 HIGH SCHOOL COMPLETE
    4 POST HIGH SCHOOL BUSINESS OR TRADE SCHOOL
    5 1-3 YEARS OF COLLEGE
    6 4 YEARS OF COLLEGE
    7 POSTGRADUATE SCHOOL

84. Do you happen to know from which country or part
    of the world <u>(NEIGHBOR'S)</u> ancestors came from?
    2 YES
    1 NO
    IF "YES," SHOW CARD AND ASK Q. 85.

85. Looking at this card, from which countries or
    part of the world did (NEIGHBOR'S) ancestors come
    from? (RECORD COUNTRY CODE FROM CARD)
    IF "MORE THAN ONE COUNTRY," ASK Q. 86.

86. With which one of these countries would
    (NEIGHBOR) be associated most closely? (RECORD
    COUNTRY CODE FROM CARD)

87. How many neighbors do you rely on for help in
    emergencies? (RECORD ACTUAL NUMBER)
    IF "NONE," SKIP TO Q. 89.

88. In general, about how old are these neighbors you
    rely on in emergencies--are all of them about 60
    years old or older, most of them about 60 or
    older, most of them younger than 60, or all of
    them younger than 60?
    5 ALL ABOUT 60 OR OLDER
    4 MOST 60 OR OLDER
    3 HALF OLDER; HALF YOUNGER (VOLUNTEERED RESPONSE)
    2 MOST YOUNGER THAN 60
    1 ALL YOUNGER THAN 60

89. About how frequently do you spend some time with
    any of your neighbors? That is, how often do you
    go to see them, or they come to see you, or you
    go out to do things together?
    6 ONCE A DAY OR MORE
    5 2 TO 6 DAYS A WEEK
    4 ONCE A WEEK
    3 AT LEAST ONCE A MONTH
    2 SEVERAL TIMES A YEAR
    1 ONCE A YEAR OR LESS

90. How often do you usually talk to your neighbors
    on the telephone?
    6 ONCE A DAY OR MORE
    5 2 TO 6 DAYS A WEEK
    4 ONCE A WEEK
    3 AT LEAST ONCE A MONTH
    2 SEVERAL TIMES A YEAR
    1 ONCE A YEAR OR LESS

91. In general, do you get together with neighbors
     about as often as you would like, or would you
     like to get together with them more often or less
     often?
     3 GET TOGETHER WITH THEM OFTEN AS WOULD LIKE
     1 WOULD LIKE TO GET TOGETHER WITH THEM MORE OFTEN
     2 WOULD LIKE TO GET TOGETHER WITH THEM LESS OFTEN

92. Have you found it difficult to make close friends
     in this neighborhood?
     2 YES
     1 NO
     IF "NO," SKIP TO Q. 94.

93. Why would you say this is so? (PROBE: Why do
     you think it has been difficult? PROBE FOR
     DETAILS.)

94. How much do you have in common with your
     neighbors -- a lot, some, or not much at all?
     3 A LOT
     2 SOME
     1 NOT MUCH AT ALL

95. Which of the following things have you ever done
     for your neighbors?

		RESPONDENT HAS:	
		DONE	NOT DONE
a.	Look in on them to see how they are doing	2	1
b.	Give them rides to the doctor, shopping, etc.	2	1
c.	Get things for them at the store	2	1
d.	Talk to them about their personal concerns and problems	2	1
e.	Look after the house or apartment when they are away	2	1
f.	Lend them things (other than money)	2	1

96.   Which of these things have your neighbors ever done <u>for you</u>?

		NEIGHBORS HAVE:	
		DONE	NOT DONE
a.	Look in on you to see how you are doing	2	1
b.	Give you rides to the doctor, shopping, etc.	2	1
c.	Get things for you at the store	2	1
d.	Talk to you about your personal concerns and problems	2	1
e.	Look after the house or apartment when you are away	2	1
f.	Lend you things (other than money)	2	1

97.   Now I would like to ask questions about your friends who do <u>not</u> live in this neighborhood. How many friends do you have who live in the Albany-Schenectady-Troy area, but not in your neighborhood? (RECORD ACTUAL NUMBER) IF "NONE," SKIP TO Q. 99.

98.   Would you say that <u>all</u> of these friends are about 60 years old or older, <u>most</u> of them are about 60 or older, <u>most</u> of them are <u>younger</u> than 60, or <u>all</u> of them are <u>younger</u> than 60?
      5   ALL ABOUT 60 OR OLDER
      4   MOST 60 OR OLDER
      3   HALF OLDER; HALF YOUNGER (VOLUNTEERED RESPONSE)
      2   MOST YOUNGER THAN 60
      1   ALL YOUNGER THAN 60

99.   How many <u>new</u> friends have you made during the past year, <u>either</u> in your neighborhood or outside of your neighborhood? (RECORD ACTUAL NUMBER) IF "NONE," SKIP TO Q. 102.

100. Are these new friends <u>all</u> <u>about</u> <u>60</u> years old or older, <u>most</u> <u>about</u> <u>60</u> or older, <u>most</u> <u>younger</u> than 60, or <u>all</u> <u>younger</u> than 60?
    5 ALL ABOUT 60 OR OLDER
    4 MOST 60 OR OLDER
    3 HALF OLDER; HALF YOUNGER (VOLUNTEERED RESPONSE)
    2 MOST YOUNGER THAN 60
    1 ALL YOUNGER THAN 60

101. How many of these new friends are neighbors? (RECORD ACTUAL NUMBER)

102. Do you think of yourself as young, middle-aged, elderly, or old?
    1 YOUNG
    2 MIDDLE-AGED
    3 ELDERLY
    4 OLD

103. Is there anybody among your friends, relatives, or neighbors who is a good example of what a person should be like in his or her old age? IF "NO," SKIP TO Q. 108.

104. What is this person's relationship to you?
    1 PARENT
    2 BROTHER/SISTER
    3 AUNT/UNCLE
    4 SPOUSE
    5 OTHER RELATIVE (Specify)
    6 NEIGHBOR FRIEND
    7 NON-NEIGHBOR FRIEND
    8 OTHER (Specify):

105. About how old is this person?   (RECORD ACTUAL AGE)

106. Is this person a man or a woman?
    1 MAN
    2 WOMAN

107. What do you admire about him or her?   (PROBE: Is there anything else you admire about him/her?)

108. Do you ever go to a Senior Center or any other club or organization for older people?
    2 YES
    1 NO
    IF "NO," SKIP TO Q. 111.

109. How often do you go there?
    6 SEVERAL TIMES A WEEK OR MORE
    5 AT LEAST ONCE A WEEK
    4 SEVERAL TIMES A MONTH
    3 AT LEAST ONCE A MONTH
    2 LESS THAN ONCE A MONTH
    1 LESS THAN ONCE A YEAR

110. About how many blocks from your home is this club or organization? (IF R GOES TO MORE THAN ONE CLUB/ORGANIZATION/ETC., RECORD RESPONSE FOR THE ONE ATTENDED MOST FREQUENTLY.)
    1 ONE-3 BLOCKS
    2 4-6 BLOCKS
    3 7-10 BLOCKS
    4 11-20 BLOCKS
    5 MORE THAN 20 BLOCKS
    6 IF ANSWER IS IN MILES, SPECIFY EXACT NUMBER

111. Have you ever taken any action on behalf of older people -- such as going to meetings, writing letters, demonstrating, and so forth?
    2 YES
    1 NO
    IF" YES," ASK Q. 112.

112. What did you do? (PROBE FOR A COMPLETE RESPONSE.)

113. With regard to the following, would you say you are better off, about the same, or worse off than most other persons your age?

	BETTER	SAME	WORSE
a. Relationships with your family	3	2	1
b. Social contacts other than with your family	3	2	1
c. Your health	3	2	1
d. Your financial situation	3	2	1

114. Would you personally prefer to spend most of your
      time with people your own age, with people
      younger than yourself, or with people of
      different ages?
      3 PEOPLE OWN AGE
      1 YOUNGER PEOPLE
      2 PEOPLE OF DIFFERENT AGES
      4 PEOPLE OLDER THAN I AM (VOLUNTEERED RESPONSE)
      5 AGE DOESN'T MATTER (VOLUNTEERED RESPONSE)

115. Why is that?   (PROBE: Are there any other
      reasons?)

116. If it were up to you, would you prefer to live in
      housing limited to people your own age, or in
      housing with people of different ages?
      2 PEOPLE OWN AGE
      1 PEOPLE OF DIFFERENT AGES

117. Do you see as much of people your own age as you
      would like to, or would you like to see more of
      people you own age; or less of people your own
      age?
      3 SEE AS MUCH AS WOULD LIKE TO
      1 WOULD LIKE TO SEE MORE
      2 WOULD LIKE TO SEE LESS

118. Do you see as much of younger people (that is,
      younger families, people under 40) as you would
      like to, or would you like to see more of younger
      people, or less of younger people?
      3 SEE AS MUCH AS WOULD LIKE TO
      1 WOULD LIKE TO SEE MORE
      2 WOULD LIKE TO SEE LESS

119. As people grow older, they often face changes in
      their lives and feelings. Have you found people
      of your own age at all helpful in offering advice
      and support about changes in your life as you
      have grown older?
      2 YES
      1 NO
      IF "NO," SKIP TO Q. 123.

120. With what changes or concerns have people your
     own age been helpful? (PROBE FOR A COMPLETE
     RESPONSE.)

121. Among those your own age, who would you say has
     helped you the <u>most</u> -- relatives, friends,
     neighbors, or just who? (PROBE FOR <u>ONE</u> RESPONSE.)
     1 RELATIVES
     2 FRIENDS
     3 NEIGHBORS
     4 SPOUSE
     5 OTHER (Specify)

122. Are those who helped you all (same sex as
     respondent), mostly (same sex), mostly (other
     sex) or all (other sex)?
     5 ALL SAME SEX
     4 MOSTLY SAME SEX
     3 HALF SAME SEX; HALF OTHER SEX (VOLUNTEERED
        RESPONSE)
     2 MOSTLY OTHER SEX
     1 ALL OTHER SEX

123. Now we would like to know how you would describe
     <u>most</u> older people--aged 65 and older. For each
     word I read, please tell me if you feel most
     older people are very, somewhat, or hardly at all
     described by that word. The first word is
     (INSERT WORD). Do you feel that older people are
     very, somewhat, or hardly at all (INSERT WORD)?
     (REPEAT FOR EACH WORD UNTIL YOU HAVE COMPLETED
     THE LIST.)

		VERY	SOMEWHAT	HARDLY AT ALL
a.	wise	3	2	1
b.	trustworthy	3	2	1
c.	sick	1	2	3
d.	friendly	3	2	1
e.	flexible	3	2	1
f.	tolerant	3	2	1
g.	selfish	1	2	3
h.	effective	3	2	1
i.	active	3	2	1
j.	sad	1	2	3
k.	dependent	1	2	3

124. Now we would like to know how you would describe
most younger people--those in their 20's. Again,
for each word I read, please tell me if you feel
most younger people are very, somewhat, or hardly
at all described by that word. The first word is
(TRUSTWORTHY). Do you feel that most younger
people are very, somewhat, or hardly at all
(TRUSTWORTHY). (REPEAT FOR EACH WORD LISTED.)

		VERY	SOMEWHAT	HARDLY AT ALL
a.	trustworthy	3	2	1
b.	friendly	3	2	1
c.	selfish	1	2	3
d.	tolerant	3	2	1

125. Now I would like to read some statements that
people sometimes make about life in general. As
I read each statement, please tell me how you
feel about it yourself. That is, do you strongly
agree, agree somewhat, disagree somewhat, or
strongly disagree with each statement.

		STRONGLY AGREE	AGREE SOMEWHAT	DISAGREE SOMEWHAT	STRONGLY DISAGREE
a.	Little things bother me more this year	1	2	3	4
b.	Things keep getting worse as I get older	1	2	3	4
c.	I see enough of my friends and relatives	4	3	2	1
d.	I have little control over the things that happen to me	1	2	3	4
e.	I sometimes worry so much that I can't sleep	1	2	3	4
f.	I have as much pep as I had last year	4	3	2	1

g.	I sometimes feel that life isn't worth living	1	2	3	4
h.	There is really no way that I can solve some of the problems I have	1	2	3	4
i.	I am afraid of a lot of things	1	2	3	4
j.	As you get older, you are less useful	1	2	3	4
k.	Life is hard for me much of the time	1	2	3	4
l.	There is little I can do to change many of the important things in life	1	2	3	4
m.	I get mad more than I used to	1	2	3	4
n.	As I get older, things are better than I thought they would be	4	3	2	1
o.	I have a lot to be sad about	1	2	3	4
p.	I often feel helpless in dealing with the problems of life	1	2	3	4
q.	I take things hard	1	2	3	4
r.	I am as happy now as when I was younger	4	3	2	1
s.	Sometimes I feel that I am being pushed around in life	1	2	3	4
t.	I get upset easily	1	2	3	4

u. What happens to   4   3   2   1
    me in the future
    depends upon me

v. I can do just   4   3   2   1
    about anything
    I set my mind to
    do

126. How often do you feel lonely? Would you say a
      great deal, sometimes, not much, or not at all?
      1 A GREAT DEAL
      2 SOMETIMES
      3 NOT MUCH
      4 NOT AT ALL

127. How satisfied are you with your life today? Are
      you very satisfied, satisfied, dissatisfied, or
      very dissatisfied?
      4 VERY SATISFIED
      3 SATISFIED
      2 DISSATISFIED
      1 VERY DISSATISFIED

128. You have been very cooperative. I would like to
      ask you just a few more questions to finish the
      interview. We need this information for
      statistical purposes.
      How old were you on your last birthday? (RECORD
      ACTUAL AGE)

129. What is your religious preference--is it
      Protestant, Catholic, Jewish, some other
      religion, or no religion?
      1 PROTESTANT
      2 CATHOLIC
      3 JEWISH
      4 SOME OTHER RELIGION
      5 NO RELIGION

130.   How important is religion in your life? Is it
       very important, somewhat important, or hardly
       important at all?
       3 VERY IMPORTANT
       2 SOMEWHAT IMPORTANT
       1 HARDLY IMPORTANT AT ALL

131.   From what countries or part of the world did your
       ancestors come? (RECORD COUNTRY CODE FROM CARD)
       IF "MORE THAN ONE COUNTRY," ASK Q. 132.

132.   Which one of these countries do you feel closer
       to? (RECORD COUNTRY CODE FROM CARD)

133.   How would you say your health is at the present
       time--would you say excellent, good, fair, poor,
       or very poor?
       5 EXCELLENT
       4 GOOD
       3 FAIR
       2 POOR
       1 VERY POOR

134.   Now we would like to ask you about some of the
       activities of daily living, things that we all
       need to do as part of our daily lives. As I read
       each item, will you please tell me if you can do
       it without difficulty by yourself, if you have
       some difficulty but can still manage by yourself,
       or if you cannot do it without the help of
       another person.

		WITHOUT DIFFI- CULTY	SOME DIFFI- CULTY	NEED HELP
a.	Going outdoors	3	2	1
b.	Walking up and down stairs	3	2	1
c.	Getting around the house/apartment/ room	3	2	1
d.	Doing the cleaning and other household chores	3	2	1

135.   We would also like to know something about how
       you manage financially. Please tell me which <u>one</u>
       of these statements best describes the position
       you (and your husband/wife) find yourself
       (yourselves) in.
       1   I/we really can't make ends meet
       2   I/we just about manage to get by
       3   I/we have enough to get along, and even a
             little extra
       4   Money is not a problem, I/we can buy pretty
             much anything I/we want

136.   Do you <u>own</u> this apartment/house, <u>rent it</u>, <u>rent a</u>
       <u>room</u>, or do you <u>live with family or friends</u>?
       1   OWN THIS APARTMENT/HOUSE
       2   RENT THIS APARTMENT/HOUSE
       3   RENT A ROOM
       4   LIVE WITH FAMILY/FRIENDS
       5   OTHER (Specify)

137.   For statistical purposes, we need to know your
       total family income for 1979 <u>before taxes</u>. This
       should include all sources of income that you
       (and your spouse) received during 1979. Look at
       this card and tell me the letter of the income
       group that includes you.
       01   A   LESS THAN $1,000
       02   B $1,000–$1,999
       03   C $2,000 – $2,999
       04   D $3,000 – $3,999
       05   E $4,000 – $4,999
       06   F $5,000 – $6,999
       07   G $7,000 – $9,999
       08   H $10,000 – $14,999
       09   I $15,000 – $24,999
       10   J $25,000 OR MORE

138.   Looking at the card again, please try to tell me
       approximately how much your major <u>possessions</u>,
       such as property, stocks, bonds, and savings are
       worth altogether. We don't need to know the

exact amount; just give me the letter next to the
appropriate amount on the card that indicates
your best estimate.

01   A   LESS THAN $1,000
02   B $1,000 - $1,999
03   C $2,000 - $2,999
04   D $3,000 - $3,999
05   E $4,000 - $4,999
06   F $5,000 - $6,999
07   G $7,000 - $9,999
08   H $10,000 - $14,999
09   I $15,000 - $24,999
10   J $25,000 OR MORE

139.   How far did you go in school?
1   0-4 YEARS
2   5-8 YEARS
3   SOME HIGH SCHOOL
4   HIGH SCHOOL COMPLETE
5   POST HIGH SCHOOL BUSINESS OR TRADE SCHOOL
6   1-3 YEARS OF COLLEGE
7   4 YEARS OF COLLEGE
8   POSTGRADUATE SCHOOL

INTERVIEWER: RECORD THE FOLLOWING FROM YOUR PERSONAL
OBSERVATION.

140.   SEX: 1   MALE
0   FEMALE

141.   RACE: 1   WHITE
2   BLACK
3   OTHER (Specify)

142.   NEIGHBORHOOD:
1   ENTIRELY RESIDENTIAL
2   MORE THAN HALF RESIDENTIAL
3   LESS THAN HALF RESIDENTIAL

143. TYPE OF HOUSING ON BLOCK RESPONDENT LIVES ON:
    1 MOSTLY SINGLE FAMILY HOUSES
    2 MOSTLY APARTMENT HOUSES OR GARDEN APARTMENTS
       (1 OR 2 STORIES)
    3 MOSTLY HIGH-RISE APARTMENTS (4 STORIES OR MORE)
    4 MIXED

144. PLEASE NOTE THE GENERAL PHYSICAL CONDITION OF THE
    RESPONDENT:

		YES	NO	CAN'T TELL
a.	HANDS SHAKE	1	0	8
b.	IMMOBILIZED--CANNOT WALK WITHOUT HELP	1	0	8
c.	DIFFICULTY HEARING	1	0	8
d.	DIFFICULTY SEEING	1	0	8
e.	PARALYSIS	1	0	8
f.	CANE	1	0	8
g.	WALKER	1	0	8
h.	WHEELCHAIR	1	0	8
i.	CONFINED TO BED	1	0	8

Appendix B Tract Data

Characteristics of tract population and housing were included in the data for individual respondents. Population age is from 1980 tract statistics, and other characteristics are from 1970 tract statistics.

Population characteristics
 1. Percentage black
 2. Sex ratio (Males/Females)
 3. Percentage aged 60 +
 4. Percentage of families with both husband and wife
 5. Percentage married, widowed, and single
 6. Percentage native parentage
 7. Median years of schooling
 8. Percentage living in same house in 1965 and 1970
 9. Percentage of workers who take a bus to work
10. Percentage males aged 16 + and females aged 16 + in labor force
11. Median family income
12. Percentage of families with income below poverty level

Housing characteristics
1. Percentage of housing units vacant year round
2. Percentage of housing units with one person per room or less
3. Median value owner-occupied housing units
4. Median contract rent
5. Median gross rent
6. Percentage of year-round housing units built before 1940

References

Adams, B. 1967. "Interaction theory and the social network." *Sociometry* 30:575–597.

Adams, R. 1985. "People would talk: Normative barriers to cross-sex friendship for elderly women." *Gerontologist* 25:605–611.

Adams, R. 1986. "Emotional closeness and physical distances between friends. Implications for elderly women living in age segregated and age integrated settings." *International Journal of Aging and Human Development* 22 (1): 55–76.

Anderson, W., and Anderson, N. 1978. "The politics of age exclusion: The Adults Only Movement in Arizona." *Gerontologist* 18:6–12.

Antonucci, T. 1985. "Personal characteristics, social support, and social behavior." In R. Binstock and E. Shanas (eds.), *Handbook of Aging and the Social Sciences*, 2d ed. New York: Van Nostrand Reinhold.

Arling, G. 1976. "The elderly widow and her family, neighbors, and friends." *Journal of Marriage and the Family* 38:757–768.

Babchuk, N. 1978. "Aging and primary relations." *International Journal of Aging and Human Development* 9:137–51.

Barker, R. 1968. *Ecological Psychology.* Stanford, Calif.: Stanford University Press.

Baum, S., and Boxley, R. 1983. "Age identification in the elderly." *Gerontologist* 23:532–537.

Bengtson, V., and DeTerre, E. 1980. "Aging and family relations." *Marriage and Family Review* 3 (1–2): 51–76.

Bennett, R., and Eckman, J. 1973. "Attitudes toward aging: A critical examination of recent literature and implications for future research." In C. Eisdorfer and M. P. Lawton (eds.), *The Psychology of Adult Development and Aging*. Washington, D.C.: American Psychological Association.

Berghorn, F., Schafer, D., Steere, G., and Wiseman, R. 1978. *The Urban Elderly: A Study of Life Satisfaction*. Montclair, N. J.: Allanheld, Osmun.

Bild, B., and Havighurst, R. 1976. "Senior citizens in great cities: The case of Chicago." *Gerontologist* 16 (1, Pt. 2): 1–88.

Binstock, R. 1974. "Aging and the future of American politics." In E. Eisele (ed.), *Political Consequences of Aging*. Annals of the American Academy of Political and Social Science 415:199–212.

Birch, D. 1971. "Toward a stage theory of urban growth." In R. Yin (ed.), *The City in the Seventies*. Itasca, Ill.: Peacock.

Blau, P. 1977. *Inequality and Heterogeneity: A Primitive Theory of Social Structure*. New York: Free Press.

Blau, Z. 1956. "Changes in status and age identification." *American Sociological Review* 21:198–205.

Blau, Z. 1973. *Old Age in a Changing Society*. New York: New Viewpoints.

Booth, A. 1972. "Sex and social participation." *American Sociological Review* 37:183–193.

Booth, A., and Hess, E. 1974. "Cross-sex friendships." *Journal of Marriage and the Family* 36:38–47.

Bradburn, N. 1969. *The Structure of Psychological Well-Being*. Chicago: Aldine.

Branco, K., and Williamson, J. 1982. "Stereotyping and the life cycle: Views of aging and the aged." In A. Miller (ed.), *In the Eye of the Beholder: Contemporary Issues in Stereotyping*. New York: Praeger.

Brubaker, T., and Powers, E. 1976. "The stereotype of 'old'—A review and alternative approach." *Journal of Gerontology* 31:441–447.

Bultena, G., and Powers, E. 1978. "Denial of aging: Age identification and reference group orientations." *Journal of Gerontology* 33:748–754.

Bultena, G., and Wood, V. 1969. "The American retirement community: Bane or blessing?" *Journal of Gerontology* 24:209–217.

Burt, R., Wiley, J., Minor, M., and Murray, J. 1978. "Structure of well-being: Form, content, and stability over time." *Sociological Methods and Research* 6:365–407.

Cantor, M. 1975. "Life space and the social support system of the inner city elderly of New York." *Gerontologist* 15:23–26.

Cantor, M. 1979. "Neighbors and friends: An overlooked resource in the informal support system." *Research on Aging* 1:434–463.

Cantor, M. 1983. "Strain among caregivers: A study of experience in the United States." *Gerontologist* 23:597–604.

Carp, F. 1975. "Life style and location within the city." *Gerontologist* 15:27–34.

Carp, F. 1976. "Housing and living environments of older people." In R. Binstock and E. Shanas (eds.), *Handbook of Aging and the Social Sciences*. New York: Van Nostrand Reinhold.

Carp, F., and Carp, A. 1981. "It may not be the answer, it may be the question." *Research on Aging* 3:85–100.

Chevan, A. 1982. "Age, housing choice, and neighborhood age structure." *American Journal of Sociology* 87:1133–1149.

Cobb, S. 1976. "Social support as a moderator of life stress." *Psychosomatic Medicine* 38:300–314.

Cobb, S. 1979. "Social support and health through the life course." In M. Riley (ed.), *Aging from Birth to Death: Interdisciplinary Perspectives*. Boulder, Colo.: Westview Press.

Coward, R., and Rathbone-McCuan, E. 1985. "Delivering health and human services to the elderly in rural society." In R. Coward and G. Lee (eds.), *The Elderly in Rural Society*. New York: Springer.

Cowgill, D. 1974. "Aging and modernization: A revision of the theory." In J. Gubrium (ed.), *Late Life: Communities and Environmental Policies*. Springfield, Ill.: Charles C. Thomas.

Cowgill, D. 1978. "Residential segregation by age in American metropolitan areas." *Journal of Gerontology* 33:446–453.

Cowley, M. 1982. *The View from 80.* New York: Penguin Books.

Cumming, E., and Henry, W. 1961. *Growing Old: The Process of Disengagement.* New York: Basic Books.

Cutler, N. 1979. "Age variations in the dimensionality of life satisfaction." *Journal of Gerontology* 34:573–578.

Daum, M. 1978. "The correlates and dimensions of age identification." Paper presented at annual meeting of Gerontological Society, Dallas.

Dean, A., and Lin, N. 1977. "The stress-buffering role of social support." *Journal of Nervous and Mental Disease* 165:403–417.

Dono, J., Falbe, C., Kail, B., Litwak, E., Sherman, R., and Siegel, D. 1979. "Primary groups in old age: Structure and function." *Research on Aging* 1:403–433.

Dowd, J. 1980a. *Stratification among the Aged.* Monterey, Calif.: Brooks/Cole.

Dowd, J. 1980b. "Exchange rates and old people." *Journal of Gerontology* 35:596–602.

Eckert, J. 1980. *The Unseen Elderly.* San Diego: Campanile Press.

Eisdorfer, C., and Altrocchi, J. 1961. "A comparison of attitudes toward old age and mental illness." *Journal of Gerontology* 16:340–343.

Elder, G. 1981. "History and the life course." In D. Bertaux (ed.), *Biography and Society: The Life History Approach in the Social Sciences.* Beverly Hills, Calif.: Sage.

Feld, S. 1981. "The focused organization of social ties." *American Journal of Sociology* 86:1015–1035.

Ferraro, K. 1980. "Self-ratings of health among the old and the old-old." *Journal of Health and Social Behavior* 21:377–382.

Firey, W. 1945. "Sentiment and symbolism as ecological variables." *American Sociological Review* 10:140–148.

Fischer, C. 1975. "Toward a subcultural theory of urbanism." *American Journal of Sociology* 80:1319–1341.

Fischer, C. (ed.). 1977. *Networks and Places.* New York: Free Press.

Fischer, C. 1981. "The public and private worlds of city life." *American Sociological Review* 46:306–316.

Fischer, C., and Jackson, R. 1976. "Suburbs, networks and attitudes." In B. Schwartz (ed.), *The Changing Face of the Suburbs.* Chicago: University of Chicago Press.

Fischer, C., and Jackson, R. 1977. "Suburbanism and localism." In C. Fischer (ed.), *Networks and Places.* New York: Free Press.

Fischer, C., and Stueve, C. 1977. "Authentic community: The role of place in modern life." In C. Fischer (ed.), *Networks and Places.* New York: Free Press.

Fitzpatrick, K., and Logan, J. 1985. "The aging of the suburbs, 1960–1980." *American Sociological Review* 50:106–116.

Foner, A. 1974. "Age stratification and age conflict in political life." *American Sociological Review* 39:187–196.

Foner, A. 1979. "Ascribed and achieved bases of stratification." In A. Inkeles, J. Coleman, and R. Turner (eds.), *Annual Review of Sociology.* Vol. 5. Palo Alto, Calif.: Annual Reviews.

Ford, R. 1950. "Population succession in Chicago." *American Journal of Sociology* 56:156–160.

Freidson, E. 1961. *Patients' Views of Medical Practice.* New York: Russell Sage Foundation.

Friedman, S. 1975. "The resident welcoming committee: Institutionalized elderly in volunteer service to their peers." *Gerontologist* 15:362–367.

Gans, H. 1962. *The Urban Villagers.* New York: Free Press.

George, L. 1979. "The happiness syndrome: Methodological and substantive issues in the study of social psychological well-being in adulthood." *Gerontologist* 19:210–216.

George, L. 1980. *Role Transitions in Later Life*. Monterey, Calif.: Brooks/Cole.

George, L., and Bearon, L. 1980. *Quality of Life in Older Persons: Meaning and Measurement*. New York: Human Sciences Press.

Gerson, K., Stueve, C., and Fischer, C. 1977. "Attachment to place." In C. Fischer (ed.), *Networks and Places*. New York: Free Press.

Glass, R. 1948. *The Social Background of a Plan*. London: Routledge and Kegan Paul.

Glenn, N., and McClanahan, S. 1981. "The effects of offspring on the psychological well-being of older adults." *Journal of Marriage and the Family* 43:409–421.

Goffman, E. 1963. *Stigma: Notes on the Management of Spoiled Identity*. Englewood Cliffs, N.J.: Prentice-Hall.

Golant, S. 1979. "Central city, suburban, and nonmetropolitan area migration patterns of the elderly." In S. Golant (ed.), *Location and Environment of Elderly Population*. Washington, D.C.: V. H. Winston.

Golant, S. 1984. *A Place to Grow Old: The Meaning of Environment in Old Age*. New York: Columbia University Press.

Gould, J. 1964. "Neighborhood." In J. Gould and W. Kolb (eds.), *Dictionary of the Social Sciences*. New York: Free Press.

Granovetter, M. 1973. "The strength of weak ties." *American Journal of Sociology* 78:1360–1380.

Granovetter, M. 1974. *Getting a Job: A Study of Contacts and Careers*. Cambridge, Mass.: Harvard University Press.

Gubrium, J. 1973. *The Myth of the Golden Years: A Socio-Environmental Theory of Aging*. Springfield, Ill.: Charles C. Thomas.

Guptill, C. 1969. "A measure of age identification." *Gerontologist* 9:96–102.

Hawley, A. 1950. *Human Ecology: A Theory of Community Structure*. New York: Ronald.

Herzog, A., and Rodgers, W. 1981. "Age and satisfaction: Data from several large surveys." *Research on Aging* 3:142–165.

Hess, B. 1972. "Friendship." In M. Riley, M. Johnson, and A. Foner (eds.), *Aging and Society*. Vol. 3: *A Sociology of Age Stratification*. New York: Russell Sage Foundation.

Hess, B. 1976. "Self-help among the aged." *Social Policy* 7 (3): 55–62.

Hess, B. 1979. "Sex roles, friendship, and the life course." *Research on Aging* 1:494–515.

Hochschild, A. 1973. *The Unexpected Community*. Englewood Cliffs, N.J.: Prentice-Hall.

Homans, G. 1950. *The Human Group*. New York: Harcourt Brace Jovanovich.

Hoyt, D., Kaiser, M., Peters, G., and Babchuk, N. 1980. "Life satisfaction and activity theory: A multidimensional approach." *Journal of Gerontology* 35:935–941.

Hoyt, G. 1954. "The life of the retired in a trailer park." *American Journal of Sociology* 59:361–370.

Hunter, A. 1975. "The loss of community: An empirical test through replication." *American Sociological Review* 40:537–552.

Jackson, R. 1977. "Social structure and process in friendship choice." In C. Fischer (ed.), *Networks and Places*. New York: Free Press.

Jackson, R., Fischer, C., and Jones, L. 1977. "The dimensions of social networks." In C. Fischer (ed.), *Networks and Places*. New York: Free Press.

Johnson, S. 1971. *Idle Haven: Community Building among the Working-Class Retired.* Berkeley, Calif.: University of California Press.

Johnston, R. 1971. *Urban Residential Patterns.* New York: Praeger.

Johnston, R. 1972. "Activity spaces and residential preferences." *Economic Geography* 48:199–211.

Kahana, E. 1982. "A congruence model of person-environment interaction." In M. P. Lawton, P. Windley, and T. Byerts (eds.), *Aging and the Environment.* New York: Springer.

Kahana, E., Liang, J., Felton, B., and Fairchild, T. 1977. "Perspectives of aged on victimization, 'ageism,' and their problems in urban society." *Gerontologist* 17: 121–129.

Kahn, R. 1979. "Aging and social support." In M. Riley (ed.), *Aging from Birth to Death: Interdisciplinary Perspectives.* Boulder, Colo.: Westview Press.

Kaplan, B., Cassel, J., and Gore, S. 1977. "Social support and health." *Medical Care* 15 (5, Suppl.): 47–58.

Karp, D., and Yoels, W. 1982. *Experiencing the Life Cycle: A Social Psychology of Aging.* Springfield, Ill.: Charles C. Thomas.

Kasarda, J., and Janowitz, M. 1974. "Community attachment in mass society." *American Sociological Review* 39:328–339.

Keller, S. 1968. *The Urban Neighborhood.* New York: Random House.

Kennedy, J., and DeJong, G. 1977. "Aged in cities: Residential segregation in 10 U.S.A. central cities." *Journal of Gerontology* 32:97–102.

Kennedy, L. 1978. "Environmental opportunity and social contact: A true or spurious relationship." *Pacific Sociological Review* 21:173–186.

Kessler, R. 1979. "A strategy for studying differential vulnerability to the psychological consequences of stress." *Journal of Health and Social Behavior* 20:100–107.

Kessler, R., and Essex, M. 1982. "Marital status and depression: The importance of coping resources." *Social Forces* 61:484–507.

Kivett, V. 1985. "Aging in rural society: Non-kin community relations and participation." In R. Coward and G. Lee (eds.), *The Elderly in Rural Society.* New York: Springer.

La Gory, M. 1982. "Toward a sociology of space: The constrained choice model." *Symbolic Interaction* 5:65–78.

La Gory, M., and Pipkin, J. 1981. *Urban Social Space.* Belmont, Calif.: Wadsworth.

La Gory, M., Ward, R., and Juravich, T. 1980. "Explanations of the age segregation process in American cities." *Urban Affairs Quarterly* 16:59–80.

La Gory, M., Ward, R., and Mucatel, M. 1981. "Patterns of age segregation." *Sociological Focus* 14:1–13.

Larson, R. 1978. "Thirty years of research on the subjective well-being of older Americans." *Journal of Gerontology* 33:109–125.

LaRue, A., Bank, L., Jarvik, L., and Hetland, M. 1979. "Health in old age: How do physicians' ratings and self-ratings compare?" *Journal of Gerontology* 34:687–691.

Laumann, E. 1966. *Prestige and Association in an Urban Community.* Indianapolis: Bobbs-Merrill.

Laumann, E. 1973. *Bonds of Pluralism: The Form and Substance of Urban Social Networks.* New York: Wiley-Interscience.

Lawton, M. P. 1970. "Ecology and aging." In L. A. Pastalan and D. H. Carson (eds.), *The Spatial Behavior of Older People.* Ann Arbor, Mich.: Institute of Gerontology.

Lawton, M. P. 1975. "The Philadelphia Geriatric Center Morale Scale: A revision." *Journal of Gerontology* 30:85–89.

Lawton, M. P. 1980. *Environment and Aging*. Belmont, Calif.: Wadsworth.

Lawton, M. P. 1982. "Competence, environmental press, and the adaptation of older people." In M. P. Lawton, P. Windley, and T. O. Byerts (eds.), *Aging and the Environment*. New York: Springer.

Lawton, M. P. 1983a. "Environment and other determinants of well-being in older people." *Gerontologist* 23:349–357.

Lawton, M. P. 1983b. "The suprapersonal neighborhood context of older people: Age heterogeneity and well-being." Philadelphia, Pa.: Philadelphia Geriatric Center.

Lawton, M. P., and Kleban, M. 1971. "The aged resident of the inner city." *Gerontologist* 11:277–283.

Lawton, M. P., and Nahemow, L. 1973. "Ecology and the aging process." In C. Eisdorfer and M. P. Lawton (eds.), *The Psychology of Adult Development and Aging*. Washington, D.C.: American Psychological Association.

Lawton, M. P., and Nahemow, L. 1979. "Social areas and the well-being of tenants in housing for the elderly." *Multivariate Behavioral Research* 14:463–484.

Lawton, M. P., and Simon, B. 1968. "The ecology of social relationships in housing for the elderly." *Gerontologist* 8:108–115.

Lee, B., Oropesa, R., Metch, B., and Guest, A. 1984. "Testing the decline of community thesis: Neighborhood organization in Seattle, 1929 and 1979." *American Journal of Sociology* 89:1161–1188.

Lee, G., and Cassidy, M. 1985. "Family and kin relations of the rural elderly." In R. Coward and G. Lee (eds.), *The Elderly in Rural Society*. New York: Springer.

Lee, T. 1970. "Urban neighborhood as socio-spatial schema." In H. Proshansky, W. Ittelson, and L. Rivlin (eds.), *Environmental Psychology*. New York: Holt, Rinehart, and Winston.

Lemon, B., Bengtson, V., and Peterson, J. 1972. "An exploration of the activity theory of aging: Activity types and life satisfaction among in-movers to a retirement community." *Journal of Gerontology* 27:511–523.

Liang, J., Dvorkin, L., Kahana, E., and Mazian, F. 1980. "Social integration and morale: A reexamination." *Journal of Gerontology* 35:746–757.

Linn, M., and Hunter, K. 1979. "Perception of age in the elderly." *Journal of Gerontology* 34:46–52.

Litwak, E. 1985. *Helping the Elderly*. New York: Guilford Press.

Litwak, E., and Szelenyi, I. 1969. "Primary group structures and their functions: Kin, neighbors, and friends." *American Sociological Review* 34:465–481.

Lofland, L. 1985. *A World of Strangers: Order and Action in Urban Public Space*. Prospect Heights, Ill.: Waveland Press.

Longino, C., McClelland, K., and Peterson, W. 1980. "The aged subculture hypothesis: Social integration, gerontophilia, and self-conception." *Journal of Gerontology* 35:758–767.

Lopata, H. 1975. "Support systems of elderly urbanites: Chicago of the 1970s." *Gerontologist* 15:35–41.

Lopata, H. 1979. *Women as Widows: Support Systems*. New York: Elsevier.

Lowenthal, M., and Haven, C. 1968. "Interaction and adaptation: Intimacy as a critical variable." *American Sociological Review* 33:20–31.

Lowenthal, M., and Robinson, B. 1976. "Social networks and isolation." In R. Binstock and E. Shanas (eds.), *Handbook of Aging and the Social Sciences*. New York: Van Nostrand Reinhold.

Lowenthal, M., Thurnher, M., and Chiriboga, D. 1975. *Four Stages of Life*. San Francisco: Jossey-Bass.

McKinlay, J. 1973. "Social networks, lay consultation, and help-seeking behavior." *Social Forces* 51:275–292.

McTavish, D. 1971. "Perceptions of old people: A review of research methodologies and findings." *Gerontologist* 11:90–101.

Maddox, G., and Wiley, J. 1976. "Scope, concepts, and methods in the study of aging." In R. Binstock and E. Shanas (eds.), *Handbook of Aging and the Social Sciences*. New York: Van Nostrand Reinhold.

Mangum, W. 1973. "Retirement villages." In R. Boyd and C. Oakes (eds.), *Foundations of Practical Gerontology*. Columbia, S.C.: University of South Carolina Press.

Markides, K., and Boldt, J. 1983. "Change in subjective age among the elderly: A longitudinal analysis." *Gerontologist* 23:422–427.

Marshall, V. 1975. "Socialization for impending death in a retirement village." *American Journal of Sociology* 80:1124–1144.

Marshall, V. 1978. "No exit: A symbolic interactionist perspective on aging." *Aging and Human Development* 9:345–358.

Matthews, S. 1979. *The Social World of Old Women: Management of Self-Identity*. Beverly Hills, Calif.: Sage.

Messer, M. 1967. "The possibility of age-concentrated environment becoming a normative system." *Gerontologist* 7:247–250.

Michelson, W. 1976. *Man and His Urban Environment*. Reading, Mass.: Addison-Wesley.

Milgram, S. 1970. "The experience of living in cities." *Science* 167:1461–1468.

Miller, A., Gurin, P., and Gurin, O. 1980. "Age consciousness and political mobilization of older Americans." *Gerontologist* 20:691–700.

Montgomery, R. 1982. "Impact of institutional care policies on family integration." *Gerontologist* 22:54–88.

Mumford, J. 1956. "For older people—not segregation but integration." *Architectural Record* 119:191–194.

Mutran, E., and Burke, P. 1979a. "Feeling 'useless': A common component of young and old adult identities." *Research on Aging* 1:137–212.

Mutran, E., and Burke, P. 1979b. "Personalism as a component of old age identity." *Research on Aging* 1:37–63.

Mutran, E., and Reitzes, D. 1981. "Retirement, identity, and well-being; Realignment of role relationships." *Journal of Gerontology* 36:733–740.

National Council on the Aging. 1975. *The Myth and Reality of Aging in America*. Washington, D.C.

Neugarten, B., Moore, J., and Lowe, J. 1965. "Age norms, age constraints, and adult socialization." *American Journal of Sociology* 70:710–717.

Newcomer, R. 1976. "An evaluation of neighborhood service convenience for elderly housing project residents." In P. Suefeld and L. Russell (eds.), *The Behavioral Basis of Design*. Book 1. Stroudsburg, Pa.: Dowden, Hutchinson, and Ross.

Nie, N., Hull, C., Jenkins, J., Steinbrenner, K., and Bent, D. 1975. *Statistical Package for the Social Sciences*. 2d ed. New York: McGraw-Hill.

O'Brien, J., and Wagner, D. 1980. "Help seeking by the frail elderly: Problems in network analysis." *Gerontologist* 20:78–83.

Offenbacher, D. I., and Poster, C. H. 1985. "Aging and the baseline code: An alternative to the 'normless' elderly." *Gerontologist* 25:526–531.

O'Gorman, H. 1980. "False consciousness of kind: Pluralistic ignorance among the aged." *Research on Aging* 2:105–128.

Osgood, N. 1982. *Senior Settlers*. New York: Praeger.

Pampel, F., and Choldin, H. 1978. "Urban location and segregation of the aged: A block-level analysis." *Social Forces* 56:1121–1139.

Park, R., and Burgess, E. 1925. *The City*. Chicago: University of Chicago Press.

Peach, C. (ed.). 1975. *Urban Social Segregation*. New York: Longman.

Pearlin, L., Lieberman, M., Menaghan, E., and Mullan, J. 1981. "The stress process." *Journal of Health and Social Behavior* 22:337–356.

Pearlin, L., and Schooler, C. 1978. "The structure of coping." *Journal of Health and Social Behavior* 19:2–21.

Perkinson, M. A. 1980. "Alternate roles for the elderly: An example from a midwestern retirement community." *Human Organization* 39:219–226.

Peters, G. 1971. "Self-conceptions of the aged, age identification, and aging." *Gerontologist* 11:69–73.

Phillips, B. 1957. "A role theory approach to adjustment in old age." *American Sociological Review* 22:212–217.

Pihlblad, C., and Adams, D. 1972. "Widowhood, social participation, and life satisfaction." *International Journal of Aging and Human Development* 3:323–330.

Powers, E., and Bultena, G. 1976. "Sex differences in intimate friendships of old age." *Journal of Marriage and the Family* 38:739–747.

Ragan, P., and Dowd, J. 1974. "The emerging political consciousness of the aged: A generational interpretation." *Journal of Social Issues* 30:137–158.

Rapoport, A. 1977. *Human Aspects of Urban Form: Towards a Man-Environment Approach to Urban Form and Design*. New York: Pergamon.

Regnier, V. 1975. "Neighborhood planning for the urban elderly." In D. Woodruff and J. Birren (eds.), *Aging: Scientific Perspectives and Social Issues*. New York: Van Nostrand.

Regnier, V. 1976. "Neighborhoods as service systems." In M. P. Lawton, R. Newcomer, and T. Byerts (eds.), *Community Planning for an Aging Society: Designing Services and Facilities*. Stroudsburg, Pa.: Dowden, Hutchinson, and Ross.

Regnier, V. 1981. "Neighborhood images and use: A case study." In M. P. Lawton and S. Hoover (eds.), *Community Housing Choices for Older Americans*. New York: Springer.

Riley, M. 1976. "Age strata in social systems." In R. Binstock and E. Shanas (eds.), *Handbook of Aging and the Social Sciences*. New York: Van Nostrand Reinhold.

Riley, M. 1978. "Aging, social change, and the power of ideas." *Daedalus* 107(4): 39–52.

Riley, M., Johnson, M., and Foner, A. (eds.). 1972. *Aging and Society*. Vol. 3: *A Sociology of Age Stratification*. New York: Russell Sage Foundation.

Rose, A. 1965a. "The subculture of aging: A framework for research in social gerontology." In A. Rose and W. Peterson (eds.), *Older People and Their Social World*. Philadelphia, Pa.: Davis.

Rose, A. 1965b. "Group consciousness among the aging." In A. Rose and W. Peterson (eds.), *Older People and Their Social World*. Philadelphia, Pa.: Davis.

Rosenberg, G. 1970. *The Worker Grows Old*. San Francisco: Jossey-Bass.

Rosencranz, H., and McNevin, T. 1969. "A factor analysis of attitudes toward the aged." *Gerontologist* 9:55–59.

Rosow, I. 1967. *Social Integration of the Aged*. New York: Free Press.

Rosow, I. 1974. *Socialization to Old Age*. Berkeley, Calif.: University of California Press.

Rosow, I. 1976. "Status and role change through the life span." In R. Binstock and E. Shanas (eds.), *Handbook of Aging and the Social Sciences*. New York: Van Nostrand Reinhold.

Rosow, I. 1978. "Social psychology and gerontology: A discussion." *International Journal of Aging and Human Development* 9:153–161.

Ross, J. 1977. *Old People, New Lives.* Chicago: University of Chicago Press.

Rowles, G. 1978. *Prisoners of Space? Exploring the Geographical Experience of Older People.* Boulder, Colo.: Westview Press.

Rowles, G. 1979. "The last new home." In S. Golant (ed.), *Location and Environment of Elderly Population.* New York: Wiley.

Sarbin, T. 1970. "The culture of poverty, social identity, and cognitive outcomes." In V. Allen (ed.), *Psychological Factors in Poverty.* Chicago: Markham.

Schooler, K. 1969. "The relationship between social interaction and morale of the elderly as a function of environmental characteristics." *Gerontologist* 9:25–29.

Schooler, K., Pastorello, T., Comen, A., and Clark, C. 1981. "The relative impact of objective and subjective social integration on morale: A replication." Paper presented at annual meeting of Gerontological Society of America, Toronto.

Schrank, H. T., and Waring, J. M. 1983. "Aging and work organizations." In M. W. Riley, B. Hess, and K. Bond (eds.), *Aging and Society: Selected Reviews of Recent Research.* Hillsdale, N.J.: Erlbaum.

Schutz, M. 1982. "Residential segregation of age groups in Hamburg, 1961, 1970, 1977." In Jurgen Friedrichs (ed.), *Spatial Disparities and Social Behaviour: A Reader in Urban Research.* Hamburg: Christians.

Schwirian, K. 1974. *Comparative Urban Structure: Studies in the Ecology of Cities.* Lexington, Mass.: Heath.

Seguin, M. 1973. "Opportunity for peer socialization in a retirement community." *Gerontologist* 13:208–214.

Seltzer, M., and Atchley, R. 1971. "The concept of old: Changing attitudes and stereotypes." *Gerontologist* 11:226–230.

Shanas, E. 1979. "The family as a social support system in old age." *Gerontologist* 19:169–174.

Shanas, E., Townsend, P., Wedderburn, D., Friis, P., and Stehouwer, J. 1968. *Old People in Three Industrial Societies.* New York: Atherton Press.

Sherman, E., Newman, E., and Nelson, A. 1976. "Patterns of age integration in public housing and the incidence and fears of crime among elderly tenants." In J. Goldsmith and S. Goldsmith (eds.), *Crime and the Elderly: Challenge and Response.* Lexington, Mass.: Lexington Books.

Sherman, S. 1971. "The choice of retirement housing among the well-elderly." *International Journal of Aging and Human Development* 2:118–138.

Sherman, S. 1972. "Satisfaction with retirement housing: Attitudes, recommendations, and moves." *International Journal of Aging and Human Development* 3:339–366.

Sherman, S. 1975a. "Patterns of contacts for residents of age-segregated and age-integrated housing." *Journal of Gerontology* 30:103–107.

Sherman, S. 1975b. "Mutual assistance and support in retirement housing." *Journal of Gerontology* 30:479–483.

Sherman, S. 1979. "The retirement housing setting: Site permeability, service availability, and perceived community support in crises." *Journal of Social Service Research* 3:139–157.

Sherman, S., Ward, R., and La Gory, M. 1984. "Gender differences in role models and confidants." Paper presented at Annual Meeting of Gerontological Society of America.

Sherman, S., Ward, R., and La Gory, M. 1985. "Socialization and aging group consciousness: The effect of neighborhood age concentration." *Journal of Gerontology* 40:102–109.

Shevky, E., and Bell, W. 1955. *Social Area Analysis.* Stanford, Calif.: Stanford University Press.

Shulman, N. 1975. "Life-cycle variations in patterns of close relationships." *Journal of Marriage and the Family* 37:813–821.

Simpson, I., Back, K., and McKinney, J. 1966. "Exposure to information on preparation for and self-evaluation in retirement." In I. Simpson and J. McKinney (eds.), *Social Aspects of Aging.* Durham, N.C.: Duke University Press.

Singer, E. 1981. "Reference groups and social evaluations." In M. Rosenberg and R. Turner (eds.), *Social Psychology: Sociological Perspectives.* New York: Basic Books.

Snider, E. 1980. "Factors influencing health service knowledge among the elderly." *Journal of Health and Social Behavior* 21:371–376.

Snow, D., and Gordon, J. 1980. "Social network analysis and intervention with the elderly." *Gerontologist* 20:463–467.

Stea, D. 1970. "Home range and use of space." In L. Pastalan and D. Carson (eds.), *Spatial Behavior of Older People.* Ann Arbor, Mich.: University of Michigan–Wayne State University Institute of Gerontology.

Stinchcombe, A. R., R. Adams, C. Heimer, K. Sheppale, J. Smith, and G. Taylor. 1980. *Crime and Punishment: Changing Attitudes in America.* San Francisco, Calif.: Jossey-Bass.

Streib, G. 1976. "Social stratification and aging." In R. Binstock and E. Shanas (eds.), *Handbook of Aging and the Social Sciences.* New York: Van Nostrand Reinhold.

Streib, G., and Schneider, C. 1971. *Retirement in American Society.* Ithaca, N.Y.: Cornell University Press.

Struyk, R., and Soldo, B. 1980. *Improving the Elderly's Housing: A Key to Preserving the Nation's Housing Stock and Neighborhoods.* Cambridge, Mass.: Ballinger.

Stueve, A., and Gibson, K. 1977. "Personal relations across the life-cycle." In C. Fischer (ed.), *Networks and Places.* New York: Free Press.

Sussman, M. 1976. "The family life of old people." In R. Binstock and E. Shanas (eds.), *Handbook of Aging and the Social Sciences.* New York: Van Nostrand Reinhold.

Suttles, G. 1972. *The Social Construction of Communities.* Chicago: University of Chicago Press.

Taietz, P. 1975. "Community complexity and knowledge of facilities." *Journal of Gerontology* 30:357–362.

Taub, R., Surgeon, G., Lindholm, S., Otti, P., and Bridges, A. 1977. "Urban voluntary associations, locality based and externally induced." *American Journal of Sociology* 83:425–442.

Taueber, K., and Taueber, A. 1965. *Negroes in Cities: Residential Segregation and Neighborhood Change.* New York: Atheneum.

Teaff, J., Lawton, M. P., Nahemow, L., and Carlson, D. 1978. "Impact of age integration on the well-being of elderly tenants in public housing." *Journal of Gerontology* 33:126–133.

Thoits, P. 1982. "Conceptual, methodological, and theoretical problems in studying social support as a buffer against life stress." *Journal of Health and Social Behavior* 23:145–159.

Tibbitts, C. 1979. "Can we invalidate negative stereotypes of aging?" *Gerontologist* 19:10–20.

Timms, D. 1971. *The Urban Mosaic*. New York: Cambridge University Press.

Trela, J. 1972. "Age structure of voluntary associations and political self-interest among the aged." *Sociological Quarterly* 13:244–252.

Trela, J. E., and Jackson, D. J. 1979. "Family life and community participation in old age." *Research on Aging* 1:233–251.

U.S. Bureau of the Census. 1983. 1980 Census of Population and Housing. Census Tracts. Albany-Schenectady-Troy, N.Y., SMSA. Washington, D.C.: U.S. Government Printing Office.

U.S. Public Health Service. 1981. "Current estimates from the National Health Interview Survey: United States, 1980." *Vital and Health Statistics*, series 10, no. 139, National Center for Health Statistics. Washington, D.C.: U.S. Government Printing Office.

Unruh, D. R. 1983. *Invisible Lives: Social Worlds of the Aged*. Beverly Hills: Sage.

Verbrugge, L. 1977. "The structure of adult friendship choices." *Social Forces* 56:576–597.

Wagner, D., and Keast, F. 1981. "Informal groups and the elderly: A preliminary examination of the mediation function." *Research on Aging* 3:325–332.

Ward, R. 1977a. "The impact of subjective age and stigma on older persons." *Journal of Gerontology* 32:227–232.

Ward, R. 1977b. "Services for older people: An integrated framework for research." *Journal of Health and Social Behavior* 18:61–70.

Ward, R. 1977c. "Aging group consciousness: Implications in an older sample." *Sociology and Social Research* 61:496–519.

Ward, R. 1979. "The meaning of voluntary association participation to older people." *Journal of Gerontology* 34:438–445.

Ward, R. 1984a. *The Aging Experience*. New York: Harper and Row.

Ward, R. 1984b. "The marginality and salience of being old: When is age relevant?" *Gerontologist* 24:227–232.

Ward, R. 1985. "Informal networks and well-being in later life: A research agenda." *Gerontologist* 25:55–61.

Weiss, R. 1969. "The fund of sociability." *Transaction* 6:36–43.

Wellman, B. 1976. *Urban Connections*. Research Paper 84. Toronto: Center for Urban and Community Studies, University of Toronto.

Wellman, B. 1979. "The community question: The intimate networks of East Yorkers." *American Journal of Sociology* 84:1201–1231.

Wellman, B., Craven, P., Whitaker, M., Stevens, H., Shorter, A., DuToit, S., and Bakker, H. 1973. "Community ties and support systems: From intimacy to support." In L. Bourue, R. Mackinnon, and J. Simmons (eds.), *The Form of Cities in Central Canada: Selected Papers*. Toronto: University of Toronto Press.

Williamson, J., Evans, L., Powell, L., and Hesse-Biber, S. 1982. *The Politics of Aging: Power and Policy*. Springfield, Ill.: Charles C. Thomas.

Wirth, L. 1938. "Urbanism as a way of life." *American Journal of Sociology* 44:1–24.

Woelfel, J., and Haller, A. 1971. "Significant others, the self-reflexive act and the attitude formation process." *American Sociological Review* 36:74–87.

Wood, V. 1971. "Age-appropriate behavior for older people." *Gerontologist* 11:74–78.

Wood, V., and Robertson, J. 1978. "Friendship and kinship interaction: Differential effect on the morale of the elderly." *Journal of Marriage and the Family* 40:367–375.

Zipf, G. 1949. *Human Behavior and the Principle of Least Effort*. New York: Hafner.

Index

254

About the Authors

Russell A. Ward is associate professor of sociology at the State University of New York at Albany. He received his doctorate and master's degree in sociology from the University of Wisconsin and his bachelor's degree in chemistry from the University of Rochester.

Mark La Gory is associate professor of sociology at the University of Alabama at Birmingham. He received his bachelor's, master's, and doctoral degrees from the University of Cincinnati.

Susan R. Sherman is associate professor of social welfare at the State University of New York at Albany. She received her doctorate from the University of California at Berkeley and her bachelor's degree from the University of Chicago.